Migration, Minorities and Modernity

Volume 7

Series Editors
Thomas Geisen, Trier, Germany
Zvi Bekerman, The Hebrew University of Jerusalem, Jerusalem, Israel
Pat Cox, SSWCC, University of Central Lancashire, Preston, UK

This series explores the often complex relationships between migration, society and democracy. With a focus on local and regional aspects, the studies presented in this series discuss migration itself, including questions related to forced migration and resettlement, and offer new insights on the connections between established groups and newcomers in modern societies, especially with regard to their potential impact on social and democratic development. The scope of the series encompasses distinct fields such as migration/minorities and democracy, migration/minorities and law, migration/minorities and social organisation, migration/minorities and education, migration/minorities and the labour market, migration/minorities and high-tech capitalism, migration/minorities and racism, in addition to the intersections of these distinct fields with each other, for example: migration/minorities, citizenship, law, and democracy. This series adopts an international and interdisciplinary approach to seek better understandings of the complexity of migration/minorities and reveal the fruitful outcomes of migration/minorities as well as examine more interwoven and problematic issues of migration/minorities, societies and democracies.

Jennifer Martin · Dharma Arunachalam ·
Helen Forbes-Mewett

Identity and Belonging Among Chinese Australians

Phenotype, Ethnic Language and Cultural Values

Jennifer Martin
Department of Sociology and Anthropology
Monash University
Melbourne, VIC, Australia

Dharma Arunachalam
Department of Sociology and Anthropology
Monash University
Melbourne, VIC, Australia

Helen Forbes-Mewett
Department of Sociology and Anthropology
Monash University
Melbourne, VIC, Australia

ISSN 2522-0713   ISSN 2522-0721   (electronic)
Migration, Minorities and Modernity
ISBN 978-3-031-47861-1   ISBN 978-3-031-47862-8   (eBook)
https://doi.org/10.1007/978-3-031-47862-8

© The Editor(s) (if applicable) and The Author(s), under exclusive license to Springer Nature Switzerland AG 2023

This work is subject to copyright. All rights are solely and exclusively licensed by the Publisher, whether the whole or part of the material is concerned, specifically the rights of translation, reprinting, reuse of illustrations, recitation, broadcasting, reproduction on microfilms or in any other physical way, and transmission or information storage and retrieval, electronic adaptation, computer software, or by similar or dissimilar methodology now known or hereafter developed.
The use of general descriptive names, registered names, trademarks, service marks, etc. in this publication does not imply, even in the absence of a specific statement, that such names are exempt from the relevant protective laws and regulations and therefore free for general use.
The publisher, the authors, and the editors are safe to assume that the advice and information in this book are believed to be true and accurate at the date of publication. Neither the publisher nor the authors or the editors give a warranty, expressed or implied, with respect to the material contained herein or for any errors or omissions that may have been made. The publisher remains neutral with regard to jurisdictional claims in published maps and institutional affiliations.

This Springer imprint is published by the registered company Springer Nature Switzerland AG
The registered company address is: Gewerbestrasse 11, 6330 Cham, Switzerland

Paper in this product is recyclable.

Preface

Ethnicity is arguably one of the key factors shaping identity development especially when the individual or group in question is visibly different from the mainstream population. The Chinese diaspora in Australia is a diverse group yet, at face value, is commonly perceived as being a homogeneous group. Not only may they be grouped by their physical appearance, the Chinese diaspora may also be defined by ethnic languages spoken. This book explores the process of ethnic identity construction among a specific cohort of the Chinese diaspora in Australia, the multi-generation Australian-born Chinese. As with other visibly different ethnic groups, identity construction among multi-generation Australian-born Chinese is multi-dimensional and influenced by a range of social, political and historical conditions. In consideration of the situational context, ethnic identity construction is in a constant state of re-negotiation.

This book considers what 'being Chinese' means to Australian-born Chinese in terms of how 'Chineseness' is perceived, constructed and understood. Using a social constructivist theoretical framework, 28 semi-structured in-depth interviews were conducted with multi-generation Australian-born Chinese living across three states or territories in Australia. To understand how identity development occurred for second- and higher-generation Australian-born Chinese, their ethnic identity construction was examined in terms of 'being' and 'feeling' Chinese in relation to two main signifiers of an ethnic group's identity—that of phenotype and ethnic language. This research also examined 'doing' Chinese and the different ways in which Chineseness is manifested.

Three key findings emerged from this study. First, it is difficult to ignore phenotype in the construction of Chineseness. Not only did it have a pervasive influence on the way in which Australian-born Chinese saw themselves, but it also informed the public perception of Chineseness. Second, ethnic language retention was perceived as an important ethnic identity marker for second-generation Australian-born Chinese but became less relevant for the third-generation and beyond. Importantly, ethnic language was used as a tool for communication and not necessarily a tool for the transmission of cultural values and traditions. Third, Chineseness is enacted in a variety of ways, and this was influenced by generational status, social and historical context and family relationships. Changing environmental and social conditions in the Australian population means that Chineseness like other ethnic identities is no longer fixed; rather it is in a constant state of change.

Melbourne, Australia   Jennifer Martin
Melbourne, Australia   Dharma Arunachalam
Melbourne, Australia   Helen Forbes-Mewett

Contents

1	**Introduction**	1
	Background to This Study	2
	Construction of Chinese Identity	3
	Positioning Australian-Born Chinese in the Global Context	8
	Study Participants	13
	The Scope and Limitations of the Book	15
	References	18
2	**White Australia: Nationalism and National Identity**	21
	Nationalism and National Identity	22
	How 'White' is Australia?—The Racialisation of Australian National Identity	25
	What Is Australia's National Identity?	30
	Multiculturalism: Friend or Foe?	34
	Conclusion	40
	References	42
3	**Race and Ethnicity in Identity**	47
	Introduction	47
	The Racialisation of Identity	49
	Schoolyard Memories	49
	'Us' Versus 'Them'	53
	Objectification and Stigma	57
	Stereotypes	60
	Being the 'Other'	64
	The Family as a Reinforcer of Difference	66
	Internalising and Normalising Racism Within the Family	67
	Being Half and Half	70
	Fostering Chineseness	71
	Embracing Chineseness	73
	Importance of Filial and Social Support	78

	Discussion	80
	References	82
4	**Language and Ethnic Identity**	85
	Language as a Marker of Identity	86
	"You'd Be Less Chinese If You Didn't Speak the Language"	86
	"It Doesn't Matter What Language You Speak"	87
	"You're Chinese in Your Heart"	89
	Family Dynamics and Language Use	92
	"We Would Reply in English to Our Parents"	93
	"Chinese Is What Keeps Me Really Connected with My Parents"	95
	"Me and My Dad Don't Really Have Conversations"	97
	Social Acceptability of Parental Languages	102
	Discussion	105
	References	108
5	**Performing Chineseness**	111
	You Are What You Eat	113
	Chinese Community Associations as Centres of Chineseness	117
	Chinese New Year and Doing Chinese	119
	Marrying Chinese	123
	Educational Achievement	126
	Going Home	129
	Discussion	131
	References	134
6	**Conclusion**	137
	Overview	137
	Phenotype and Identity	141
	To Speak or not to Speak Chinese	143
	The Enactment of Chineseness	145
	References	147

About the Authors

Jennifer Martin is Research Affiliate at the School of Social Sciences, Monash University. Dr. Martin is a second-generation Chinese Australian. She has extensive experience in the education, public and community sectors, and she is an advocate for Culturally and Linguistically Diverse (CALD) communities.

Dharma Arunachalam is Professor of Sociology, School of Social Sciences, Monash University. His current research focuses on migration, identity and social cohesion in Australia and family formation in India and Australia. He recently coedited a volume on *Creating Social Cohesion in an Interdependent World: Experiences of Australia and Japan* (Healy, E. J., Arunachalam, D., Mizukami, T., eds., Palgrave Macmillan, 2016).

Helen Forbes-Mewett is Associate Professor of Sociology, School of Social Sciences, Monash University. She is Editor-in-Chief of the *Journal of Sociology*, the official *journal of The Australian Sociological Association.* In 2022, she was awarded the A. Noam Chomsky North Star Medal of Lifetime Achievement. Her books include: *International Student Security* (Marginson, Nyland, Sawir, & Forbes-Mewett, Cambridge Uni Press 2010), *International students and Crime* (Forbes-Mewett, McCulloch & Nyland, Palgrave Macmillan 2015); *The New Security: Individual, Community and Cultural Experiences* (Forbes-Mewett, Palgrave Macmillan 2019); *Vulnerability in a Mobile World* (Forbes-Mewett, ed. Emerald 2020).

Chapter 1
Introduction

This book explores the diverse ways in which 'Chineseness' is perceived, constructed and understood among Australian-born Chinese. Ethnic identities, like other identities, are fluid and context dependent. Ethnicity sits alongside other identities, including gender, occupation and religion, and thus, may or may not be central to individual constructions of identity among Australian-born Chinese.

The Western idea of 'being Chinese' often meant some form of racial collectivism based on a shared imagining of a 'Chinese' homeland and stereotypical physical characteristics (Ngan & Chan, 2012) or what Ang (1993, p. 8) termed as the 'corporeal malediction' of Chineseness where the 'fact of yellowness' was characterised by 'slanted eyes'. Representations of Chinese people in the media often reinforce stereotypical images such as those of Chinese partaking in cultural festivals and food events, of Chinese being studious as well as having distinguishable visible features and speaking with an accent. Historical and social contexts tend to be ignored or considered in a limited way.

These views are also, to some extent, reinforced by diasporic Chinese. Although flawed as a concept, certain aspects of Chineseness relating to homeland, history and culture still serve as important identifiers that help diasporic Chinese make sense of their lives. While there is no universal Chinese identity, the essentialised notions of 'race' and 'ethnicity' still play a role in establishing a hierarchy of identities in Western hegemonic societies as well as within cultural groups. Language proficiency, for example, has been used as a measure of Chinese authenticity (Ang, 1993) with Mandarin being at the top of the hierarchy of Chinese dialects. Ang (1993) also suggests that there is a tendency within Chinese culture to consider itself unique and to view all non-Chinese as 'foreign devils', 'barbarians' or 'ghosts'.

Yet, Chineseness like any other identity is a shifting entity and is political in nature. It connotes different meanings across diasporic communities as well as within them. What Chineseness entails in Malaysia may differ from that in mainland China or in Australia. What it means to be Chinese within one family may differ between parents and children—individuals who grew up when the Immigration Restriction Act 1901, commonly known as the White Australia Policy, was in force would presumably have different experiences compared to individuals growing up in multicultural Australia. Even at the micro-level, siblings are also prone to having different views within the one family (Song, 1997). Identity is thus not only a fluid concept (Bauman, 1996), it also is only one of many groupings to which a person may belong (Ngan & Chan, 2012). Situational factors including social, economic and historical circumstances all influence identity formation (Rosenthal & Feldman, 1992a).

This book demonstrates that the category of Australian-born Chinese is wide-ranging and diverse by providing a detailed account of how Australian-born Chinese construct their identity and demonstrates the multi-faceted nature of identity construction in the broader sense.

Background to This Study

Chinese immigrants first arrived in Australia in the early 1850s. There was a huge influx of Chinese immigrants during the Gold Rush period, and by the 1880s, there were about 10,000 Chinese men and 100 Chinese women (Washington, n.d.). At the time, there was strong anti-Chinese sentiment and when Australia became a federation, the introduction of the Immigration Restriction Act 1901 resulted in a significant drop in the size of the Chinese population. In the first two decades after the Second World War, Australia's relatively mono-cultural population, a remnant of the White Australia Policy and the subjugation of indigenous Australians, was gradually changing with the relaxation of immigration laws. In the 1970s, there was a large influx of Indochinese refugees following the Vietnam War and in 1989, following the Tiananmen Square uprising, more than 42,000 Chinese students in Australia were reportedly granted permanent visas (Banham, 2003). In recent times, mainland China has emerged as the largest source of international student migration to Australia. These trends and events resulted in greater diversity among the Australian-born Chinese in terms of the first-generation's country of origin, socio-economic status, socio-political position and socio-cultural outlook among other features.

The growth and diversity of the Chinese population has also increased its visibility. In Australia, Asian identity is often equated with Chinese identity in the public sphere. This perhaps stems from the 'racialization of "Asians" in the dominant cultural imaginary: the lumping together and homogenization of a group of people on the basis of a phenotypical discourse of "race"'(Ang, 2001, p. 113). Since the 1970s, when the White Australia Policy was abolished and a policy of multiculturalism established, the discourse changed from one of 'race' to one of ethnicity. Ethnicity is characterised by some key features such as native language, religion and birthplace. However, this did not prevent racialist undertones from re-surfacing as invoked by some political leaders. Thus, Asianness and Chineseness have become interchangeable, at least, in the public domain. In the 1980s, there was debate over the rate of Asian immigration fuelled by comments made by the historian, Geoffrey Blainey, and the then opposition leader, John Howard. In the 1990s, in her maiden speech to Parliament, the One Nation political party leader, Pauline Hanson, claimed that Australia was being 'swamped by Asians'. The precariousness of ethnic identity in relation to the mainstream identity was reinforced by visible difference.

While increased numbers of ethnic minorities may invoke a perceived fear of being 'swamped' by others in some members of the community, one other outcome of an increased Asian population is the ability among the ethnic group minority to build a sense of solidarity. If individuals feel supported, whether it be from within the home and/or in the public arena, they may be more inclined to embrace their ethnic identity. As the book shows, situational context appeared to be an integral force in identity construction for Australian-born Chinese and indeed for the population at large.

A key signifier of identity is phenotype or visible physical characteristics which also serve to differentiate one group from another. Essentialised notions of ethnic identity are largely racialised and have the effect of categorising people into groups based on visual cues. The proliferation of such categorical approaches is problematic to our understanding of identity as a concept with multiple and hybridised meanings. The lived experiences of multi-generation Australian-born Chinese highlighted the diverse ways in which Chineseness was constructed and how this was sometimes at odds with essentialised constructions of Chineseness. The act of framing an identity is to differentiate it from 'other' identities and to some extent, define these 'other' identities. This is problematic as identity is fluid and context-driven, and it is often external agencies that dictate what constitutes the 'other'. This book investigates the difficulty of current hybridised notions of identity to reconcile with this development and the extent to which external constructions played a role in identity construction among Australian-born Chinese. So, how is construction of identity is understood?

Construction of Chinese Identity

Identity construction among Australian-born Chinese is multi-dimensional and influenced by a range of contextual factors including environmental, historical and social conditions. Ethnicity is arguably one of the key factors shaping identity development especially when the individual or group in question is visibly different from the mainstream population. An ethnic group is defined primarily through its relationship with others and is designed from within or from the perspective of its members (Eriksen, 2010). Given the dynamic nature of identity construction, Bauman's (1996) concept of a 'liquid society' in conjunction with the social constructivist theory of Barth (1994) underpins this research.

The central tenet behind identity construction is the differentiation between one person or group and another. It is this process of establishing boundaries that has been problematised by several theorists. Boundaries imply a fixity which is rigid and solid and this is contrary to the concept of a 'liquid society'. In the establishment of boundaries, questions also arise as to who is responsible for their establishment and by what authority and on what basis are they created? Are these boundaries effectively barriers of inclusion and exclusion created by those in power?

To understand how Australian-born Chinese navigate their identity, understanding the situational context is fundamental. The social, environmental and political conditions in 1950s Australia were markedly different to conditions over the decades up to the present day. In the first half of the twentieth century, mainstream Australia was arguably mono-cultural by design and nationalism was perhaps used as a tool by those in power to reinforce what Anderson (1991) termed as an 'imagined community', of a 'white', Anglo-Celtic Australia. It is important to acknowledge that this community was couched in a history of invasion and oppression imposed on indigenous Australians by 'white' colonialists. Like Gellner (1983) believed that nations were ideological constructions that created imagined communities.

In the context of postmodern society, Bauman (1996) explains how 'liquid' life has become and how identity is constantly in a state of flux. It is an era of liquid modernity and 'identities can be adopted and discarded like a change of costume' (Bauman, 1996, p. 23) and it is the activity of choosing more than what is being chosen that matters. Barth's (1969) social constructivist perspective on ethnic identity is also useful in highlighting the fluidity of ethnicity. Ethnicity is recognised as situationally defined and ethnic boundaries are permeable. Self-perceptions as well as the perceptions of other persons play roles in defining one's identity. This fluidity, in turn, is reflected in the idea of 'groupness' as explored by Brubaker (2004a).

Anderson (1983) refers to ethnic groups as 'imagined communities' which are based on a sense of commonality with others. This commonality can exist in two ways—by the construction of a group 'origin' and by an 'imaginary' common culture, language or other characteristics factors shared by members of the group. Ethnic groups involve the establishment of boundaries that are both internally constructed or externally imposed and these boundaries can determine who can and cannot belong. They may include birth place, cultural practices, common language and so on. How the boundary is constructed is diverse and contextual (Anthias, 1992). Australian identity in the first half of the twentieth century was arguably influenced by the mainstream population's shared British ancestry and shared historical experiences. With the Immigration Restriction Act 1901 in place, non-European immigrants, particularly Chinese, were largely excluded from entry into Australia. Until the Act was repealed in 1959, the State's drive to homogenisation served to stigmatise 'otherness'. One language was standardised and an imagined community created based on a shared culture, one that was constituted in relation to others.

This book examines the experiences of multi-generation Australian-born Chinese born in the second half of the twentieth century. As such, it is important to understand the context which those participants born in Australia faced when the White Australia Policy was still in place and national identity was inherently centred around an imagined community to which they did not belong. This period of modernity was characterised by a sense of nationalism much like that described by Anderson (1983) and Gellner (1983). This sense of nationalism continued to have some influence even with the shift towards postmodernity. A number of key events and features in

Australia's recent history had a profound bearing on the everyday lives of the multi-generation Australian-born Chinese study participants including the aftermath of the White Australia Policy, increased diversity in the immigrant population, the influx of refugees following the Vietnam War and the rise of Pauline Hanson and her One Nation political party. Moreover, the Chinese migrated to Australia from many countries, resulting in a diverse array of cultural, economic and political backgrounds. The socio-political environment in which the first generation initially settled in Australia has also changed over time and this, in turn, has impacted on the second and later generation experiences of growing up in Australia. Barth (1969) considers ethnic identity as an aspect of social organisation rather than of culture. However, ethnicity is a form of social organisation and a form of organising cultural difference. It is not so much the cultural traits that make up this difference but the actual boundaries that are created. It is the process of dichotomisation or the behaviour that maintains group boundaries rather than the traits themselves. That is, ethnic identities are based on ascription and self-ascription rather than on the cultural attributes one may have.

In the creation of boundaries, the distinction between 'we' and 'them' does not include a hegemonic view of the 'other' as a stranger but a view of the 'other' as a familiar co-resident. In terms of ascription and self-ascription, our identity is developed by acting in the world and interacting with others. Culture is an individual, fluid proposition and is influenced by our experiences both within and across the boundary (Barth, 1994). Being situational, ethnic groups and their features are influenced by interactional, historical, economic and political circumstances (Barth, 1994; Brubaker, 2004a, 2004b; Verdery, 1994). Barth (1994) argued that the modern state can play an important role in influencing identity development and the boundaries that are constructed. The State has the capacity to exercise some control over boundary maintenance through public laws and policies, allocation of public goods, regulation of lives and movements and among other factors, political processes. Barth (1994) identifies three levels at which these processes operate. At the micro level, identity formation is influenced by individual experiences and interpersonal relations (Barth, 1994). Our exposure to symbols, events, values, self-value and lived experiences informs our identity. At the meso level, collective identities are created and groups are mobilized by the wider community including through the words of politicians and the rhetoric that creates stereotypes. Self-perceptions and the perceptions of others are influenced by external forces. Stereotypes like the 'Tiger mother' and the 'model minority' may not be embedded in government policies at the macro level but they have the potential to influence opinions in everyday life. Such collective attitudes are arguably 'harmless' insofar as they do not impinge on citizen rights. Yet, they do have the potential to cast doubt on one's sense of belonging by highlighting difference in a negative way. At the macro level, State policies and narratives may be selectively employed to control imagined communities.

At all these levels, ethnicity is fluid and constantly changing. The social world can rarely be divided into fixed groups with clear boundaries and group categories can no longer be based on ethnicity alone given that ethnic group boundaries are relative and vary situationally (Eriksen, 2010). Multiple communities and allegiances are reflected in, among other things, diversity in place of origin, religion, place of residence and socio-economic position. Even in the face of essentialised constructions of Chineseness, Australian-born Chinese exercise agency in their navigation around these constructions to arrive at an identity of their own choosing.

Pieterse (1994) and Bhabha (1990) see hybridity as an alternative option to the singular, universalist view of culture/ethnicity. For Pieterse, hybridity is an unremarkable concept in that it has deep historical roots. It has only become an issue because of the strength of boundaries that have been imposed in recent times. For Bhabha (1990), the third space is like a re-creation or re-construction of existing spaces much like the 'global mélange' that Pieterse (1994) refers to. Ang (2001) speaks about the importance of the third space of hybridity and argues 'for the importance of hybridity as a means of bridging and blurring the multiple boundaries which constitute 'Asian' and 'Western' identities as mutually exclusive and incommensurable' (p. 193). Ang goes further to describe her personal position as one of 'hybrid in-betweenness': 'neither truly Western nor authentically Asian; embedded in the West yet always partially disengaged from it' (p. 194). Those marginalised from the white or Western hegemony can gain power by 'claiming one's difference and turning it into symbolic capital' (Ang, 2003, p. 141). While race may be conceptualised as an ethnic cue, race also allows a range of ethnic options as characterised by 'symbolic ethnicity' (Kibria, 2000) or what Gans (1979, p. 1) calls 'an ethnicity of last resort'. Gans (1979) claims that 'ethnics have some choice about when and how to play ethnic roles' (p. 8) and this is particularly so among third-and fourth-generations but also the second generation. Hybridity affords one a sense of agency.

Hybridity, however, requires further qualification. Lo (2000) distinguishes between 'happy hybridity' and 'intentional hybridity'. 'Happy hybridity' celebrates cultural difference where there is a sense of political in-difference to underlying issues of political and economic power. At the same time, this celebration of culture difference masks and perpetuates structural inequities or what Lo claims are a 'whitewash' for the status quo. In contrast, 'intentional hybridity' challenges hegemonic relations because it focuses on negotiation and contestation between cultures. Hybridity is not perceived as a 'natural' outcome of cultural mixing but rather as a form of political intervention. It is this strategic intentional hybridity that is of relevance to this research. Noble et al. (1999) discuss the construction of ethnic identity in terms of strategic essentialism and strategic hybridity. Drawing on their study among male Arabic-speaking youth in South-western Sydney, they demonstrate how this group uses its ethnicity for political leverage. They do this by recognising that their ethnic identity is a given, characterised by both their parents' background as well as their experiences in Australian society.

For Brubaker and Cooper (2000), 'identity' tends to mean too much when understood in a strong sense, too little when understood in a weak sense or, nothing at all because of its ambiguity. From a constructivist stance on identity where identities are constructed, fluid and multiple, there is no rationale for discussing 'identities' at all and to examine 'hard' dynamics and essentialist claims of contemporary identity politics. 'Soft' constructivism allows 'identities' to proliferate. But as 'identities' proliferate, the term loses its strength. If identity is everywhere, it is nowhere in particular. Brubaker and Cooper (2000) argue if it is fluid, how can self-understandings harden? If it is multiple, how can we understand the singularity that politicians use to transform mere categories into unitary, exclusive groups?

Brubaker and Cooper (2000) see 'identity' as: (i) a ground or basis of social or political action; (ii) a specifically 'collective' phenomenon; (iii) a core aspect of individual or collective 'selfhood'; (iv) a product of social or political action; and (v) the product of multiple and competing discourses that highlights the multiple and fragmented nature of the contemporary 'self'. While the first point has overarching application to the concept of 'identity', the second and third points reflect a 'strong' conception of identity that implies a fundamental sameness. It is a 'collective' phenomenon and a core aspect of individual or collective 'selfhood'. The fourth and fifth points reject notions of sameness and reflect a 'weak' conception of 'identity'. However, both 'strong' and 'weak' conceptions of identity are problematic for several reasons. Strong conceptions of identity entail problematic assumptions: identity is something all people have/ought to have; identity is something all groups have/ought to have; identity is something people and groups can have without being aware of it; and strong notions of collective identity imply strong notions of group boundedness and homogeneity. But, not all people have a fixed, singular notion of their identity, conscious or otherwise. 'Weak' understandings of 'identity', on the other hand, break consciously with the everyday meaning of the term. It is unclear why weak conceptions of 'identity' are conceptions of identity at all if core meanings are repudiated; and weak conceptions may be too weak to do useful theoretical work.

Brubaker and Cooper (2000) propose alternative terms that might stand in for 'identity': (i) *Identification and categorisation*: Identification of oneself and others is intrinsic to social life while identity in the strong sense is not. Identification is situational and contextual; relational (by friendship or kinship) and categorical (by race, ethnicity, or language); and there is a distinction between self-identification and identification of oneself by others. (ii) *Self-understanding and social location:* Self-understanding doesn't imply a homogeneous, bounded, unitary entity but a sense of who one is can take many forms; may be variable across time or persons and does not imply sameness like 'identity'; is like 'self-representation' and 'self-identification'; and is limited to one's own understanding of who one is. (iii) *Commonality, connectedness, groupness*: Commonality denotes the sharing of some common attribute; connectedness is the relational ties that link people; both communality and connectedness together engender groupness (the sense of belonging to a distinctive, bounded solidary group. Central to these alternative terms is self-identification and agency as well as subjectivity and situational context. In support of their argument for a revision of the concept of 'identity', Brubaker and Cooper (2000) draw on several case studies to highlight deficiencies in the concept of identity.

Apart from the need to reformulate the concept of 'identity', it is also important to review the meaning of other associated terms. In their review of developments in identity formation among the Chinese diaspora, Benton and Gomez (2014) highlight identity changes across generations and the need to reformulate the meaning of 'nation' insofar as studies of the Chinese diaspora show the emergence of multiple and complex identities not bounded by a fixed idea about 'nation'. Through her analysis of the Chinese in Australia, Ang (2014) also argues that terms such as assimilation, multiculturalism and diaspora do not fully capture the experiences of Chinese Australians. Ang questions the 'groupness' of the 'Chinese' and of the 'Australian' and proposes a more flexible understanding where 'ethnic' and 'national' identities are constantly evolving and mutually related.

New identities are emerging among local-born generations along class, sub-ethnic and generational differences which challenge the idea of a collective identity among ethnic minorities. Benton and Gomez (2008) noted that many long-term British Chinese residents were found to frown upon new migrants. Similarly, using Singapore as an example, the ethnic Chinese population in Singapore distinguish themselves from recent immigrants from mainland China. The identity of migrants may be rooted in their countries of origin. Local-born generations, however, develop their identities by combining parts of their heritage and their local culture. Third and fourth generations have even more complex identities as they are likely to attach importance to their Chinese heritage. Multi-generations are also inclined to 'reclaim a 'Chinese' identity … on their own terms, selecting what appeals to them, and they are secure in their national identities' (Benton & Gomez, 2014, p. 1159).

Despite the emergence of diverse new identities, the State has a propensity to treat 'minorities as static categories' and the host society to see them as 'outsiders'. There is a general disregard by governments for both inter-generational and intra-generational differences in identity formation. As Benton and Gomez (2014, p. 1160) observed:

> Ethnic Chinese are segmented into those rich and poor in skills and resources, and by cleavages of provenance, generation, sub-ethnicity, length of residence and so on. Each segment is shaped less by cultural and national features than by its reception, resources and spatial distribution.

States ignore this segmentation clinging to fixed categories, thus alienating fluid, multiple identities of the second generation and beyond.

Further, studies have shown that there is ambivalence among new generations about their Chineseness and national identities and with the creation of more complex identities, there is a need to de-homogenise new generations. There may be renewed interest in Chineseness among later generations but this is reclaimed on their terms. With the emergence of hybrid and hyphenated identities, these new forms of identification imply new ways of belonging to a national space as well as the multi-layeredness of identity among Chinese.

Positioning Australian-Born Chinese in the Global Context

To gain a broader understanding of how the Australian experience sits within the Chinese diaspora globally, it is worth exploring other places where the Chinese have settled. Because this book has examined the role of phenotype, ethnic language maintenance and the cultural manifestation of Chineseness, it makes sense to consider these same factors in English-speaking and culturally similar settings like the United States and Great Britain as a starting point. From an historical perspective, both Australia and the United States are similar in terms of being settler societies. In addition, from the commencement of white settlement in Australia, affinity with British identity was strong. However, further examination of the historical context of both the US and Britain and the Chinese experience in these countries will reveal the uniqueness of the Australian-born Chinese experience.

American history, like Australian history, is rooted in a mythology around the white settler experience of migration to seek a new life and to build a new nation. According to Tuan (2002), white ethnics could exclusively claim this collective memory of the pioneering experience unlike African Americans brought on slave ships and Native Americans forced to incorporate into this American life. While Asian immigrants also arrived voluntarily, they experienced exclusion and rejection which was similar to the experiences of the Chinese in nineteenth century Australia and well into the twentieth century. Asian Americans were thus not seen as 'real' Americans and their experiences of early migration were erased from collective memory.

Both the US and Australia enacted legislation to specifically exclude Chinese. According to Wang et al. (2021), all Asian Americans have experienced discrimination in US history. It is pointed that from 1865 to 1869, over 20,000 Chinese laborers helped construct the country's railroad networks with little recognition. In 1882, the Chinese Exclusion Act was enacted to prohibit Chinese immigrants from entering the United States to work in a number of industries like construction despite the need for workers. In 1913, the Alien Land Law Act in California blocked Asian immigrants from citizenship or owning land. Similar discriminatory laws across other US states restricted Asian property rights in the following decades. During the 1940s and 1950s, at the height of McCarthyism when people suspected of being Communists were accused of treason, Chinese Americans "wrestled with the sense that being Chinese is itself a crime" (Wang et al., 2021, p. ii). Wang et al. (2021) also claim that anti-Asian racism continued into the twenty-first century with Chinese American scholars suspected, under the Trump administration, of espionage and stealing State secrets and the anti-Asian movement continued with the COVID-19 outbreak at the end of 2019 when President Trump first labelled it the Chinese virus in 2020. Between March and May 2020, more than 1700 anti-Asian hate incidents were documented across the United States (Le et al., 2020, p. 1371). Further, the association between disease, racism and Asian Americans is not new in US history. Xenophobia and discriminatory acts against Asian Americans were evident in the nineteenth century as typified by the introduction of the Chinese Exclusion Act in 1882, the first racial exclusion law in American history.

Asian Americans also struggle with the "perception that all Asians, irrespective of generational status, are foreigners in this country" (Tuan, 2002, p. 209). There is an underlying expectation in their encounters with non-Asians that Asian Americans should be closer to their ethnic roots than their American ones. Conversely, in their interactions with Asian immigrants, American-born Asians also contend with not being seen as Asian enough. Asian Americans continue to struggle against externally-imposed stereotypical labels and the question of "cultural authenticity" (Tuan, 2002). American identity is shaped by ethnic or racial markers (Sorrell et al., 2019; Tuan, 2002) and Asian Americans find that how they choose to identify is not a private affair in the same way as it is for 'white ethnics'. Tuan (2002) observed that the public is unable to distinguish between Asian Americans and Asians and, hence, their status in society is affected by "changing social, political and economic conditions beyond their personal control" (p. 216). These sentiments were reflected in the experiences of Chinese Australians included in the current study. An interesting distinction is that, unlike Chinese Americans being subsumed into one race-based Asian American category, Chinese Australian identity arguably still manages to stand alone. Pan-ethnic categories, like Asian American, were initially externally imposed and conveniently based along racial lines by dominant members of society. These categories eventually take on a life of their own and ethnic distinctions become increasingly secondary with the emergence of racial consciousness (Tuan, 2002).

Sorrell et al. (2019) assert that "immigrant narratives continue to reify the United States as a white nation, thus leading to their exclusion by default" (p. 1). Their findings reveal that immigrants understand their identity in America in terms of how they think others perceive them. The centrality of race in the United States was evident in many immigrants perceiving their physical appearance a barrier to identifying as American because they believed that other Americans did not recognise them as such. Many in Sorrell et al.'s (2019) study used nationalities interchangeably with racial or ethnic categories: "if you're not white, then you're something else, you're not American" (p. 7). The strength of outsiders' perceptions in shaping the way American immigrants identify reflects a heightened sense of the racialized American self which is in contrast to the experiences of Australian immigrants today. As this book shows Australian-born Chinese have agency when it comes to how they identify themselves in contrast to the racialized Asian American experience.

"Cultural authenticity" is something that Asian Americans must involuntarily contend with as they become more removed from the immigrant generation. They can be deemed inauthentically American as well as not being seen as Chinese enough. Later generation white ethnics, or white Americans, on the other hand, can personally choose to identify along ethnic lines or not. However, stereotypes still abound and resonate with both Chinese Australians and Chinese Americans alike. There is an assumption encountered by Chinese Americans of Chinese language fluency and surprise over their fluency in English by non-Chinese Americans (Tuan, 2002). However, among Chinese Australians, while Chinese language fluency raised questions of authenticity, it was not deemed to be essential as an identity marker. Future research into the significance of ethnic language maintenance among Chinese in other English-speaking locations like the US and the UK and how it is used as a marker of identity would expand our understanding of the relationship between language proficiency and ethnic identity.

Other Chinese stereotypes that seem to persist across nation-states include the model minority myth. The model minority stereotype has a negative impact on American Asian students. Their over-representation on US campuses due to hard work has seen them racialized as "yellow peril foreigners" and subject to anti-Asian racism on campuses (Wang et al., 2021). While there was no evidence in Australia of hostilities associated with the model minority label, the stereotype still persisted. Nonetheless, as argued in this book Australian-born Chinese have the capacity to express agency in their formation of identity. In the US case, it is difficult to surmount the assumptions that arise from the race-based nature of society and thus, even harder to dispel stereotypes, particularly when political and societal structures persist in perpetuating racial differences.

From an historical perspective, Britishness figured prominently in the national identity of Australians until the 1970s: "Australians gloried in their possession of a 'British soul'" (McGregor, 2006, p. 493). Britishness provided an ethnic core and laid the base for a nationalism that was both Australian and British. McGregor claimed that Britishness in its northern hemisphere home was distinct from the British amalgam in Australia where immigrants from all over the British Isles intermingled more than they did in Britain. According to McGregor, this 'consolidated ethnic Britishness' was reinforced by a perceived threat to British-Australians' continued possession of Australia. Like other British settlement colonies on the Pacific Rim, there were fears of an Asian invasion or what was termed the 'yellow peril' (p. 500). Further, Britishness provided a source of history, culture and symbols connecting Australia to a glorious past. At the same time, Australia's political and legal institutions established after Federation were exclusively Australian although founded on British institutions. The White Australia Policy cemented the British-Australian ethos while in force by admitting white non-Britishers on the understanding that they would assimilate into the British-Australian nation. From the 1970s, the large intake of non-British immigrants helped to reorientate "Australian nationalism from the ethno-cultural toward the civic/territorial pole" (p. 508). This, in part, gives context to the Chinese immigrant experience in Australia. However, the Chinese experience in Great Britain is somewhat different and warrants further attention.

According to Hsiao (2020), early settlement of Chinese in Britain began with Chinese sailors arriving in British ports in the eighteenth century with a later shift to laundry businesses. During this early stage of settlement, most Chinese people in Britain were single men and few Chinese women. For various reasons, including the 1914 Aliens Restriction Act and the recession in the shipping industry, there was a decline in the Chinese population in Britain. Like the Chinese population numbers experiencing a decline in Britain, Chinese in Australia experienced a similar situation when the White Australia Policy was in force. In the 1950s, there was a second wave of Chinese immigrants to Britain who were largely rural farmers from the New Territories of Hong Kong. The *Birmingham Mail* reported that during the 1950s and 1960s, major social upheaval caused a wave of mainland Chinese crossing the border into Hong Kong which led to unemployment, homelessness and poverty. This resulted in Chinese people leaving Hong Kong for Britain in search of better prospects. As Hong Kong was still a British Dependent Territory, Hong Kong Chinese were entitled to seek jobs in England. Many Chinese entered the take-away industry which led to the Chinese becoming widely dispersed (Mail, 2014). Most second-generation British Chinese people are descendants of the 1950s Chinese immigrants (Hsiao, 2020).

Hsiao noted that second-generation British Chinese children who help out in the family business and work at take-aways are positioned where cultures meet and racial confrontations are frequent. Hsiao claims that second-generation young people are confused about their identity and must contend with the "strangers' gaze" as well as parents' perspectives, who usually identify themselves with Chinese people (p. 39). Stereotypes were forced upon the second generation in their encounters with other British people including "the delicate and docile China Doll, the physically weak but intelligent yellow boy who eats strange food, sexually inferior Oriental men" (Hsiao, 2020, p. 40) resulting in a sense of inferiority. It is argued that helping out in the Chinese take-away may cause a distaste for being Chinese and drive the second-generation away from their Chineseness into assimilation into British society due to the "intensive labor, parental control and direct cultural confrontations" (Hsiao, 2020, p. 42). Hsiao does acknowledge that her research is limited to the few literary writings from second-generation British Chinese and even fewer writings from the third-generation. From this perspective, Hsiao's observations are somewhat limited and stigmatizing as she is quick to label this cohort as "catering-tainted Chinese" (p. 44) in her comparison to the "new immigrants" arriving in Britain after the late 1970s who were more highly educated, wealthier professionals.

Despite Hsiao's observations being somewhat limited, they expose elements of similarity and universal truths in the experiences of emigrant Chinese and their offspring. Pai (2005) believes that British Chinese are subject to attack because they are few in number and isolated insofar as they are geographically dispersed and have limited social contact when they retire. The dispersal of the Chinese population in Britain as well as the relatively low population numbers arguably affects their capacity to have a voice. Britain's Chinese were long seen as a silent minority in politics and wider society (The Economist, 2016). They were also perceived to be culturally inward-looking, highly dispersed and their efforts at trying to be self-sufficient only served to isolate them.

Contrary to perceptions of a voiceless minority with a static identity, Chinese people in Britain do have multi-dimensional identities. According to Parker (1995), young Chinese people in Britain have a range of identifications than a simple binary position. Most young Chinese people grow up in isolation from one another so there is little social cohesion. However, Chinese identity can be held within an inner space. The meaning of being Chinese can be relatively open rather than a single monolithic British Chinese identity. Song (1997) observed that "cultural identities are not static or unitary, and are not effectively captured by dichotomous either-or categories such as Chinese or British" (p. 351). "Although ethnic minority individuals cannot fully control the ways in which they are ethnically constructed by others" (Song, 1997, p. 357), they can adopt an interiorised sense of self and belonging.

Parker and Song (2009), in their analysis of online discussion forums produced by British Chinese young people, have found that the emergence of such media has provided wider access to the means of representation as well as the opportunity to speak for oneself, and thus, express and transform British Chinese identities. Rather than adopt a binary approach to identity formation as with the 'old' ethnicities where there was a negotiation between allegiances to Britain and past affiliations to a country of origin, the 'new' ethnicities are multi-dimensional and progressive in character. This analysis supports the notion that, given the right opportunities, ethnic Chinese in their adopted countries have the capacity for agency in the way they choose to identify.

However, identity formation is contextual and in many ways, Australian-born Chinese are uniquely different to their US and UK counterparts abroad. What seems to be common, in light of the COVID-19 pandemic, is the precariousness of ethnic Chinese sense of place. In the case of the US, on the face of it, the race-based nature of that society means that factors such as phenotype play a central role in identity formation. In the UK, it would appear that agency is strongly related to having a voice. Clearly, there is a need for further research into Chinese identity studies as contemporary reports of discrimination continue to persist. For example, the precariousness of being Chinese in the US is of concern because it relegates non-White Americans to a subservient position. When The Guardian spoke to five Black and Asian Britons in the TV industry about their experiences of discrimination, one film-maker remarked on how often British-born Chinese people are forced to pretend that English is not their first language and that they must fake a Chinese accent (Mistlin, 2021). In light of these cross-context differences, this book explores identity construction among Australian-born Chinese by critically examining the rich life experiences and practices of a small number of second or multi- generation Australian-born Chinese.

Study Participants

This book is based on the life experiences and views of 28 Chinese Australians. They ranged from second- to fourth-generation Australian-born Chinese. The youngest participant was 21 years of age and the oldest was 65 years of age. Hence, the study cohort spanned multiple decades from modern society to the advent of post-modern society. Semi-structured in-depth interviews were conducted by the first author in 2014 and 2015. The majority of participants were female—18 females and 10 males. All participants resided in Australia. Many participants were either university students or university educated and were working. Only seven participants were not tertiary-educated or had indicated that they were working in a semi-skilled capacity or were retired from the workforce.

This study was unique in targeting participants from two specific states in Australia. The objective was to determine whether location played any role in the ways in which Australian-born Chinese engaged in ethnic identity construction. Tasmania was selected for several reasons: first, the lead author had connections to the Chinese community in Hobart; second, proximity to Melbourne; and third, the population demographic in terms of cultural mix was perceived to be a contrast to that of Melbourne. Victoria was chosen purely for logistical reasons given that the first author was located in Melbourne. The regional centre of Bendigo was also targeted because there was a historically significant Chinese presence in the area. By chance, there was an opportunity to interview a participant in Darwin which also had a historically significant Chinese population. While the study cohort was not designed to represent Australian-born Chinese as a whole, it did provide a snapshot of the group in different settings.

The study participants had families who originated from China but also other places including South Africa, New Zealand, East Timor, Malaysia, and Vietnam. The common thread was that despite their families' place of origin, all participants identified as Australian-born Chinese.

It is not feasible to expect commonality based on place of birth alone. Even for those participants whose families had recently migrated from China, their idea of China may have evolved politically, economically and socially from the long-established Australian-born Chinese whose families migrated in the first half of the twentieth century. China in the 1940s was vastly different in many ways to China in the 1990s. Recent immigrants to Australia from mainland China may be different from post-World War II immigrants in terms of education, economic and political position among other factors.

Second-generation Australian-born Chinese who were born in the latter part of the twentieth century and who were participants in this study came from a range of different national backgrounds, different socio-economic circumstances or had parents who lived in a different host society prior to coming to Australia. The study cohort also included fourth-generation Australian-born Chinese of mixed ethnicity who identified as Chinese and participants whose families had initially resided in China before settling in other countries prior to migrating to Australia. There are few studies that capture this diversity and that are comparative in nature.

The first step in the recruitment process was to identify the parameters of the target population. The following parameters were outlined: potential participants must be 2nd or 3rd generation Australian-born Chinese; born after 1945; and either parents or grandparents born in China and were ethnically Chinese.

At the completion of each interview, study participants were asked to encourage others to participate in the study. There were some who did not meet the participation criteria but had seen the recruitment flyer and encouraged others from their friendship circles to volunteer for the study.

In the initial stages of this study, the focus was on both parents and grandparents being ethnically Chinese. However, these criteria would have served to limit the study and exclude those who identified as Australian-born Chinese as well as other identities. Seven of the participants were from mixed marriages but acknowledged that at least part of their identity was Chinese. Ethnicity-wise, Billie in this research also had Sri Lankan heritage; Brenda and Gabrielle had European heritage; and Doris, Faye, Heather and Holly had British heritage. Being of mixed parentage, these participants added another dimension to the way in which an Australian-born Chinese could be defined.

Semi-structured interviews were conducted in English given that all participants were born in Australia and the development of the interview questions was framed around the key research aim which was to explore how Chineseness was perceived, constructed and understood by Australian-born Chinese. The interview questions served as a guide and were not strictly adhered to due to the semi-structured nature of the interview process. This approach yielded responses that were broad and represented many perspectives.

Approximately 26 h of recordings were transcribed into text. Privacy was maintained and data was de-identified by attributing pseudonyms to each recording. After transcribing to text, the data was collated, coded and analysed. This involved colour-coding quotes into key themes in the research. The key themes centred around phenotype as an identity marker, the role of language in identity development and ways in which Chineseness was performed. Interesting and relevant quotes were further grouped around a range of topics including: marriage; relationships; customs; assimilation; Australian identity; Chinese identity; racism; language; culture; values; food; phenotype; filial piety (a sense of respecting and looking after one's parents); cultural differences; bullying; belongingness; family; generational conflict; stereotypes; strategic essentialism; education; homeland; resilience; and hybridity.

The Scope and Limitations of the Book

This study considers what 'being Chinese' means to multi-generation Australian-born Chinese in terms of how 'Chineseness' is perceived, constructed and understood. In the process of ethnic identity construction, the perceptions and actions of others both within the home and outside the home count towards this process. The extent to which external perceptions impact on self-perceptions depends upon the level of uncertainty one has about their ethnic status or role. Sometimes, it can be a real challenge to ignore collectivist constructions of ethnicity. At the same time, essentialised constructions of Chineseness may also be embraced. Historical antecedents, family circumstances, place of origin, age, generation, and length of settlement are some of the factors that shape identity construction. With all these factors to consider, identity is in a constant state of re-negotiation.

The chapters in this book on Chineseness are framed around the concepts of being, feeling and doing (Verkuyten & de Wolf, 2002). These concepts are all intertwined. To understand how second-generation and long-established Australian-born Chinese develop their identity, this study examined ethnic identity construction in terms of 'being' and 'feeling' Chinese in the context of two of the main signifiers of an ethnic group's identity—that of phenotype and ethnic language maintenance. These signifiers are seen to represent what it means to be Chinese both in terms of ethnic self-definitions as well as public perceptions.

Being Chinese is often defined in biological terms not only by phenotype but also by whether someone is born of two Chinese parents (Verkuyten & de Wolf, 2002)—thus suggesting the status of 'real' Chinese. While it is acknowledged that identity is a fluid concept, external perceptions can have a powerful influence. Under these terms, it is easy to homogenise Chineseness. However, this is problematic given the hybridised nature of identity in the postmodern age. Similarly, 'real' Chinese may be expected to have Chinese language skills and, accordingly, may be regarded as a 'fake' Chinese if one is unable to speak or understand the Chinese language. This group-defining attribute, like phenotype, is a deterministic account of Chineseness which denies personal agency and the possibility of change (Verkuyten & de Wolf, 2002).

Both signifiers were problematised but were found, in this book, to exert influence on identity construction to differing degrees. It was also found that personal agency was more of a key determinant in ethnic identity construction. Following on from this, the role of personal agency in how Chineseness is performed in everyday life was also examined. The lived experiences of Chinese Australians, this book argues, supports Bauman's (1996, p. 23) claim that 'identities can be adopted and discarded like a change of costume' and that identity is a fluid construction.

The book also explores the performance of Chineseness or 'doing' Chinese. In examining the myriad of ways in which Chineseness is enacted, one can discern some degree of agency in the choices that Australian-born Chinese make in displaying their Chineseness. The principal focus of this book centres around how Chineseness is perceived, constructed and understood by Australian-born Chinese. In addressing this question, the book examines how social and environmental factors shape identity construction and the roles of age, family circumstances, history, socio-economic conditions, location and generation in the process. In establishing the nature of Chineseness in its varied forms, how important is it as a marker of identity, if at all? Can one escape Chineseness? What new forms of hybridity are emerging?

There are relatively few studies on multi-generation Australian-born Chinese although many studies on other ethnicities. Second-generation and long-established Australian-born Chinese also have unique experiences in terms of their phenotype or visible difference that sets them apart from the mainstream or the majority Anglo-Celtic population. Their experiences may be different from those immigrant groups such as Italians who are able to physically assimilate. The Chinese were one of the few groups who were faced with legislation specifically targeted at keeping them from entering Australia and historically, being Chinese was viewed negatively during the Gold Rush period.

There are oral histories on long-established Australian-born Chinese, the most notable collection in the National Library of Australia, a culmination of the work of oral historian, Diana Giese. Other researchers like Ngan and Chan (2012) and Tan (2003) also wrote about long-established Australian-born Chinese but there are few comparative studies that look at both long-established Australian-born Chinese and the more recent Australian-born Chinese whose family origins are from the wider Chinese diaspora. In addition, there are arguably few studies that include 'mixed-race' Chinese Australians in the Australian-born Chinese category. This study is unique in that it traverses and compares multi-generation Australian-born Chinese in times of 'solid' and 'liquid' modernity.

A common theme that runs through studies of identity formation is a 'between two cultures' approach or one of identity conflicts' (Parker, 1995). Invariably, it is often the dominant identity that prevails insofar as the dominant identity has the capacity to define the 'other'. Historically, being Chinese in Australia was stigmatised in the nineteenth century and in the first half of the twentieth century. Chinese people were excluded from entry into Australia through the Immigration Restriction Act 1901. Chineseness may be perceived as a 'corporeal malediction' (Ang, 1993, p. 8) in much of the literature but this book hopes to show that being Chinese is embraced and seen as a positive virtue among multi-generation Australian-born Chinese. This book contributes to debates around essentialist and pluralist features of contemporary ethnic identities.

This book comprises six chapters flanked by an introductory chapter and a concluding chapter. Chapter two provides an historical and political context for the development of Australia's national identity from the post-World War Two period up to the present day. Australian identity directly after the Second World War continued to be influenced by the White Australia Policy. With the racialisation of national identity up until the abolition of the White Australia Policy, Australian-born Chinese had to contend with 'outsider' status and the way in which they navigated this was dependent upon situational context. As Australia's population became more culturally diverse with the advent of multicultural policies, the Chinese population not only grew in number but also grew in diversity in terms of their country of origin. How the historical and political changes in Australian society impacted on Australia's national identity allows one to understand the context in which Australian-born Chinese had to contend with in forming their own identities.

Chapter three examines the role of phenotype in the way Chineseness as an identity is constructed both in the public and private sphere. Essentialised constructions of Chineseness are contrasted with hybridised constructions of Chineseness. The chapter problematises the homogeneity of Chineseness yet recognises that stereotypes and ethnic group categories persist and inform our everyday lives. Framed around Brubaker's (2004a) *Ethnicity without groups* and Barth's (1969) *Ethnic groups and boundaries*, this chapter shows how bounded ethnic groups continue to be treated as entities and, at the same time, recognises that such ethnic boundaries are permeable. Phenotype or physical features are perpetuated and reinforced as markers of ethnic identity among Australian-born Chinese through the racialisation of identity, the perceived stigma of being Chinese, the fostering of stereotypes and being perceived as a perpetual outsider. How the individual reacts to the essentialisation of ethnic identity depends upon the intersectionality of a range of conditions and accordingly results in various outcomes of ethnic identity construction.

Chapter four examines what is arguably one of the main signifiers of an ethnic group's identity alongside phenotype, namely ethnic language retention and maintenance. Ethnic language maintenance in immigrant families may serve both a practical and a symbolic function. Language may help to facilitate intergenerational transmission of cultural practices and values between the first- and second-generation. It may also provide a level of authenticity to one's claim of ethnicity. There are two questions that arise—whether ethnic language maintenance is perceived as an important signifier of ethnic identity for first- and second-generation Chinese Australians, and whether ethnic language maintenance is less important, if at all, for third- and fourth-generations. The notion that ethnic language maintenance contributes to the successful transmission of cultural practices and values is juxtaposed against the idea that ethnic language is primarily a medium of communication between the first- and second-generation and its role is only functional in nature. This chapter also explores the role of family dynamics in ethnic language retention as well as the perceived social acceptability of parental language use and its impact on language retention or loss.

Chapter five explores the creative ways in which Chineseness is interpreted and acted out through a range of practices including the process of eating Chinese food, participation with other Chinese community members in Chinese-themed events, lifestyle choices and visits to the 'homeland'. Drawing on generational, historical, spatial and socio-economic factors, this chapter discusses seven performances: the act of sharing food; membership of Chinese community associations; participation in Chinese cultural festivals and events; ancestor worship; marriage partner choice; educational achievement; and visits to the 'homeland'. In previous chapters, key markers of identity and the extent to which these markers of identity impacted on personal constructions of identity were examined. Sense of agency plays an important role in how the individual navigates external forces when constructing their identity. Similarly, the level of agency that one has will likely impact on how Chineseness is displayed. For Bauman (1998, p. 211), 'the opportunity to pick and choose one's "true self"…has come to signify freedom". It is the activity of choosing rather than what is being chosen that matters more. This principle underlies the ways in which Chineseness is manifested in everyday life in 'White Australia'.

References

Anderson, B. R. O. G. (1991). *Imagined communities: Reflections on the origin and spread of nationalism* (Rev. and extended ed.). Verso.

Anderson, B. R. O. G. (1983). *Imagined communities: Reflections on the origin and spread of nationalism*. Verso.

Ang, I. (1993). To be or not to be Chinese: Diaspora, culture and postmodern ethnicity. *Southeast Asian Journal of Social Science, 21*(1), 1–17. https://doi.org/10.1163/030382493x00017

Ang, I. (2001). *On not speaking Chinese: Living between Asia and the West*. Routledge.

Ang, I. (2003). Together-in-difference: Beyond diaspora, into hybridity. *Asian Studies Review, 27*(2), 141–154. https://doi.org/10.1080/10357820308713372

Ang, I. (2014). Beyond Chinese groupism: Chinese Australians between assimilation, multiculturalism and diaspora. *Ethnic and Racial Studies, 37*(7), 1184–1196. https://doi.org/10.1080/01419870.2014.859287

Anthias, F. (1992). Connecting 'Race' and Ethnic Phenomena. *Sociology, 26*(3), 421–438. https://doi.org/10.1177/0038038592026003004

References

Banham, C. (2003, December 26). Children of the revolution. *Sydney Morning Herald*. Retrieved from https://www.smh.com.au/national/children-of-the-revolution-20031226-gdi1qx.html

Barth, F. (Ed.). (1969). *Ethnic groups and boundaries: The social organization of culture difference*. Little, Brown and Company.

Barth, F. (1994). Enduring and emerging issues in the analysis of ethnicity. In H. Vermeulen & C. Govers (Eds.), *The anthropology of ethnicity: Beyond 'Ethnic groups and boundaries'* (pp. 11–32). Amsterdam: Het Spinhuis Publishers.

Bauman, Z. (1998). Identity—Then, now, what for? *Polish Sociological Review, 123*, 205–216. Retrieved from http://www.jstor.org.ezproxy.lib.monash.edu.au/stable/41274679

Bauman, Z. (1996). From pilgrim to tourist—or a short history of identity. In S. Hall & P. du Gay (Eds.), *Questions of cultural identity* (pp. 18–36). London: Sage.

Benton, G., & Gomez, E. T. (2008). *Transnationalism, Economy and Identity: The Chinese in Britain, 1800–Now*. Palgrave.

Benton, G., & Gomez, E. T. (2014). Belonging to the nation: Generational change, identity and the Chinese diaspora. *Ethnic and Racial Studies, 37*(7), 1157–1171. https://doi-org.ezproxy.lib.monash.edu.au, https://doi.org/10.1080/01419870.2014.890236

Bhabha, H. K. (Ed.). (1990). *Nation and narration*. Routledge.

Brubaker, R., & Cooper, F. (2000). Beyond "identity". *Theory and Society, 29*(1), 1–47. Retrieved from http://www.jstor.org/stable/3108478

Brubaker, R. (2004a). *Ethnicity without groups*. Harvard University Press.

Brubaker, R. (2004b). In the name of the nation: Reflections on nationalism and patriotism. *Citizenship Studies, 8*(2), 115–128. https://doi.org/10.1080/1362102042000214705

Eriksen, T. H. (2010). *Ethnicity and nationalism: Anthropological perspectives* (3rd ed.). Pluto Press.

Gans, H. J. (1979). Symbolic ethnicity: The future of ethnic groups and cultures in America. *Ethnic and Racial Studies, 2*(1), 1–20. https://doi.org/10.1080/01419870.1979.9993248

Gellner, E. (1983). *Nations and nationalism*. Basil Blackwell.

Hsiao, Y.-H. (2020). "Take-away" my childhood: The second-generation British Chinese in the catering trade. *Journal of Ethnic and Cultural Studies, 7*(3), 34–47. https://doi.org/10.29333/ejecs/341

Kibria, N. (2000). Race, ethnic options, and ethnic binds: Identity negotiations of second-generation Chinese and Korean Americans. *Sociological Perspectives, 43*(1), 77–95. https://doi.org/10.2307/1389783

Le, T. K., Cha, L., Han, H.-R., & Tseng, W. (2020). Anti-Asian xenophobia and Asian American COVID-19 disparities. *American Journal of Public Health, 110*(9), 1371–1373. https://doi.org/10.2105/AJPH.2020.305846

Lo, J. (2000). Beyond happy hybridity: Performing Asian-Australian identities. In I. Ang, S. Chalmers, L. Law, & M. Thomas (Eds.), *alter/asians: Asian-Australian identities in art, media and popular culture*. Annandale: Pluto Press Australia Ltd.

Mail, B. (2014, September 20). The highs and lows of settling in city: Carl continues to look at the lives of Chinese settlers in Birmingham. Retrieved from https://www.proquest.com/newspapers/highs-lows-settling-city/docview/1563426491/se-2

McGregor, R. (2006). The necessity of Britishness: Ethno-cultural roots of Australian nationalism. *Nations and Nationalism, 12*(3), 493–511. https://doi.org/10.1111/j.1469-8129.2006.00250.x

Mistlin, A. (2021). 'I've never experienced such abject racism': What it's really like to work in TV as a person of colour. The Guardian (Online), Guardian News & Media Limited. Retrieved from https://www.proquest.com/docview/2605428391/19CF630A39ED4D30PQ/1?accountid=12528

Ngan, L.L.-S., & Chan, K.-b. (2012). *The Chinese face in Australia: Multi-generational ethnicity among Australian-born Chinese*. Springer.

Noble, G., Poynting, S., & Tabar, P. (1999). Youth, ethnicity and the mapping of identities: Strategic essentialism and strategic hybridity among male Arabic-speaking youth in South-Western Sydney. *Communal/plural, 7*(1), 29–44.

Pai, H.-H. (2005). Comment & Debate: Isolated and vulnerable: The Chinese in Britain do well at school, but that does not mean our lives aren't afflicted by racism. *The Guardian*. Retrieved from https://www.proquest.com/newspapers/comment-debate-isolated-vulnerable-chinese/docview/246353206/se-2

Parker, D. (1995). *Through different eyes: The cultural identity of young Chinese people in Britain*. Ashgate Publishing Ltd.

Parker, D., & Song, M. (2009). New ethnicities and the Internet: Belonging and the negotiation of difference in multicultural Britain. *Cultural Studies, 23*(4), 583–604. https://doi.org/10.1080/09502380902951003

Pieterse, J. N. (1994). Globalisation as hybridisation. *International Sociology, 9*(2), 161–184. https://doi.org/10.1177/026858094009002003

Rosenthal, D. A., & Feldman, S. S. (1992a). The nature and stability of ethnic identity in Chinese youth: Effects of length of residence in two cultural contexts. *Journal of Cross Cultural Psychology, 23*(2), 214–227. Retrieved from http://search.proquest.com/docview/57767453?accountid=12528

Song, M. (1997). 'You're becoming more and more English': Investigating Chinese siblings' cultural identities. *Journal of Ethnic and Migration Studies, 23*(3), 343–362. https://doi.org/10.1080/1369183x.1997.9976596

Sorrell, K., Khalsa, S., Ecklund, E. H., & Emerson, M. O. (2019). Immigrant identities and the shaping of a racialized American self. *Socius: Sociological Research for a Dynamic World, 5*, 1–12. https://doi.org/10.1177/2378023119852788

Tan, C. (2003). Living with 'difference': Growing up 'Chinese' in white Australia. *Journal of Australian Studies, 27*(77), 101–108.

The Economist. (2016). Raise the red lantern; the Chinese in Britain. *The Economist, November 5*(421), 25–49.

Tuan, M. (2002). Second-generation Asian American identity: Clues from the Asian ethnic experience. In P. G. Min (Ed.), *The second generation: Ethnic identity among Asian Americans* (pp. 209–237). Altamira Press.

Verdery, K. (1994). Ethnicity, nationalism, and state-making: Ethnic groups and boundaries: Past and future. In H. Vermeulen & C. Govers (Eds.), *The anthropology of ethnicity: Beyond 'Ethnic groups and boundaries'* (pp. 33–58). Amsterdam: Het Spinhuis Publishers.

Verkuyten, M., & De Wolf, A. (2002). Being, feeling and doing: Discourses and ethnic self-definitions among minority group members. *Culture & Psychology, 8*(4), 371–399. Retrieved from https://search.proquest.com/docview/60454240?accountid=12528

Wang, C., Wang, J., & Lin, M. (2021). COVID-19 and Asian phobia: Anti-Asian racism and model minority myth. *New Waves, 24*(2), i–iv. Retrieved from https://www.proquest.com/scholarly-journals/covid-19-asian-phobia-anti-racism-model-minority/docview/2603457789/se-2

Chapter 2
White Australia: Nationalism and National Identity

Nationalism is one of the key features of modern society—it has the capacity to define who we are, where we belong and who we belong with. It also has the power to exclude. Nationalism, coupled with a collective national identity and a strong sense of belonging can lead to a sense of obligation to other members within the same community (Moran, 2005a). Individuals can become quite protective of their community by resisting any attempts to change its national identity, that is, its cultural traditions, history, beliefs, and qualities of character and inherited way of life (Parekh, 2008). Australian national identity has long been shaped by its colonial past. Up until the end of the Second World War and prior to the onset of migration from non-British countries to Australia, the majority population was likely to have had a common British ancestry. It wasn't until post-World War Two changes in immigration policies and the introduction of multiculturalism as official government policy in Australia that there was a shift away from a predominantly British-oriented population and hence, a challenge towards Australia's inherently 'white' identity. Yet, despite several decades of multiculturalist policies in Australia, there still appears to be resistance society towards altering the conception of a 'white' Australian identity.

Historically, Australia's national identity was inherently race-based. This book focuses on twentieth century events up until the present day. However, it is important to acknowledge that the history of 'white' settlement from 1788 was peppered with acts of domination including the subjugation of indigenous Australians, the introduction of slave labour among South Sea Islanders and riots against Chinese on the goldfields. Bearing this in mind, it is not surprising that up until the end of the Second World War, Australia's population was predominantly Anglo-Celtic in origin with 99% being 'white' and 96% claiming British and Irish ancestry (Colic-Peisker, 2011). With a common British ancestry, Australia's mainstream population was relatively homogeneous. Ethnic minority groups did not figure prominently in the national psyche at the time. With the advent of multiculturalism as official government policy, ethnic minority communities proliferated and multiculturalism became a key feature of Australia's national identity (Moran, 2011) and ethnicity became a core aspect of this identity. At the same time, Australia's racialised and racist past weighs heavily on Australia's culturally diverse present (Stratton, 2006) and therefore warrants discussion. This chapter examines the concept of nationalism, how this is manifested in Australia, the notion of 'whiteness' as a part of Australia's national identity and the impact of cultural diversity on Australia's sense of self. Other related questions are why national identities are formed in the first place and why Australia's national identity is so inherently 'white'. To properly understand and contextualise the construction of national identity, one must consider the driving forces behind national identity formation as well as the historical context and the depth of influence that Australia's past has had on its identity formation. Other forces that shape national identity including the power of government action and policy as well as popular culture will also form part of this discourse. This chapter provides a contextual base upon which to understand how long-established Australian-born Chinese and younger Australian-born Chinese formulate their identities over the course of time. It also demonstrates how important historical antecedents are in shaping one's present and one's future as well as the importance of reflecting on the dominant position of the host society as it influences the ways those outside that group formulate their identities.

Nationalism and National Identity

> Nationalism is a discursive formation that gives shape to the modern world. It is a way of talking, writing, and thinking about the basic units of culture, politics, and belonging that helps to constitute nations as real and powerful dimensions of social life. (Calhoun, 2007, p. 27)

At its best, nationalism, as a key feature of modern and postmodern democracies, provides solidarity and recognition. At its worst, it can be used to justify crimes against humanity. Historically, religious and monarchical systems defined the 'old' communities and battles were fought in defence of these systems. These feudal societies were also agrarian communities that to some extent were not unitary in nature. According to Gellner (2006), the shift away from agrarian society to an industrialised society coincided with the emergence of nationalism. For Gellner (2006, p. 132), cultural homogeneity, literacy and anonymity are key traits of nationalism:

> culturally homogeneous, based on a culture striving to be a high (literate) culture … large enough to sustain the hope of supporting the educational system which can keep a literate culture going … their populations are anonymous … the individual belongs to them directly, in virtue of his cultural style, and not in virtue of nested sub-groups.

As Elder (2007, p. 24) confirms 'nationalism resulted from "the organisation of human groups into large, centrally educated, culturally homogenous units".' With the organisation of groups into culturally homogenous units and with political authority in the hands of a large and well-centralized state 'which monopolizes legitimate culture' (Gellner, 2006, p. 134), the development of a central, homogenised national identity seemed an inevitable outcome.

When nationalism originated is debatable. The issue of importance here though is not when nationalism emerged but what impact it has had on the formation of a nation state and on national identity which is embedded within it. Some believe that nationalism and nationalist sentiment first emerged in modern times while others, such as Benedict Anderson, believed that the emergence of nationalism was evident in Western Europe during the eighteenth century. Anderson's (1991) *Imagined Communities* is regarded by some as a seminal work on the rise and spread of nationalism (Reid, 1985; Sears, 1994). However, critics considered it an 'evocative' work that 'relies more on highly subjective interpretations of nationalist poetry than on statistics of social mobilization' (Haas, 1986). Despite this, Anderson attempts to explain how nationalism has evolved and spread globally. He points out that 'since World War II every successful revolution has defined itself in national terms' (Anderson, 2006, p. 2). To conceptualise the origin and spread of nationalism, Anderson defined nation as 'an imagined political community', imagined because 'members of even the smallest nations will never know most of their fellow members ... yet in the minds of each lives the image of their communion' (Anderson, 2006, p. 6). Furthermore, it is a community because 'the nation is always conceived as a deep, horizontal comradeship' (Anderson, 2006, p. 7). For Anderson, nations are constructed rather than a given and its citizens share a common imaginary or a common set of stories that fosters a connection with shared values where they might not actually exist (Elder, 2007). The essence of what nationalism is about, as represented by Anderson's *Imagined Communities*, seems to be defined not so much by the existence of physical borders but by the privilege of sharing common stories. Thus, while the citizens of Australia may all live on the same continent, it may not necessarily follow that they all share the same common stories.

In Australia's case, the narratives of Australians descended from the British played an important role in nation formation. According to Elder (2007, p. 26), 'nationalism is ... the belief that citizens of an Australian nation will share a common understanding of being Australian, and that this understanding—seen to have historical roots—bonds them together in a common love for their shared nation. Over time, the dominant story or representational codes become naturalized and come to stand as common-sense'. Based on the principle that story-telling is instrumental in defining who we are and that these stories result in a shared history, it follows then that we have the capacity to have a shared identity or a national identity. In Australia, the creation of stories, myths and symbols has been a central way in which being Australian is expressed. For Elder (2007), ideas of being Australian are invented and these inventions are centred on a desire for the land and a fear of others taking over the land. Moreover, stories about being Australian are produced in relation to space and in contrast to others being either different or the same. In a basic sense, the Australian identity is focused on land ownership with a strong desire to uphold ownership by keeping different others at arm's length. Elder (2007, p. 16) remarked that, 'many of the dominant stories of being Australian reflect a white diasporic loyalty, that is, many of the strongest cultural, political, economic and military alliances Australia has in this globalising world are with other "white" nations…transnational loyalties among populations that subscribe to the kinship of whiteness.' For example, Australia continues to foster ties with Britain both in its allegiance with the Queen via the Governor-General and through its institutional structures. Australia also has military allegiances with both Britain and the US. While both these nations are multicultural in nature, it is the values and stories of their dominant white culture that seems to predominate. Nationalism might help make stories of being Australian and even if these stories continue in the national psyche, such as the ANZAC tradition, they reflect the power of the story or the power of the story makers rather than the truth (Elder, 2007). The myths and legends of the Anzac and of the digger are deeply entwined in the Australian national identity and continue to be upheld each year in the national calendar (Seal, 2004).

Often, it is the powerful or those with agency who have the capacity to influence the direction in which the nation evolves. As Lin (2008, p. 1) noted, it is usually the powerful that have the 'capital and resources for constructing…advantageous identities. It (identity) presupposes certain cultural forms of knowing, acting, and orientations towards social relations.' The Australian Government is, by and large, comprised of politicians from predominantly European, Anglo-Celtic backgrounds. In Federal politics, while there are a few politicians with either an indigenous background or a cultural and linguistically diverse background, they are not in significant numbers. The media is also largely controlled by media barons with European, Anglo-Celtic backgrounds. While media representations include images of Australia as a multicultural State, it could be argued that this is tokenistic in nature. For example, Australian TV shows like "Neighbours" and "Home and Away" depict mainly European, Anglo-Celtic, English-speaking families as if this is the norm in Australia. So, in our consideration of what constitutes an Australian identity, one must always be both mindful of hegemonic influences as well as the lack of universality in the notion of an Australian identity. The same can be said in our consideration of the success or failure of multiculturalist policies in shaping a new Australian identity—government action and policies as well as the media are instrumental in this process.

For Moran (2005a, 2005b, p. 170), 'White Australia emerged as the dream of Australian nationalists in the latter half of the nineteenth century.' Historically, various governments sought to actively exclude non-European people from entering Australia. Based on a notion of racial superiority, the Australian Government implemented the Immigration Restriction Act 1901 (or what is better known as the beginning of the official White Australia Policy) to exclude non-white immigration, with a focus on Asian immigrants. This period also marked the beginning of Federation where all the colonies came together as a nation and it was also a point at which Australia could begin to define itself. The Australian Government could conceal any racist intent by introducing the Dictation Test where immigrants were required to pass a language test in any European language. This test could be applied to anyone entering Australia, but in practice, it was not generally applied to those of European background. Hence, it was by design that Australia's population remained predominantly 'white' up until the mid-twentieth century.

How 'White' is Australia?—The Racialisation of Australian National Identity

> The genesis of an Australian national identity dates back to the time of early European settlement whereby influences on the developing culture at that time comprised a composite of British or Anglo-Saxon heritage. (Craven & Purdie, 2005, p. 3)

Australia's national identity has been largely shaped by its colonial past, its ties with Britain, as well as the myths and symbols that have arisen from its colonial and British past. Originally based on the doctrine of *terra nullius*, Australian identity was founded on the subjugation of the Indigenous land owners and an overwhelming desire to distance itself from its Asian neighbours and other non-Europeans. While it is beyond the scope of this book to focus on the position of Indigenous Australians in the discourse on Australian national identity, it is important to acknowledge the racial inequities that figured so prominently in the early development of this settler society. This chapter demonstrates how 'race' continued to play a significant role in Australia's identity formation throughout its short history as a settler society.

Australia was arguably one of only a few nations in the world settled by Europeans that enacted legislation to exclude potential immigrants based on physical characteristics, namely race or more specifically skin colour. The White Australia Policy as a national immigration policy also remained unchallenged until the 1960s (Batrouney & Goldlust, 2005). By the end of the nineteenth century and as a consequence of the Gold Rush period, there were 30,000 Chinese in Australia but between 1901 and 1947, that figure had depleted to 6900 due in part to natural attrition but mainly due to legislation. Fear of polluting 'white' Australia was evident as early as the nineteenth century as illustrated in depictions of Chinese people in 'The Bulletin'. In 1886, the ugly threat of Chinese invasion was exemplified by the 'Mongolian Octopus'—not only was there a fear of disease and vice, there was also a fear of the Chinese polluting the purity of the 'white race' as well as its morality (Fig. 2.1).

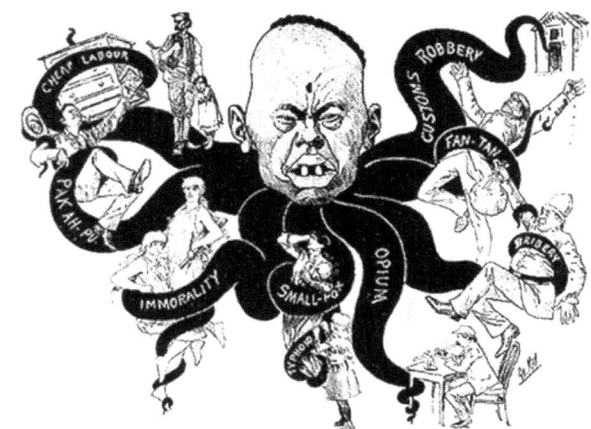

Fig. 2.1 The Mongolian Octopus. *Source* May, 1886, *The Mongolian Octopus—his grip on Australia*, *The bulletin*. National Library of Australia. Retrieved September 13, 2023, from http://nla.gov.au/nla.obj-507911285

Ronald (1901), the Labour Member for Southern Melbourne at the time, spoke on the effect that contact with 'inferior' races would have upon white women:

> We do not object to these aliens because of their colour. We object to them because they are repugnant to us from our moral and social stand-points … I want to say, however that our intention in regard to these alien races is perfectly honourable, and that we have no racial hatred or antipathy towards them. We wish them all well; we desire to do them good, but we do not believe that by allowing them to come among us we shall do anything to elevate them. It is just like that which very often happens. Some pure-minded, noble woman marries some degenerate debauchee, with the hope of reclaiming him; but the almost inevitable result is that the man drags her down to his level. So with these inferior races.

Racist propaganda was not just confined to the Chinese. Southern Europeans, in particular, Southern Italians were differentiated from other Italians on the basis of skin colour. Where Chinese were depicted as the Yellow Peril, Southern Italians were assessed as 'black' by some immigration officials in their enforcement of the Immigration Restriction Act 1901 and therefore, excluded from entry in the early twentieth century. The following images negatively portray both Chinese and Southern Italians (Fig. 2.2):

The way 'whiteness' was assessed was also highly controversial. Pugliese (2002) noted the dubious nature in which immigration officials used 'apartheid screening practices' in their assignation of race and to keep Australia white. One litmus test for whiteness was based on the cuticles of fingernails and another test of whiteness was the colour of one's backside. The body was effectively segmented into parts and the assessment of whiteness became a highly subjective one. This was

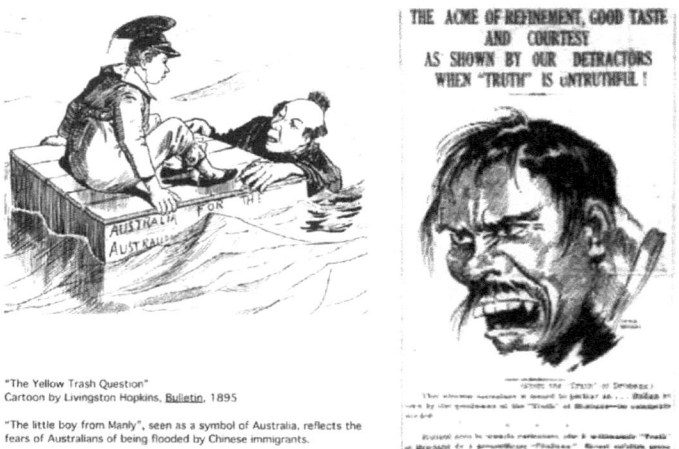

Fig. 2.2 Portrayal of Chinese. *Source* Hopkins (1895), The yellow trash question, *The Bulletin*. National Library of Australia. Retrieved September 13, 2023, from http://nla.gov.au/nla.obj-490 373413; and Bresson (1932, June 4). The acme of refinement, good taste and courtesy as shown by our detractors when "truth" is untruthful!. *Il Giornale Italiano* (Sydney, NSW: 1932–1940), p. 1. National Library of Australia. Retrieved September 13, 2023, from http://nla.gov.au/nla.news-article83028371

also evident in the determination of whiteness by officials towards the Aboriginal population when deciding whether children should be removed from their families and shipped to institutions to be assimilated into 'white' society. The use of calipers to measure different parts of the body and the use of colour filters to identify exact colouration was also noted (Pugliese, 2002). Discrimination was not just about skin colour—religious preference was also a source of discrimination, as was evident with negative sentiments expressed against Irish Catholics and Jews. In recent times, this discrimination has manifested again with people of Islamic faiths being targeted in the media. It is, however, fair to say that discrimination based on physical features was and continues to be an easily identifiable source of division.

It was by racial exclusion that the Australian population remained predominantly Anglo-Celtic up until the end of World War II (Colic-Peisker, 2011). After the Second World War, Australia was compelled to introduce immigration from non-English speaking countries because it could neither sustain its population nor its economy from British migration alone. Immigrants from ethnically 'white' countries such as the Netherlands, Italy and Greece were still the preferred options as opposed to those from Asia. Assimilation to the Australian way of life was still the driving force up until at least the abolition of the White Australia Policy. It was the fear of an 'Asian invasion' that was the original impetus for the White Australia Policy, a policy primarily focused on assimilation.

Britishness was central to Australian identity and it was the only source of myths, memories and symbols that could lay the foundations for a nation (McGregor, 2006). Citing Smith (1986), author of 'The ethnic origins of nations', McGregor (2006, p. 499) declared that 'no "nation-to-be" can survive without a homeland or a myth of common origins and descent'. Further, 'Australians gloried in their possession of a "British soul"', particularly in the Federation era which was a crucial period of nation-building. This was reinforced at the time of Federation by Henry Parkes who declared that 'the crimson thread of kinship runs through us all'. Australia's civic institutions were modelled on the British system and colonial governments sought to establish British culture and promote British norms of behaviour (Mason, 2010). Today, ties with Britain remain as Australians continue to celebrate the bestowal of Queens Birthday awards and the Royal family attracts much attention from both the public and the media. Australians who had parents or grandparents of British origin were also given rights to residency in the UK. Robertson (2011, p. 1338) noted that one of Benedict Anderson's arguments 'with respect to nationalism is that it has been through extensive "networking" often across long distances that nationalist sentiments have been created.' As long as ties with Britain can be maintained, whether it is via citizenship rights or reverence towards and identification with British customs and traditions, the British influence on Australian nationalist sentiments may continue.

British immigrants came from a range of ethnic identities including English, Scottish and Irish but these became an 'amalgamated Britishness' in Australia, thereby fostering a collective identity (Ref?). There are various reasons for this amalgamation and one of these might have been the fact that these groups were similar in terms of culture (ie cultural closeness as opposed to cultural distance). It could also have been the geographical isolation from the 'homeland' and the need to derive unity as a protective mechanism against the threat of Asia. Proximity to the 'yellow peril' served to strengthen Australians' sense of their British heritage in the face of a perceived threat from their Asian neighbours (McGregor, 2006). The effect of promoting this 'consolidated ethnic Britishness' was to racialise Australian nationalism. Race became a defining feature of Australian nationhood. The introduction of the Dictation Test and the White Australia Policy were specifically designed to curb the number of Asians arriving in Australia.

Until World War II, the source of the Asian threat came mainly from Japan with its modernisation, its military domination of the Western Pacific and its increasing recognition on the world stage illustrated by its presence at international conferences (Meaney, 1995). This fear of invasion was compounded by Japan's advancement across Asia during World War II—the 'Yellow Peril' was too close for comfort and in the decade or so after World War II, Australia adopted a restrictive immigration policy based on a principle of 'populate or perish' to preserve its 'white' British character. Australia's race-based policy drew criticism from other countries, particularly in Asia which resulted in a shift away from the language of race to one of assimilation and culture. Despite this shift in language, sentiments were still firmly rooted in the preservation of a mono-cultural 'white' Australia.

It was not until the end of the 1960s when there was an Allied withdrawal from the Asian region that Australia was forced to concede that its 'home' was neighbouring Asia. In 1971, Prime Minister John Gorton introduced the idea of a 'multi-racial society' and declared to the Singaporeans:

> I think if we build up gradually inside Australia a proportion of people who are not of white skin, then as that is gradually done, so there will be a complete lack of consciousness of difference between races. (Meaney, 1995, p. 182)

The Whitlam and Fraser governments continued to embrace this 'multi-racial' and 'multicultural' focus and by the 1980s, Asian migrants represented more than one third of the total intake. While multiculturalist policies were embraced during this time, there was still some confusion about what it meant, whether it represented a tolerance of minority cultures or whether it meant that all cultures were equal (Meaney, 1995). As previously mentioned, the huge influx of Asians also attracted several critics including Geoffrey Blainey and John Howard who expressed concerns over Australia's social cohesion. The language again shifted back to respect for a set of 'common values' but there was some confusion about what these were. Further discussion on the embracement of a multicultural agenda and its impact will follow but the point to be made here is that it had the effect of highlighting race and cultural differences and at the same time, creating a sense of unease around its purported effect on national unity.

Despite the abolition of the White Australia Policy, politicians and prominent others, in recent times, have espoused negative views about specific ethnic groups, at the same time declaring that they are not racist. Pauline Hanson, in her maiden speech to Parliament in 1996 declared:

> Immigration and multiculturalism are issues that this government is trying to address, but for far too long ordinary Australians have been kept out of any debate by the major parties. I and most Australians want our immigration policy radically reviewed and that of multiculturalism abolished. I believe we are in danger of being swamped by Asians. Between 1984 and 1995, 40 per cent of all migrants coming into this country were of Asian origin. They have their own culture and religion, form ghettos and do not assimilate. Of course, I will be called racist but, if I can invite whom I want into my home, then I should have the right to have a say in who comes into my country. A truly multicultural country can never be strong or united ("Pauline Hanson's, 1996 maiden speech", 2016).

While Pauline Hanson tried to distance herself from being labelled a 'racist', she nonetheless espoused views against multiculturalism in the belief that Asians were different from 'ordinary Australians', effectively, racialising the multiculturalism debate. By creating an 'us' and 'them' dichotomy, one is effectively creating an environment of inclusion and exclusion, a place of belonging or not, and in this case, based on race.

While legislation protects citizens from race-based discrimination, it cannot prevent individuals from thinking about racial differentiation or even feeling racially superior over others. There are politicians that would engage in race denial to further their arguments when targeting particular communities. Pauline Hanson, for example, argued that the fabric of Australian society was being eroded by the large influx of 'Asians'. The removal of young indigenous Australians from their families was built on the premise that they would have a better life if they were assimilated with the 'white' Australian community, the benchmark for 'normality'. The social welfare argument was used when, it could be argued, it was clearly a matter of racial politics. John Howard, when he was Prime Minister of Australia, refused to issue a formal apology to Indigenous Australians for the policy of removing Indigenous children from their families possibly because he did not believe that an apology was warranted. Tascon (2008, p. 255) states that 'race as a distinct discourse that has a history of harm associated with it, in the Australian context, has been silenced as a lens for analysis in the everyday, and appears in places where its association with harm and discrimination are distanced and abstracted.' Given that Australia was founded as a 'white man's country' (Lake, 2003, p. 346), that it enacted legislation to exclude non-white immigration and that politicians draw on racial categories yet deny that race is the primary issue, it is difficult to accept that race does not matter when it comes to defining the Australian national identity.

Race difference also manifests itself in seemingly innocuous yet powerful ways in what Tascon (2008, p. 255) calls a 'blindness to white privilege'. Tascon (2008) analysed interviews that had been conducted with volunteers and activists who had either provided assistance to or were politically lobbying for refugees at the time of the 'boat people' crisis in Australia from 1999 to 2002. Tascon (2008, p. 257) found that even these volunteers who had sought to help others were blind towards 'their own racialised privilege and others' under-privilege' and maintained a sense of goodness by the privilege of 'pretending'. In other words, their privileged position was taken for granted and normalised because it had been built into the fabric of the nation-state, a nation-state founded on 'whiteness'.

The benchmark for 'normality' seems to be related to race or in Western settler democracies, 'whiteness'. Baz Luhrmann's 2008 film *Australia* was examined for its racialised discourse on Australian national identity (Hogan, 2010). In her analysis, Hogan found that the film reinforced the image of the 'white' man as embodying Australianness and that this white male image continues to dominate the national imaginary when it comes to defining Australianness. It is universally accepted that figures like the digger, the Man from Snowy River, Crocodile Dundee, and Don Bradman represent Australianness. Luhrmann's film also used negative Asian stereotypes which only served to reinforce Asian 'otherness' (Hogan, 2010). While this film is a work of fiction, it still serves to reinforce existing stereotypes in the national imaginary. Moreton-Robinson (2005) commented on both the 'perseverance of a white national identity' in Australia as well as the nation being created as a 'white' possession. She also remarks on the racialisation of Britishness whereby the different ethnicities of the English, Irish, Scottish and Welsh are melded into one 'white' race. Significantly, this blanket of 'whiteness' masks the heterogeneity of Britishness and, at the same time, serves to strengthen the solidarity of British roots as a foundation for Australian national identity which is explored in the following section.

What Is Australia's National Identity?

> National identity is not a fixed property assigned at birth but an emergent and constantly evolving sense of what it means to be Australian (Jones, 1997, p. 302)

National identity is indeed a dynamic concept that is subject to change depending upon current circumstances (Walsh & Karolis, 2008). It is also a highly subjective concept whose definition is dependent upon who one asks. It may include a commitment to parliamentary democracy, rule of law, individual freedom, freedom of speech, religious tolerance, equality of opportunity (Jones, 1997), sporting prowess and diversity (Purdie & Wilss, 2007). However, its features are variable—for instance, values of religious tolerance and equality of opportunity are more likely to be upheld in good economic times rather than in economic downturns (Jones, 1997). In the previous section, it was established that one of the key characteristics of the Australian national identity was its 'whiteness'. While national identity is a highly subjective concept, in the Australian context, it could be argued that 'whiteness' as one of the features of Australian identity is a given.

Only a few empirical studies on how Australians construct their identities have been published (Jones, 1997). While there is no one model that is definitive, they each bring one somewhat closer to identifying some of the parameters of identity formation. One of these was Phillips (1996) who developed a Durkheimian fourfold-typology based on two dimensions: friends/enemies and internal/external to conceptualise the symbolic boundaries of the Australian national community. Phillips (1996) investigated the relationship between one's emotional attachment to Australian national community and one's attitude towards monarchism, aboriginality and multiculturalism. He also suggested three factors of influence: socio-demographic location; political orientation and exposure to civil discourse. Phillips (1996) found that the four-fold model was confirmed—that social categories of 'internal friends', 'external friends', 'internal enemies' and 'external enemies' existed. He also found that Australians who were right-wing, strongly religious, older, less educated, identified strongly with a political party, paid little attention to politics and watched more television were more likely to have a strong attachment to symbolic boundaries of the Australian national community and this, in turn, influenced their attitudes towards national issues like multiculturalism and Aboriginal assistance.

One of the enduring images of what 'real Australia' is seems to emanate from the bush (Moran, 2005a, 2005b). Characters such as Crocodile Dundee, the Jolly Swagman, Ned Kelly and the Digger represent a stereotype of the quintessential Aussie bloke who is a bit of a larrikin, has strong ties to the land and who possesses a bit of a fighting spirit. These images are reinforced in our social lives through literature and the creative arts. While they may not be the only images depicting an 'Australian', these imaginings are real on the world stage. Tranter and Donoghue (2007) examined colonial and post-colonial figures such as convicts, free settlers, bushrangers and ANZACs to see if they were associated with national identity in Australia. Unlike other Australian empirical research on national identity, Tranter and Donoghue (2007) adopted an approach grounded in history and investigated the link between actual individuals or groups to national identity as opposed to the use of abstract concepts such as how important it was to be born in Australia as a measure of 'attachment' to Australia. The relevance of these actual individuals or groups to one's understanding of Australia has also been reinforced in our everyday lives through events such as media coverage of sportspeople and sports, annual commemoration of ANZAC Day and Gallipoli, and media idolisation of Ned Kelly. Tranter and Donoghue (2007) found that ANZACs and sporting heroes were very important influences in the way Australians saw themselves. Some Australians are or were related to a digger and some claim to have convict ancestry, whether real or imagined. What is important to note is that these figures are all quintessentially 'white' and they continue to endure despite the cultural and ethnic shift in the population.

It may be fair to say that, at least, up until the end of the Second World War, many Australians shared a common history and could identify with bush characters such as the Swagman and Ned Kelly. Many 'white' Australians had relatives or forebears who either fought in the world wars, came off the land or were transported to Australia from Britain as either convicts or settlers. It is this collective identity that ties communities together and that continues to persist in the Australian psyche. Phillips and Smith (2000) asked their study participants to think about and identify what they considered to be 'Australian' and why they made such choices. They found that traditional, past-oriented symbols and images of Australia featured prominently in what the participants chose to represent 'Australianness', for example, older white men associated with politics, sport, business and culture industries, the CWA and the RSL, rural imagery, the barbecue and mateship. These symbols and images seem to emanate from personal experiences and popular culture. Smith and Phillips (2001) also found that to be 'unAustralian', you had to be 'Australian' first. In addition, 'unAustralian' meant things were 'either a violation of norms of civility and natural justice and/or are a 'foreign' influence on Australian culture' (Smith & Phillips, 2001, p. 335). Pauline Hanson, a right-wing populist Senator, was deemed 'unAustralian' as were ethnic groups, the Sydney Gay and Lesbian Mardi Gras, Chinatown and Americanisation.

The idea about being 'unAustralian' is a relatively recent phenomenon that has been used by some politicians and media personalities to target elements of individual or group behaviour. It has become one of the defining traits of what it means to be an 'Australian'. It has also become linked to one's ethnicity. Smith and Phillips (2001) considered the likelihood of ethnic groups being stigmatised as 'unAustralian' despite many years of multicultural policies. This was evidenced in events such as the 2005 Cronulla riots and in attitudes towards Muslims after the 9/11 attack. Two powerful driving forces in the perpetuation of a 'white' Australian identity and in the condemnation of 'unAustralian' acts have been the government and the media. According to Johnson (2007), John Howard's views on national identity included a desire to focus on Anglo-Celtic heritage or British values with an emphasis on assimilation.

As Jakubowicz (2002, p. 120) noted, 'myths have become amplified in a public sphere where government rhetoric has emphasized the corrupt elements among immigrants, drawing on graphic imagery designed to rouse antagonism and hatred.' In the media, the Cronulla riots were depicted as a struggle between two racially distinct groups and after the 9/11 attack, anti-Muslim sentiment increased exponentially to the point that it was deemed inappropriate to wear the hijab (Hebbani & Wills, 2012). Displays of ethnic intolerance may be attributed to a failure to include the stories of different ethnic groups, particularly those born outside Australia, in the national narrative. As some earlier studies have shown, being born in Australia is perceived as an important signifier of being 'truly Australian'. For example, Jones (1997) examined the extent to which Australians share a common civic culture that binds culturally diverse groups together. Jones developed five attitude scales – the first three consider what it means to be 'truly Australian; the fourth scale is on a form of nationalistic sentiment; and the fifth scale is on a group prejudice, or xenophobia, scale. What Jones (1997) found was that many of the study participants thought being born in Australia was fairly or very important (56%) and that having lived most of one's life in Australia was even more important (62%). These factors represent Australian nativism, one aspect of national identity. Affective civic culture, that is, respect for Australia's laws and institutions and feeling Australian, was another aspect of national identity that a majority of respondents (54%) was strongly committed to. A large minority of respondents (48%) strongly endorsed the third aspect of national identity, instrumental civic culture (importance of Australian citizenship and English language competence). But, is having been born in Australia or having lived most of one's life in Australia enough to secure one's place in the national imaginary? This may be so from the point of view of the individuals with Anglo-Celtic features but it may not necessarily follow from those individuals with phenotypically different features from the mainstream.

Studies have supported the view that Australian national identity is inherently race-based. In the last decade, other studies have encapsulated multiculturalism or cultural pluralism as a feature of national identity. For Smits (2011), national identity is characterised by cultural and ethnic diversity and is constructed in civic terms such as a commitment to common political principles, institutions and processes rather than by membership in a homogeneous ethnic community. Smits argued that cultural pluralism is consistent with a strong civic national identity that includes a commitment to political institutions and processes, social justice and egalitarianism values and the value of diversity as a public good. Moran (2011) claimed that for national identity to support multiculturalism, it must be dynamic and changing and involve ongoing discussion about national traditions. For Moran (2011), 'Australia is a new nation' and is marked by 'status anxieties' around its 'newness'. With the shift from a predominantly white, British Australia to a diverse, multi-ethnic society, it is important for Australians to engage in ongoing self-reflection about national identity. Tyrrell (2007) also reflected on the importance of direct involvement in the politics of the national state and its governance, either as participants or spectators, for the preservation of national identity in culturally diverse societies. With more groups engaged in political participation, there is less likely to be 'deep cultural homogeneity – or overt national symbolism' (Tyrrell, 2007, p. 520).

Studies on perceptions of national identity among Australia's youth are also indicative of the changing focus of Australia's national identity including the seeming shift away from 'traditional' race-based imagery (Purdie & Wilss, 2007). Purdie and Wilss (2007) invited 242 students from eight primary and secondary schools in one Australian state to write a small essay describing what they thought it meant to be an Australian. They found that nine distinct themes of what it means to be Australian had emerged—national well-being; personal well-being; democracy; agreeableness of personal characteristics; uniqueness and diversity of environment; sporting prowess; rules of citizenship; diversity; and lifestyle. A sense of national well-being in terms of national security and national prosperity was the most frequently mentioned aspect of being Australian which, according to Purdie and Wilss (2007), is an expanded pluralist view as opposed to a traditional theme.

McLeod and Yates (2003), on the other hand, explored the political beliefs and positioning around racism, national identity and the notion of 'other' developed by secondary school students of varying ethnic and class backgrounds and argued that reasoning behind race, national identity and othering as well as political beliefs were linked to identity formation and to how we imagine ourselves. Several key events in the 1990s served to highlight the focus on race and national identity including the Mabo decision, the Stolen Generations, and the emergence of Pauline Hanson and the One Nation Party. McLeod and Yates (2003) also noted 'a heritage of belief that Australia is properly a white nation' and that 'being white is a kind of invisible, unmarked, yet normative identity'. They were interested in how the students would position themselves and 'others' as white and how political debates on race and nationalism would impact on them. From the interviews conducted, some Anglo-Australian students perceived Aboriginal people as less 'other' than migrants or of having a greater claim to the nation. This is in comparison to one student from a migrant background who perceived Aboriginal people as the most 'other'. This sense of who was more properly Australian appeared to be related to a historical sense of 'already being there'.

Based on these studies, there appears to be a shift in how Australia's national identity is perceived and this is influenced by a range of factors. National identity is indeed a dynamic term and it may be characterised by a range of symbols and images that are rooted in the history and traditions of the dominant culture but it can also be influenced by personal experiences. As the population demographic changes, so too can the concept of national identity and it is important to actively engage in dialogue and debate on what constitutes identity and belonging in current contexts. One characteristic that continues to emerge in the construction of an Australian identity is the notion of 'whiteness' and this particular characteristic of the Australian identity has been reinforced by politicians and the media, both past and present. Seemingly, 'white' Australia is still a presence in our everyday lives and therefore, there will be ongoing consideration of the evolution of a 'white' Australia and the extent of its applicability in modern life. It could be argued that, to some extent, the impact of cultural diversity on the construction of Australian national identity has been somewhat stalled by the powerful 'white' imaginary reinforced by the dominant culture. The next section will consider the role that multiculturalism has played in shaping Australia's national identity and the possible barriers posed by the dominance of white 'Anglo-Australianness'.

Multiculturalism: Friend or Foe?

> Multiculturalism requires all involved to participate in a challenging context of diversity, learning about and tolerating each other's differences, but also engaging across the differences (Nye, 2007, p. 114).

Being one of the most homogeneous, European countries in the world up until the end of the Second World War, immigration from 'non-white' countries served to challenge the 'white' hegemony and with changes in the ethnic and cultural mix over the next forty years or so, the question of what constituted an Australian identity was paramount. In the 1970s, the introduction of multiculturalist policies in Australia saw a shift away from a policy of assimilation towards a policy of fostering cultural diversity, promoting social justice and political engagement for all Australians (Hogan, 2009). Multiculturalist policies and services also grew out of the failure of assimilation attempts in the 1960s (Castles, 1992). The success of multiculturalism, however, was dependent upon mutual respect and tolerance—some might argue that it was difficult to achieve such success in Australian society given its history of intolerance towards the 'Other'. However, according to Wiley et al. (2008), the endorsement of multicultural ideology can moderate the impact that others' views of a group can have on one's own views.

While Jakubowicz (2002, p. 120) stated that 'Australians have a long history of fear of invasion', the irony is that Australia's settler roots were grounded by invasion resulting in the decimation of the Aboriginal population. According to Jupp (1997, p. 30), 'Australian multiculturalism grew out of immigrant settlement, was not concerned with Aborigines...and was primarily concerned with social justice and social harmony rather than with the preservation of ethnic differences.' While Australian multiculturalism was not concerned with the plight of Aborigines, the degree of its success as a policy was directly influenced by Australia's history of oppression towards the indigenous population. For Stratton (2006, p. 663), 'the weight of Australia's racialised and racist past weighs heavily on Australia's multicultural present, both in government policy and in everyday life.' In the context of this largely homogeneous background, at least in terms of 'race', it was not surprising that the onset of multiculturalist policies as well as the change in the population mix would raise mixed emotions and possibly cause an identity crisis. Despite this, it was not until the introduction of multiculturalist policies that Australia's inherently 'white' identity started to be challenged at the national level.

It is generally agreed that multiculturalism in settler societies is an inevitable outcome. Colic-Peisker and Farquharson (2011) identified four aspects of multiculturalism: first, it is a demographic reality; second, it is an ideology that recognises ethnic diversity; third, it refers to the policies that manage cultural diversity; and, fourth, it involves the everyday practice of interacting with people from different cultural backgrounds. The extent to which society recognises and acts on these four aspects of multiculturalism will determine its success or failure. Moran (2011, p. 2168) also argued that 'diversity and multiculturalism are now key features of the national identity' alongside other features such as a commitment to a 'fair go', a commitment to civility in everyday life and commitments to equality, democracy and freedom. Multiculturalism may be an inevitable outcome and it may be a key feature of national identity but it does not necessarily follow that it will be embraced without question. As will be shown, there are a few factors that may come into play including Anglo-Celtic cultural dominance, government policy, and the condition of the global market.

The importance of having a voice or being able to share common stories is one of the main forces behind the 'success' of any group within a culturally diverse society like Australia. Australians need to continually create 'new stories of solidarity, new narratives of national identity, and explanations of what things hold them together, not simply emphasize difference and diversity' (Moran, 2011). Taylor (1994, p. 25) also argued that the need for recognition 'is one of the driving forces behind nationalist movements' and that,

> Our identity is partly shaped by recognition or its absence, often by the misrecognition of others, and so a person or group of people can suffer real damage, real distortion, if the people or society around them mirror back to them a confining or demeaning or contemptible picture of themselves. (Taylor, 1994, p. 25).

Herein lies the challenge confronted by newer arrivals to Australia, like the asylum seekers arriving by boat and people from various African nations who have escaped conflict. Mason (2010) noted that Australian multiculturalist policies have provided migrants with access to welfare and support, for example, via churches and religious establishments, as well as pathways to engage in civic society. However, articulation of migrants' past experiences and political and moral identities needs further recognition. Noble (2009) argues that there is a need for recognition across many aspects of everyday life and not just ethnicity or gender identity.

Multiculturalist policies were not without its critics and the arguments against them invariably drew on the issue of race. With the increased influx of Asian immigration associated with the Indo-Chinese refugee crisis in the late 1970s, some political conservatives disapproved of the 'Asianization' of Australia (Hogan, 2009). In the 1980s, Geoffrey Blainey, a noted historian, argued against the disproportionate preference for Asian immigration to Australia in comparison to European immigration. He commented that 'minority groups should not have the power to dictate how we should see our past and our future'. Rather than a celebration of cultural diversity, there was the perpetuation of two camps—Europeans versus the other.

For Colic-Peisker (2011, p. 565), 'multiculturalism has never been…universally accepted in liberal democracies.' And according to Ommundsen (2010), multiculturalism did not have broad popular support and was tolerated rather than embraced by much of the Australian population—ninety per cent of the population was opposed to multiculturalism when it was introduced and a 1994 poll found that 61% still disapproved of the policy. Those in favour of multiculturalism were the tertiary-educated and ethnic communities and according to Ommundsen (2010), Australian multiculturalism only flourished because of bipartisan support and post-war economic prosperity.

When economic or social circumstances change, multiculturalism can become an issue of social and political concern. This seemed evident when the job market slowed down and ethnic minorities were accused by the media of taking jobs. For example, Pauline Hanson's maiden speech used unemployment figures to fuel her argument against Asian immigration. Some also argued that immigration and multiculturalism were a threat on the welfare state. Kymlicka and Banting (2006) identified two concerns—the heterogeneity/redistribution trade-off and the recognition/redistribution trade-off. The first trade-off argues that ethnic diversity erodes the welfare state and the second trade-off argues that the way in which Western governments manage diversity through multiculturalist policies aggravates the problem. Kymlicka and Banting (2006) found very little evidence to support these hypotheses. Rather, their preliminary findings revealed that there was no relationship between the proportions of the population born overseas and social spending. There was also no evidence that countries with foreign-born populations could not sustain their social programs as well as other countries. Contrary to the notion that ethnic minorities threaten the welfare state, it could be argued that these minorities are disadvantaged by systems that do not address their needs. In recent studies on access to health services among culturally and linguistically diverse (CALD) populations, CALD people were found to have poor access to quality health services, faced multiple structural disadvantages and vulnerabilities, and faced challenges in health and social systems (Istiko et al., 2022; Khatri & Aseefa, 2022).

The role of government in determining the success or failure of policies is also fundamental. Multiculturalism is not just about the celebration of diversity – its success also hinges on how 'national politics and state management' faces the challenges and opportunities that cultural and religious diversity offers (Nye, 2007). In the 1990s, during Paul Keating's reign as Prime Minister, multiculturalism was linked to 'economic efficiency' and 'productive diversity' which stressed the market value of a diverse workforce (Joppke, 2004). Keating also emphasised the notion of Australia as being 'a part of Asia' (Jupp, 2007, p. 47). This notion was perceived as a threat to Australia's national identity which had, for a large part, been grounded in the idea of separateness from Asia. The 'old' Australia was an assimilationist and homogeneous society contrasting sharply to the 'new' Australia with its ethnic and cultural diversity. 'Ordinary' people were suddenly forced to drop their national identity, an identity founded on 'race', for one that did not embody their 'racial monopoly' (Ang & Stratton, 1998, p. 34).

In the latter part of the 1990s, Australia experienced a backlash in multiculturalism. When Pauline Hanson and the One Nation Party attracted attention in the 1990s with their racist politics, John Howard's government did not take a stand against Hanson's politics. Howard was also reluctant to embrace the term 'multiculturalism'. Multiculturalism was perceived as a threat to social cohesion—there were calls for immigrants to assimilate; the citizenship test was introduced and Anglo-Australian values were re-ignited as the core of national identity (Colic-Peisker & Farquharson, 2011). John Howard also encouraged knowledge of Australian history and tried to equate this with national inheritance (McKenna, 2009). The Howard Government also displayed a disregard of the 'Other' in its treatment of asylum seekers as highlighted by the Tampa crisis. Various Coalition MPs espoused views that demonstrated intolerance towards particular ethnic groups: Dr Brendan Nelson, the Federal Minister for Education, Science and Training at the time, was quoted in the media as saying, 'if people don't want to be Australians and they don't want to live by Australian values and understand them, well they can basically clear off' ("Accept Australian values", 2005). Nelson was referring to the Muslim population. Kevin Andrews, another Coalition MP at the time, also expressed a desire to cut immigration from Africa because of the perceived failure of Africans to integrate. Another politician, Teresa Gambarro reportedly said that new migrants should learn to use a deodorant and that they needed to learn English to avoid becoming victims of racism. When the elected governments seem more interested in assimilation and integration rather than in embracing cultural diversity, the success of multiculturalist policy is challenged. Forrest and Dunn (2010, p. 81) noted that 'Australia has in the past decade seen a decline in political support for multicultural values.'

In Australia and in recent times, many European countries have used immigration and multiculturalism as political footballs to garner support. When it is convenient for countries to extend their humanitarian hand to those in need, they will do so. However, when countries themselves face economic turmoil, there is a propensity to blame immigration and the 'others' who have entered the country. The former French president, Nicolas Sarkozy, argued for reduced immigration as part of his re-election campaign and various other politicians or political parties have espoused anti-immigration views including Marine Le Pen and the neo-Nazi group 'Golden Dawn' in Greece. As Markus, Jupp and McDonald (2009) have noted, immigration might be welcomed for economic reasons but it is also the cause of anxiety for cultural reasons. The Australian Government's treatment of asylum seekers in the last couple of decades or so reflects an arguably xenophobic fear of being invaded by the 'other'. Relative to other developed countries, Australia's asylum applications are small. It is, however, easier to shift the focus on to those who do not have a voice than to address economic woes. Kymlicka (2010, p. 106) noted two pre-conditions of multicultural citizenship—'the desecuritisation of state-minority relations and the existence of a human rights consensus'. Accordingly, when States are fearful of neighbouring enemies, they may treat their own minorities unfairly. This may in part explain the Australian government's treatment of Afghan asylum seekers and the media's portrayal of some minorities in the wake of terrorism fears in the aftermath of the 9/11 attacks.

The term 'multiculturalism' has disappeared from the Ministerial Portfolios and an emphasis has now been placed on Australian citizenship. Historically, the road to multiculturalism has not been smooth as evidenced by race debates on Asian immigration by Geoffrey Blainey in the 1980s, the backlash against multiculturalism during the 1990s with the emergence of the One Nation Party led by Pauline Hanson, and the then Prime Minister John Howard's failure to embrace the term in relation to cultural diversity. Past governments in Australia struggled with the 'boat people' crisis and in the last two decades, Australians witnessed the ugliness of the Cronulla riots, assaults on Indian students and the racist aftermath of the 9/11 attack. Given the mass media's negative portrayal of these events and ideas that ethnic difference is a threat to national unity (Jones, 1996), ethnically and culturally diverse groups in Australia would struggle to effectively use multiculturalist policy as a tool for fostering cohesion and unity. Underlying this idea of national unity is the presumption that, at least in these media portrayals, ethnically diverse groups are not members of the group that defines our national identity—a culture of us and them continues to persist. As Moran (2011) suggests, supporters of multiculturalism must engage in ongoing debates about their national identity rather than leave this to the dominant culture. This is to avoid being perpetually labelled as the 'other'.

One of the real barriers to multiculturalism is the denial of racial privilege. Multiculturalism in Australia had started off as official government policy in the 1970s to 'facilitate migrants' inclusion in Australian society, without obliging them to surrender their cultural heritage' (Mason, 2010, p. 817). It was also an opportunity to re-define Australia's national identity given that 'assimilation as a policy of integrating the minority into the majority is a failed ideology' (Wall, 2006, p. 26). Yet, it also served to highlight the differences between the Anglo-Celtic population and the ethnic 'other' because 'ordinary' or 'everyday' people did not include themselves in multiculturalism's narrative (Ang & Stratton, 1998; Tascon, 2008). Racial privilege is invisible or 'repressed' and Ang and Stratton (1998) have argued that multiculturalism in Australia does not confront this issue of 'race' and this is evident in the automatic association of multiculturalism with non-Anglo-Celtic migrants separate from the 'core culture'. In addition, Mason (2010, p. 818) noted that 'the tendency to marginalize ethnic histories within the dominant Anglo-Australian narrative is a longstanding tradition'. Denial of Anglo-cultural privilege not only differentiates the Anglo-Celtic population from the rest of society, it also results in the reinforcement of economic and social inequalities. Ethnic minorities may be misrepresented in mainstream media and Anglo Australians may be over-represented in the Australian Public Service to cite two examples (Dunn & Nelson, 2011). Thus, when one is forced into a position of 'otherness', there is an automatic hierarchical structure put in place where ethnic minorities are placed on the lower rungs and their voices are less likely to be heard.

Australia as a settler society has been dominated by European control and it is this very dominance that has shaped Australian multiculturalism. It could be argued that multiculturalism was a tool for 'white' groups to assert their superiority by having the power to manage others (Hage, 1998). Hage (1998) identified three phases in post-war immigration in Australia: expectation of assimilation; encouragement of tolerance and respect as well as access and equity; and productive diversity. For Hage (1998), white multiculturalism is about 'creating and managing an economy of otherness' or of 'fostering ethnic life and ethnic value'. This practice was presumably most pronounced during the period of the Hawke/Keating Labour Government with the rise of 'productive diversity' or the inclusion of 'economic efficiency' as a principle of multiculturalism. For Hage (1998, p. 233), 'the White nation fantasy thrives on the perception of the migrant presence as one which poses problems'. In other words, while post-war migration was driven by the need to populate and support growth in Australia's economy, 'Third-World looking migrants' were still considered separate from 'white' groups and needed to be controlled. They were relegated to a lower position or, at worst, a position of subservience. Was it a coincidence that the white population ruled? Or was race a secondary consideration? Race seems to play a significant role in the shaping of the Australian nation particularly prior to the advent of the Second World War. However, with the introduction of multiculturalist policies after the Second World War, the extent to which the race factor has played in the nation building process seems to vary. For Hage (1998), 'whiteness' seemed to have a powerful driving force for control.

Forrest and Dunn (2010) also noted an uneasy co-existence between multicultural values and the existence of racist attitudes. In the 2000s, Dunn and Nelson (2011) found widespread acknowledgment of racism in Australia. Surprisingly, non-Anglo Australians were less likely to acknowledge racism compared to those born in Australia. Furthermore, denial of racism was higher among those born in South Asia or the Middle East compared to those born in other parts of the world. There may be several explanations for this discrepancy—level of education; perception of discrimination; and social class (Forrest & Dunn, 2010), sense of citizenship and belonging; fear of criticism or of being labelled a victim among other factors. It is important to note that while there might be widespread acknowledgment of racism in Australia among the general population, there also appears to be denial of racism by governments and mainstream media (Dunn & Nelson, 2011; Jakubowicz, 2011). The Howard government denied that the Cronulla riots in 2005 were spurred on by racism and the Victorian government denied that attacks on Indian students were racist in nature.

By the twenty-first century, multiculturalism had been challenged in various ways and some have suggested that we are shifting towards a post-multicultural world (Vertovec, 2010). Some of the factors that challenged multiculturalism included 'the failure of one type of Australian-ness—Anglo-Australian-ness—to be decentred' (Elder, 2007, p. 137); a revival of Anglo-Australian nation-building myths such as Anzac Day (McKenna, 2009); defining Australian identity in terms of the pioneer past and a return to a set of 'core values' (Smolicz et al., 2001; Turner, 2008); and, increased fears of ethnic diversity and division as well as with the emergence of racist sentiments (Colic-Peisker & Farquharson, 2011). In a post-multicultural world, there is no suggestion that multiculturalism is dead (Vertovec, 2010). Rather, multiculturalism perhaps needs to be re-thought of in the context of a completely different environment to that of Australia forty years ago. Similarly, Australia's national identity needs to be adapted to reflect this changed environment.

The question is, did the introduction of multicultural policies have any influence on perceptions of Australia's national identity? It could be argued that a multicultural environment has not changed the stereotypical image of Australia being 'white'. However, the reality is that immigration has physically changed the landscape and Australians are no longer predominantly white, Anglo-Celtic people. In 2019, 30% of the Australian population was born overseas. Three per cent of Australia's total population was born in China, second to England which tops the overseas-born group at four per cent (Australian Bureau of Statistics [ABS], 2018–19). In comparison, in 1901, UK migrants made up 75% of Australia's overseas population (ABS, 2016). Given the population demographic today, it is extremely difficult for Australian politicians to continue to hang on to the stereotypical Australian identity especially with its proximity to Asia and dependence on Asia as a trading partner. As long as political and media control rests in the hands of the dominant culture, multiculturalism as an inevitable outcome for all settler societies will be contested. For Nye (2007, p. 119), 'the development of a policy of effective multiculturalism also must always be pursued within the context of national identity; it is part of the development of a national identity and not a challenge to it.'

Conclusion

Since European settlement, Australia's national identity has long been infused with images and stories reflecting its colonial ties. With the advent of multiculturalism, Australia's 'white' national identity was seriously challenged. The extent to which cultural diversity brought on by multiculturalist policies has impacted on perceptions of Australia's identity is open to debate but in post-multiculturalism Australia, one needs to re-imagine what it means to be Australian considering the changing nature of the Australian landscape.

Conclusion

This chapter has demonstrated the extent to which the modern Australian identity was entrenched in the idea of being Anglo-Celtic in origin. This identity rendered invisible the first peoples and at a later stage, early immigrants to Australia including the Chinese during the Gold Rush period. It is important to reflect on the dominant position of the host society because it impacts on the ways those outside that group formulate their identities. For multi-generation Australian-born Chinese, there is a long history of inhabiting Australia yet they were often perceived as outsiders. This book broadens perceptions of Australian identity and, at the same time, acknowledges the validity of other identities, like those of Australian-born Chinese, in the Australian context.

A core premise of this book centres around the fluidity of identity construction and how it is context-driven. This chapter examined the advent of multiculturalist policies following the abolition of the 'White Australia' policy, when Australia became an increasingly culturally diverse society. This changing demography was also reflected in the changing nature of the Australian-born Chinese population. By exploring this change in how Australian-born Chinese navigate their identities in a more culturally diverse environment, it will be possible to examine how the environment can impact on identity formation. By making comparisons across generations and between different contexts, it may also be possible to consider the roles that generational differences, history and socio-economic conditions play in identity construction.

One of the key markers of identity is phenotype or visible physical features and in the context of this book, 'race'. This book problematises the homogeneity of Chineseness and in doing so, challenge the concept of race as a group defining attribute. Race, however, continues to be an identity marker where prejudice, stereotyping and discrimination produce assumptions of 'foreignness' regardless of generational status. Chun (1996) raises the questions of what constitutes Chineseness and who are the Chinese? The term *chung-kuo* (Middle Kingdom), which predates the Chinese empire, united diverse groups with different languages, beliefs and practices. Chun notes that there was no notion in Chinese of society bounded by an ethnic group before the Nationalist Revolution of 1911. It was only then that Chinese as an ethnic category began to be associated with *chung-kuo jen* (citizens of China). The notion of what constitutes a Chinese person is highly politicised and does not necessarily equate with personal constructions of Chineseness. Chinese-language speakers are diverse in many ways: they do not all speak the same Chinese; they have varied migration experiences and therefore are not culturally homogeneous; and their level of Chinese literacy varies (Louie & Edwards, 1994). From this perspective, this book examines ethnic language as a marker of identity bearing in mind the diversity of conditions.

Race as an identity marker was a hallmark of Australia's history as a white settler society. Among other acts, Australia was founded on the subjugation of the first peoples and the denigration of Chinese gold miners culminating in the introduction of legislation designed to keep Australia 'white'. This book both acknowledges and challenges the role of historical racism as one of the factors underpinning the way in which Australian-born Chinese negotiated their Chineseness. As this book demonstrates the extent to which historical antecedents, no matter how powerful, impacts on identity construction depends on one's level of agency. Lyman and Douglass (1973, p. 365) offer a view that both ethnic groups and individual ethnics can exercise some agency in their negotiation of race and ethnicity:

> To view race and ethnicity as an unchangeable aspect of man's ascriptive estate is to ignore the important consideration that in living out their lives human actors do not merely accept a given world but rather engage regularly in the construction, manipulation, and modification of social reality.

From this perspective, race and ethnicity are variable and as Okamura (1981) claims, ethnic identity may be dependent upon the immediate social situation and the variability in the individual's perception of that situation. This is defined as situational ethnicity and is consistent although not identical with Barth (1969) who saw ethnicity as both primordial and situationally defined. How phenotype, language and cultural performance interweave with situational context in identity contruction is examined in the next three chapters.

References

Anderson, B. R. O. G. (1991). *Imagined communities: Reflections on the origin and spread of nationalism* (Rev. and extended ed.). Verso.
Anderson, B. R. O. G. (2006). *Imagined communities: Reflections on the origin and spread of nationalism* (Rev. ed.). Verso.
Ang, I., & Stratton, J. (1998). Multiculturalism in crisis: The new politics of race and national identity in Australia. *TOPIA: Canadian Journal of Cultural Studies*, (2), 22–41. https://doi.org/10.3138/topia.2.22
Australian Bureau of Statistics. (2016). Australian Historical Population Statistics (No. 3105.0.65.001). Retrieved from https://www.abs.gov.au/AUSSTATS/abs@.nsf/mf/3105.0.65.001
Australian Bureau of Statistics. (2018–19). Migration, Australia (No. 3412.0). Retrieved from https://www.abs.gov.au/ausstats/abs@.nsf/mf/3412.0
Barth, F. (Ed.). (1969). *Ethnic groups and boundaries: The social organization of culture difference.* Little, Brown and Company.
Batrouney, T., & Goldlust, J. (2005). *Unravelling identity: Immigrants, identity and citizenship in Australia.* Common Ground.
Bresson, L. (1932, June 4). The acme of refinement, good taste and courtesy as shown by our detractors when "truth" is untruthful. *Giornale Italiano* (Sydney, NSW: 1932–1940), p. 1. National Library of Australia. Retrieved from http://nla.gov.au/nla.news-article83028371
Calhoun, C. J. (2007). *Nations matter: Culture, history, and the cosmopolitan dream.* Routledge.
Castles, S. (1992). The Australian model of immigration and multiculturalism: Is it applicable to Europe? *The International Migration Review, 26*(2), 549–567. https://doi.org/10.2307/2547071
Chun, A. (1996). Fuck Chineseness: On the ambiguities of ethnicity as culture and identity. *Boundary 2: An International Journal of Literature and Culture, 23*(2), 111–138. https://doi.org/10.2307/303809
Colic-Peisker, V. (2011). A new era in Australian multiculturalism? From working-class "Ethnics" to a "Multicultural Middle-Class." *International Migration Review, 45*(3), 562–587. https://doi.org/10.1111/j.1747-7379.2011.00858.x

References

Colic-Peisker, V., & Farquharson, K. (2011). Introduction: A new era in Australian multiculturalism? The need for critical interrogation. *Journal of Intercultural Studies, 32*(6), 579–586. https://doi.org/10.1080/07256868.2011.618104

Craven, R., & Purdie, N. (2005). *What does it mean to be an Australian? The perceptions of students, senior and prominent Australians.* In Fourth International Biennial SELF Research, University of Michigan, Ann Arbor. Retrieved from http://www.aare.edu.au/05pap/cra05335.pdf

Dunn, K., & Nelson, J. K. (2011). Challenging the public denial of racism for a deeper multiculturalism. *Journal of Intercultural Studies, 32*(6), 587–602. https://doi.org/10.1080/07256868.2011.618105

Elder, C. (2007). *Being Australian: Narratives of national identity.* Allen & Unwin.

Forrest, J., & Dunn, K. (2010). Attitudes to multicultural values in diverse spaces in Australia's immigrant cities, Sydney and Melbourne. *Space and polity, 14*(1), 81–102. https://doi.org/10.1080/13562571003737791

Gellner, E. (2006). *Nations and nationalism* (2nd ed.). Blackwell Publishing.

Häas, E. B. (1986). What is nationalism and why should we study it? *International Organization, 40*(3), 707–744. Retrieved from https://www.jstor.org/stable/2706824

Hage, G. (1998). *White nation: Fantasies of White supremacy in a multicultural society.* Pluto Press.

Hanson, P. (1996). Maiden speech to Parliament. Retrieved from https://www.smh.com.au/politics/federal/pauline-hansons-1996-maiden-speech-to-parliament-full-transcript-20160915-grgjv3.html

Hebbani, A., & Wills, C. (2012). How Muslim women in Australia navigate through media (mis)representations of hijab/burqa. *Australian Journal of Communication, 39*(1), 87–100. Retrieved from https://search-proquest-com.ezproxy.lib.monash.edu.au/docview/1508226081?accountid=12528

Hogan, J. (2009). *Gender, race and national identity: Nations of flesh and blood.* Routledge.

Hogan, J. (2010). Gendered and racialised discourses of national identity in Baz Luhrmann's Australia. *Journal of Australian Studies, 34*(1), 63–77. https://doi.org/10.1080/14443050903522069

Hopkins, L. (1895). The yellow trash question. *The Bulletin.* National Library of Australia. Retrieved September 13, 2023, from http://nla.gov.au/nla.obj-490373413

Istiko, S. N., Durham, J., & Elliott, L. (2022). (Not That) Essential: A scoping review of migrant workers' access to health services and social protection during the COVID-19 pandemic in Australia, Canada, and New Zealand. *International Journal of Environmental Research and Public Health, 19*(5), 2981. https://doi.org/10.3390/ijerph19052981

Jakubowicz, A. (2002). White noise: Australia's struggle with multiculturalism. In C. Levine-Rasky (Ed.), *Working through whiteness: International perspectives* (pp. 107–125), Albany: State University of New York Press.

Jakubowicz, A. (2011). Chinese walls: Australian multiculturalism and the necessity for human rights. *Journal of Intercultural Studies, 32*(6), 691–706. https://doi.org/10.1080/07256868.2011.618111

Johnson, C. (2007). John Howard's 'values' and Australian identity. *Australian Journal of Political Science, 42*(2), 195–209. https://doi.org/10.1080/10361140701319986

Jones, F. L. (1996). National identity and social values. *People and Place, 4*(4), 17–26.

Jones, F. L. (1997). Ethnic diversity and national identity. *Journal of Sociology, 33*(3), 285–305. https://doi.org/10.1177/144078339703300302

Joppke, C. (2004). The retreat of multiculturalism in the liberal state: Theory and policy. *The British Journal of Sociology, 55*(2), 237–257. https://doi.org/10.1111/j.1468-4446.2004.00017.x

Jupp, J. (1997). Tacking into the wind: Immigration and multicultural policy in the 1990s. *Journal of Australian Studies, 21*(53), 29–39. https://doi.org/10.1080/14443059709387314

Jupp, J. (2007). *From white Australia to Woomera: The story of Australian immigration* (2nd ed.). Cambridge University Press.

Khatri, R. B., & Assefa, Y. (2002). Access to health services among culturally and linguistically diverse populations in the Australian universal health care system: Issues and challenges. *BMC Public Health, 22*(1), 1–14.https://doi.org/10.1186/s12889-022-13256-z

Kymlicka, W. (2010). The rise and fall of multiculturalism? New debates on inclusion and accommodation in diverse societies. *International Social Science Journal, 61*(199), 97–112. https://doi.org/10.1111/j.1468-2451.2010.01750.x

Kymlicka, W., & Banting, K. (2006). Immigration, multiculturalism, and the welfare state. *Ethics & International Affairs, 20*(3), 281–304. https://doi.org/10.1111/j.1747-7093.2006.00027.x

Lake, M. (2003). White man's country: The trans-national history of a national project. *Australian Historical Studies, 34*(122), 346–363. https://doi.org/10.1080/10314610308596259

Lin, A. M. Y. (2008). *Problematizing identity: Everyday struggles in language, culture, and education*. Lawrence Erlbaum Associates.

Louie, K., & Edwards, L. (1994). Chinese for Dinkum Aussies. *Asian Studies Review, 18*(2), 53–62. https://doi.org/10.1080/03147539408712995

Lyman, S. M., & Douglass, W. A. (1973). Ethnicity: Strategies of collective and individual impression management. *Social Research, 40*(2), 344–365. Retrieved from http://www.jstor.org/stable/40970142

Markus, A., Jupp, J., & McDonald, P. (2009). *Australia's immigration revolution*. Allen & Unwin.

Mason, R. (2010). Australian multiculturalism: Revisiting Australia's political heritage and the migrant presence. *History Compass, 8*(8), 817–827. https://doi.org/10.1111/j.1478-0542.2010.00721.x

May, P. (1886). The Mongolian Octopus: His grip on Australia. Retrieved from http://www.multiculturalaustralia.edu.au/library/media/Image/id/623.quotThe-Mongolian-Octopus-his-grip-on-Australiaquot

McGregor, R. (2006). The necessity of Britishness: Ethno-cultural roots of Australian nationalism. *Nations and Nationalism, 12*(3), 493–511. https://doi.org/10.1111/j.1469-8129.2006.00250.x

McKenna, M. (2009). Australian history and the Australian 'national inheritance.' *Australian Cultural History, 27*(1), 1–12. https://doi.org/10.1080/07288430902877841

McLeod, J., & Yates, L. (2003). Who is 'us'? Students negotiating discourses of racism and national identification in Australia. *Race Ethnicity and Education, 6*(1), 29–49. https://doi.org/10.1080/1361332022000044576

Meaney, N. (1995). The end of 'white Australia' and Australia's changing perceptions of Asia, 1945–1990. *Australian Journal of International Affairs, 49*(2), 171–189. https://doi.org/10.1080/10357719508445155

Moran, A. (2005a). *Australia: Nation, belonging, and globalization*. Routledge.

Moran, A. (2005b). White Australia, settler nationalism and Aboriginal assimilation. *Australian Journal of Politics & History, 51*(2), 168–193. https://doi.org/10.1111/j.1467-8497.2005.00369.x

Moran, A. (2011). Multiculturalism as nation-building in Australia: Inclusive national identity and the embrace of diversity. *Ethnic and Racial Studies, 34*(12), 2153–2172. https://doi.org/10.1080/01419870.2011.573081

Moreton-Robinson, A. (2005). The house that Jack built: Britishness and white possession. *Australian Critical Race and Whiteness Studies Association Journal, 1*(2), 21–29.

Noble, G. (2009). 'Countless acts of recognition': Young men, ethnicity and the messiness of identities in everyday life. *Social & Cultural Geography, 10*(8), 875–891. https://doi.org/10.1080/14649360903305767

Nye, M. (2007). The challenges of multiculturalism. *Culture and Religion: An Interdisciplinary Journal, 8*(2), 109–123. https://doi.org/10.1080/14755610701458915

Okamura, J. Y. (1981). Situational ethnicity. *Ethnic and Racial Studies, 4*(4), 452–465. https://doi.org/10.1080/01419870.1981.9993351

Ommundsen, W. (2010). 'She'll be right, mate': Multiculturalism and the culture of benign neglect. *Australian Cultural History, 28*(2–3), 131–139. https://doi.org/10.1080/07288433.2010.585520

References

Parekh, B. C. (2008). *A new politics of identity: Political principles for an interdependent world.* Palgrave Macmillan.

Phillips, T. L. (1996). Symbolic boundaries and national identity in Australia. *The British Journal of Sociology, 47*(1), 113–134. Retrieved from http://www.jstor.org/stable/591119

Phillips, T., & Smith, P. (2000). What is 'Australian'? Knowledge and among a gallery of contemporary Australians. *Australian Journal of Political Science, 35*(2), 203–224. https://doi.org/10.1080/713649336

Pugliese, J. (2002). Race as category crisis: Whiteness and the topical assignation of race. *Social Semiotics, 12*(2), 149–168. https://doi.org/10.1080/103503302760212078

Purdie, N., & Wilss, L. (2007). Australian national identity: Young peoples' conceptions of what it means to be Australian. *National Identities, 9*(1), 67–82. https://doi.org/10.1080/14608940601145695

Reid, A. (1985). Imagined communities. Reflections on the origin and spread of nationalism. By Benedict Anderson (book review). *Pacific Affairs, 58*(3), 497–499.

Robertson, R. (2011). Global connectivity and global consciousness. *American Behavioral Scientist, 55*(10), 1336–1345. https://doi.org/10.1177/0002764211409562

Ronald, J. (1901, September 6). 'Immigration Restriction Bill', House of Representatives, *Debates*, 4665. Retrieved from https://www.aph.gov.au/About_Parliament/Parliamentary_Departments/Parliamentary_Library/pubs/APF/monographs/Within_Chinas_Orbit/Chapterone#_ftn20

Seal, G. (2004). *Inventing Anzac: The digger and national mythology.* University of Queensland Press.

Sears, L. J. (1994). Reviews of books—imagined Communities: Reflections on the origin and spread of nationalism (revised edition) by Benedict Anderson. *Journal of the American Oriental Society, 114*(1), 129–130. Retrieved from https://search.proquest.com/docview/217139185?accountid=12528

Smith, A. (1986). *The ethnic origins of nations.* Blackwell.

Smith, P., & Phillips, T. (2001). Popular understandings of 'UnAustralian': An investigation of the un-national. *Journal of Sociology, 37*(4), 323–339. https://doi.org/10.1177/144078301128756373

Smits, K. (2011). Justifying multiculturalism: Social justice, diversity and national identity in Australia and New Zealand. *Australian Journal of Political Science, 46*(1), 87–103. https://doi.org/10.1080/10361146.2011.546051

Smolicz, J. J., Secombe, M. J., & Hudson, D. M. (2001). Family collectivism and minority languages as core values of culture among ethnic groups in Australia. *Journal of Multilingual and Multicultural Development, 22*(2), 152–172. https://doi.org/10.1080/01434630108666430

Stratton, J. (2006). Two rescues, one history: Everyday racism in Australia. *Social Identities: Journal for the Study of Race, Nation and Culture, 12*(6), 657–681. https://doi.org/10.1080/13504630601030867

Tascon, S. M. (2008). Narratives of race and nation: Everyday whiteness in Australia. *Social Identities, 14*(2), 253–274. https://doi.org/10.1080/13504630801933688

Taylor, C. (1994). *Multiculturalism: Examining the politics of recognition.* Princeton University Press.

The Age. (2005, August 25). Accept Australian values or get out. Retrieved from https://www.theage.com.au/national/accept-australian-values-or-get-out-20050825-ge0r6g.html

Tranter, B., & Donoghue, J. (2007). Colonial and post-colonial aspects of Australian identity. *The British Journal of Sociology, 58*(2), 165–183. https://doi.org/10.1111/j.1468-4446.2007.00146.x

Turner, G. (2008). The cosmopolitan city and its other: The ethnicizing of the Australian suburb. *Inter-Asia Cultural Studies, 9*(4), 568–582. https://doi.org/10.1080/14649370802386487

Tyrrell, M. (2007). Homage to Ruritania: Nationalism, identity, and diversity. *Critical Review, 19*(4), 511–522. https://doi.org/10.1080/08913810801892895

Vertovec, S. (2010). Towards post-multiculturalism? Changing communities, conditions and contexts of diversity. *International Social Science Journal, 61*(199), 83–95. https://doi.org/10.1111/j.1468-2451.2010.01749.x

Wall, P. (2006). The Aussie identity and multiculturalism: The importance of heritage values in a changing society. *AQ: Australian Quarterly, 78*(5), 25–40. Retrieved from http://www.jstor.org/stable/20638425

Walsh, M., & Karolis, A. C. (2008). Being Australian, Australian nationalism and Australian values. *Australian Journal of Political Science, 43*(4), 719–727. https://doi.org/10.1080/10361140802429296

Wiley, S., Perkins, K., & Deaux, K. (2008). Through the looking glass: Ethnic and generational patterns of immigrant identity. *International Journal of Intercultural Relations, 32*(5), 385–398. https://doi.org/10.1016/j.ijintrel.2008.04.002

Chapter 3
Race and Ethnicity in Identity

Introduction

The idea of identity as a collective concept bounded by visible features manifested through skin colour and facial features is difficult to reconcile with current hybridised notions of identity. Social scientists generally agree that race and ethnicity are social and cultural constructs that are dynamic rather than biological and fixed (Kibria, 2000; Lee & Bean, 2004). Drawing on works such as Brubaker's (2004a, 2004b) *Ethnicity without Groups*, this chapter examines the role phenotype plays in the way Chineseness as an identity is constructed both in the public and private sphere: the racialisation of identity; the perceived stigma of being Chinese; the fostering of stereotypes; and the affliction of the 'perpetual foreigner syndrome' (Cheryan & Monin, 2005). How this collective way of defining ethnic identity is perpetuated in both the public and private sphere, the social and environmental context as well as the family context will also be explored. Finally, how the individual reacts to the essentialisation of ethnic identity will be largely dependent upon the intersectionality of a range of conditions. This chapter further considers the various outcomes, including assimilation to the host society at one end of the spectrum and the successful transmission of parental cultural values at the other, recognising that these outcomes are situationally defined and not mutually exclusive.

Brubaker (2004a, 2004b) highlights the problem of 'groupism' where bounded ethnic groups continue to be treated as entities despite constructivist theorists recognising that ethnic groups have shifting boundaries and that ethnicity is responsive to everyday life (Levine, 1999). Barth (1969) postulated that ethnicity is situationally defined, ethnic boundaries are permeable, and the perceptions and definitions of the social actors play a pivotal role in ethnic ascription and subscription. Barth's model of ethnicity is transactional in nature, involving the processes of internal self-definition of identity and the processes of external definition or other-directed processes in which a person or set of persons defines the other. There exists a dichotomy between self-image and public image, between how we see ourselves and how others see us (Goffman, 1959). In this sense, identity is both variable and vulnerable. Jenkins (1994) claims that those with power and authority can make their definition of a person count and the capacity of one group to define or lay out the terms of existence for another should not be underestimated.

Group identities based on visible features such as skin colour and facial features are a clear example of how those with power and authority can include or exclude others from the mainstream population. Phenotype is an obvious marker of difference and can be perpetuated and reinforced as a marker of ethnic identity in several ways. One of the first experiences of difference encountered by study participants was their entry into the school system. It is within this system that identities can be racialised and that some study participants began to experience separation from the mainstream. It is also when their Chinese identity may be seen as a negative. The fixation with race becomes more apparent when one expresses a fear of being labeled as a member of the 'other' group on the basis of physical appearance and being Chinese becomes stigmatised. Implicit in this fear is a belief that one's ethnic identity is somehow inferior or one imagines that is how the wider society thinks. Discrimination based on appearance, ethnicity and culture'can result in social exclusion (Boese & Phillips, 2011, p. 192). The perpetuation of stereotypes both within and outside the group also serves to reinforce separation from the mainstream. With the 'model minority' stereotype, this may be construed as a positive stereotype whilesimultaneously acts as a point of difference with the mainstream. Another way in which phenotype is reinforced as a marker of identity and of difference is 'identity denial' where an individual is not recognised as a member of the in-group (Cheryan & Monin, 2005). This is typified by having to respond to the question, 'Where do you really come from?', a question that was often directed at ethnic minority members.

These essentialised ways of homogenising Chineseness based on physical difference are a constant challenge for Australian-born Chinese. One way to counter separation from the mainstream is to assimilate with the host society and the success of this is dependent upon the 'contexts of exit and reception' (Zhou, 2014). Assimilation to the host society, however, is not a foregone conclusion for Australian-born Chinese. Not only are there degrees of assimilation or adaptation, this research indicates that some Australian-born Chinese also exercise agency in constructing their identity irrespective of the limitations imposed by essentialised constructions of Chineseness. The family can play a critical role in the transmission of cultural values to their children and the more power the immigrant group has in its new setting, the less likely it is to accommodate new cultural norms (Rosenthal & Feldman, 1990). While acknowledging that intergenerational relations can play a key role in reinforcing essentialised constructions of Chineseness, the family can also play an important role in reinforcing and transferring cultural heritage to the next generation as well as providing an environment which fosters agency in identity construction.

The Racialisation of Identity

Visible physical characteristics are what strike us foremost when we first encounter an individual or group. More often than not, it may be the first criteria upon which we make an initial judgment about someone. As Bailey (2000, p. 566) states, 'phenotype is readily apparent to all, and always available for others to invoke'. When ethnicity and identity are combined and Chineseness is ethnicised, there is a risk of marginalisation and of being reduced to one particular ethnic category (Ang, 1994b). In multicultural societies like Australia, it is easy to slot people into an ethnic category and for Chineseness to become the other. The linking of 'race' and ethnicity is the most obvious tool for promoting this ethnicisation or racialisation.

Schoolyard Memories

Jenkins (1994) considers the relationship between race and ethnicity and concludes that 'racial' differentiation and racism are 'historically-specific forms' of ethnicity. Moreover, racial differentiation and racism illustrate how one ethnic group dominates another and proceeds to categorise them as immutably different and inferior. In the process of categorising the 'other', powerful groups can potentially alter the social world of the other (Jenkins, 1994; Kibria, 2000). Many ethnic minority people are not only given ethnic labels, but also racial labels and images by others (Song, 2003). Like ethnicity, race is a social construct based on subjective perceptions of other people's phenotype like skin colour or hair type. Race and ethnicity have been known to be used interchangeably and the category of race is still being used in the U.S. census despite its lack of scientific credence. Asians are often seen in racial, as opposed to ethnic terms. Furthermore, ethnic identities are often influenced by experiences of racism and discrimination. Yue (2000) argues that 'visualism marks the ideological process which reduces race and ethnicity to physical properties, so that "ways of looking" become "ways of being"' (p. 178). This visualism enforces a particular sense of Chineseness that is not only homogenising but difficult to escape. Chow (1998, p. 4) notes that, in relation to contemporary Chinese cinema, there is 'a continual tendency to stigmatize and ghettoize non-Western cultures precisely by way of ethnic, national labels'. In exploring the nature of British-Chinese identity through art, Yeh (2000) also observed that the construction of Chineseness in Britain was a product of the dominant Western social imaginary and in her fieldwork on 'British Chinese'/'Oriental' spaces, Yeh (2014) noted that the racial categorisation of Chinese included an association with the colour 'yellow'.

The fixation with colour is a modern phenomenon. Whiteness was appropriated by modern Europeans who naturalised or racialised the concept and made it a central feature of their identity (Bonnett, 1998). Whiteness was neither the sole preserve of the Europeans nor was it perceived in the same sense as in other cultures. In premodern China, for instance, the category of 'white' was used as a marker of purity and beauty distinguishing the elite from the peasantry. Ironically, 'white' was, and still is, also a signifier of death and mourning in China. But it was the racialisation of whiteness that modern Europeans used to marginalise and exclude others. This is typified by America's colour line and Australia's Immigration Restriction Act 1901 or what is better known as the White Australia Policy.

In a study on second-generation Vietnamese Americans, Thai (1999) found that there was still a belief that being 'American' meant being white and the desire to be white lead to temporary negative images of the self and of one's culture. Whiteness is still a strong factor in ascribing an Australian identity. In a separate study examining ethnic identity among young Asian-American professionals, Asian Americans were still subjected to negative stereotypes despite their multigenerational status (Min & Kim, 2000). One study participant, Brenda, is a third-generation Australian-born Chinese yet continues to remark on her sense of difference:

> I'm quite dark and you go try on clothes and they go 'Oh it looks so nice against your skin.' And it's always the white people who say that, do you know as that condescending, patronizing thing. They don't even realize that they're sort of being a bit like you're drawing attention to my ethnic colour in a way that's meant to be nice but there's something a bit off about it. I think people who make those kinds of social gaffs are really sort of highlighting their ignorance I guess and lack of cultural sensitivity. I kind of laugh about it but growing up, you're quite vulnerable. You do feel a bit sensitive about it. You think 'Are you saying that because you think I'm Chinese and you think you are superior because you're not Chinese and you kind of put me down because you're a bit racist?' I've had experiences where I've felt like that.

Brenda's interpretation of what may be a compliment to what she feels may be a racist comment highlights the volatility and the state of uncertainty of identity construction for some Australian-born Chinese. This uncertainty was also reflected in the experiences of some study participants when they first started school, an uncertainty perhaps stemming from historical circumstances such as the enforcement of the White Australia Policy. From another perspective, one could argue that Brenda has grown up in an environment where systemic racism was normalised and her insecurities were not without foundation and, indeed, they were a product of the social norms as defined by the dominant majority. Being 'over-sensitive' and second-guessing other's intentions was also a reflection of the unequal standing that the Chinese in Australia were historically subjected to. The hierarchical nature of skin colour is evident in Brenda's case as she perceives this to be what sets her apart from the store attendant. Being uncomfortable in one's own skin may also manifest in a desire to be white or more aligned to the mainstream population.

The schoolyard experiences of multi-generation Australian-born Chinese participants who grew up in a largely homogeneous white society in 1960s and 1970s Australia were similar insofar as it was the 'white' cohort who defined who they were. Dunn et al. (2004) also contend that 'old racism' which highlights inferiority was prevalent from the time of Federation in 1901 through to the early 1970s and the end of the White Australia Policy. For some of the older participants in this research, who grew up in the 1960s and 1970s, the inferiority of Chineseness was sometimes felt in everyday life and it impacted negatively on their self-identities.

The Racialisation of Identity

Before starting school, many of the study participants like other children did not think of their ethnic identity in a negative way. Many were not aware of being different until they were placed in the new social context of primary school. What became apparent was that many study participants were very much concerned with fitting in at school. Arguably, Australian-born Chinese growing up in Australia in the 1960s and 1970s were more likely to experience discrimination because of being the token Chinese at school compared to Australian-born Chinese growing up in the 1990s where schools were more culturally diverse. Harry is third-generation Australian-born Chinese in his 50s who grew up in Melbourne. Both his grandfather and father came to Australia in 1938 to set up the family business and, as was typical for Chinese immigrants at the time, his mother and two older siblings were not permitted to come to Australia until fifteen or so years later. Harry's mother never learnt to speak English so Harry always conversed in Chinese with his mother which helped to foster his fluency and interest in other languages. According to Harry, his mother was a strong woman who seemed to be comfortable living in Australia. Harry was comfortable with his cultural heritage and seemed to have a respectful relationship with his family. It was only when Harry attended school that he experienced negativity about his ethnicity:

> I was definitely more conscious of being different when I was in primary school... being outnumbered. Just being in a class where I was the only Chinese person there and of course, not so much bullying, but name-calling and things like that. I think it happened frequently with other kids calling you that.

For Harry, his pre-school years and sense of well-being were challenged when he started school and realised that there were few students of Chinese appearance in the school. In comparison to Australia in the latter part of the twentieth century, the 1960s Australia was relatively mono-cultural and it was not uncommon for children of Chinese heritage to be outnumbered in the schoolyard setting. It was also not uncommon for Chinese people to be essentialised and grouped with Japanese people. Since Japan was the enemy during the Second World War, it lent legitimacy, albeit false, to the name-callers for marginalising people of Asian appearance. This coupled with the 'White Australia' policy was the backdrop in which young Chinese people often had to contend with when navigating through their school years. In their study on Australian children's constructions of citizenship and national identity, Howard and Gill (2001) recognise the connection between schooling and national identity. Accordingly, schools in the first half of the twentieth century fostered allegiance to the nation through actions such as reciting the Oath of Loyalty, anthem singing and flag raising. These expressions of nationalistic fervour may have served to highlight cultural differences.

It could be argued that, with the abolition of the White Australia Policy and a shift in government policy towards a more culturally diverse society, there would be growing tolerance towards other ethnicities. This had not yet transpired in the schoolyards of 1970s Australia. Heather is a third-generation Australian-born Chinese of mixed background who grew up in 1970s Australia. Heather grew up in Tasmania which, in terms of cultural diversity, lagged behind Melbourne during the 1970s and, arguably, onwards. Like Harry, Heather was not aware of being different until she started school. Unlike Harry, Heather's parents did not seem as supportive when Heather was bullied and her physical difference was also reinforced by her parents during her school years. Heather's father used to refer to his daughter as a 'half-caste' and her mother would tell Heather to 'toughen up' when she experienced any bullying. Heather was teased relentlessly during her primary school years and it had a marked effect on her self-esteem:

> As soon as I went to school, it was glaringly obvious how different I was. I did get teased a lot, and that affected me very much in my younger years. I had this instance where we had an art thing at school, and they did a silhouette profile of us, and we had to paint them in, and it came to me, and everyone just laughed at me, because my profile is flat, so I got called 'Flat Face' for two years at school, and it was just horrifying to me, like I just felt so self-conscious all the time. And I still think it now; I still don't like my side profile, because people used to say, 'You look like you've been hit in the face by a wall or by a truck'.

While both Harry and Heather grew up in parts of Australia which were largely monocultural and they were the only Chinese in their respective primary schools for a time, they had different levels of support from their families and this may have impacted on their reactions towards name-calling at the time.

These schoolyard experiences of the 1960s and 1970s continue to persist in the 1990s. Frank grew up in multicultural Melbourne in the 1990s yet was also subjected to similar name-calling experiences in his first years at school. During this period, although there was a sizable Chinese population, there was still a propensity among some public figures including politicians like Pauline Hanson to deride Asian immigration and attempt to instil a fear of being 'swamped' by Asians. Despite a multicultural environment, racism can still exist, racism in terms of marking people as ethnic (Ang, 1994a, 1994b). Frank, in his 20s, was also unaware of his Chineseness until he was in Grade One:

> I funnily remember another kid calling me like 'Chinaman' or 'Ching Chong' or something like that...I don't think I took it well. I think I was a little embarrassed, or it didn't feel like a nice thing for someone to say.

Frank's experiences demonstrated that racism in school traversed generations as well as time and space. Alice, who is also second-generation but in her 60s, went to a Catholic girls' school where the student population was predominantly Anglo-Celtic. Alice and her two sisters were the only children of Asian appearance in the whole school. Alice observed that her participation in extra-curricular activities was hampered by her ethnicity:

> Well, you'd never be chosen for a main role in the school play. Well, just imagine you couldn't be a Chinese Cinderella or Snow White. So, you were never going to get that role no matter how good you were. Or you were auditioning for, um, Judas in the Jesus Christ Superstar in the Eisteddfod, I remember. And no matter how good you were, you weren't going to get the role. That's the impression I got.

For Alice, this sense of exclusion was palpable. This type of racism is subtle and is based on an unconscious white privilege that perpetuates stereotypes. Alice felt that it had an impact on her confidence and her opportunities:

I think for a lot of us growing up like that, I mean it did affect your self-esteem and confidence. I don't think we achieved to the levels we should have as a result of the discrimination and the way you were treated at school. You were treated differently and you felt different. The only thing they couldn't take away from me ... was that we were academic and they couldn't take that away from us. And so, we always did well at school academically.

Experiences of racism and discrimination especially in the early years was commonplace for some of the study participants and it served to highlight their difference. While Alice did not feel that she had much control over her social opportunities at school, she felt like she had some control over her academic pursuits. Alice's focus on academic achievement was a display of resilience as well as a way of compensating for her lack of acceptance in other areas. Denise is a second-generation Australian-born Chinese in her 60s who grew up in an environment where Chinese people were in a minority and her sense of belonging when she was growing up was compromised by her experiences of racism:

But we were always different - my two sisters and I were the only three Asians in the whole school. We used to get teased because we had flat noses. It was quite commonplace. And, also growing up in the 1950s, we were sort of experiencing I suppose a certain amount of hostility because people would see us and think, oh Japanese - we'd just been to war with Japan sort of, it was an element of that. I don't think that we really felt that we belonged anywhere - to a large extent because you didn't really fit in with white Anglo-Saxon society, although my best friend was of Irish descent and I think that sort of - that made for a much more comfortable childhood I'm sure. I played with her a lot. I went to her place a lot.

Children of ethnic minority immigrants are subject to continual 'pull–push forces' where they continually need to negotiate their identification with both the ethnic group and with mainstream culture (Asghari-Ford & Hossain, 2017). In their study on second-generation Iranians in Australia, Asghari-Ford and Hossain found that the children of ethnic minority immigrants were continually negotiating their identity both within their ethnic group as well as with mainstream society. Identity becomes situational depending on social context, time and the perception of other members of society. The socio-political context, historical processes and positions of power and privilege all serve to shape the construction of ethnic identity (Ali & Sonn, 2010). Denise grew up after the Second World War when the White Australia Policy was the backdrop to everyday life and it would appear that mainstream society either had difficulty distinguishing one Asian culture from another or it was simply easier not to make any distinctions. For Alonso (1994), ethnicity is constructed but is limited by hegemonic processes of inscription. Environmental conditions such as the political climate have the capacity to invoke feelings of uncertainty about the 'other', and the precariousness of identity is highlighted in the following section.

'Us' Versus 'Them'

The imposition of external definitions is inevitable and while it does not initially align to the self-perception of Australian-born Chinese let alone those at pre-school age, it has the power to influence and change one's identity. Hence, identity seems to have a degree of volatility driven by mainstream dominance. Lack of a sense of belonging may result from self-perceptions of being culturally different from the Anglo majority (Boese & Phillips, 2017). According to Lo (2000, p. 159), 'Australians from the various ethnic groups from Asia occupy a precarious position within the national imaginary. While their ethnicity is generally accepted as part of Australian culture, their collective status is often racialised as other whenever the political and economic power of the 'non-ethnic' centre is threatened.' Even as adults, the precariousness of identity was felt by some of the study participants. Association with other Asian people based on phenotype was something that Edward, a second-generation Australian-born Chinese in his 60s, expressed discomfort with. Edward grew up in country Victoria where the Chinese community was quite small, where everyone knew each other, and apart from the odd name-calling experiences, Edward felt like he was just a member of the wider community. As an adult living in Melbourne, Edward's awareness of his ethnic identity had become a source of uneasiness under certain political conditions:

> I wasn't very happy with Geoffrey Blainey at that stage. Then we went through the stage of the— oh, probably going back to early in the 70s when the Vietnamese refugees started coming out. I think I was a bit uncomfortable then, and then we had that Pauline Hanson episode, and again I sort of started feeling a bit uncomfortable then.

Edward highlighted these three incidences as causes of his discomfort—in 1984, Geoffrey Blainey, a highly regarded historian, claimed that the rate of Asian immigration was too high and that Australia's social cohesion was at risk; after the Vietnam War, there was a huge influx of Vietnamese refugees arriving by boat in Australia; and, in Pauline Hanson's maiden speech to the Senate as a newly elected Senator in 1996, she stated that Asians 'form ghettos and do not assimilate'. Edward perceived that all these incidences served to instil some negative sentiment towards Asian people and he wanted to disassociate himself from being grouped in the same way. In one sense, it was perhaps a reflection of Edward's own insecurities about his ethnicity and perhaps his readiness to believe the rhetoric behind these statements. Fear of racial vilification can sometimes lead to denial of cultural heritage and in some cases, racial vilification or disdain of others in the cultural group. Edward feared that the negative sentiment towards particular Asian groups would also reflect on other Asian-looking people including himself:

> By and large, I think it's become more tolerant of other races, but having said that, when it does blow up, it does get pretty uncomfortable sometimes. But people are still locked into the idea that Australia's a white— you have to be white to be Australian.

Edward perceived that the Australian identity was still inherently 'white' and his comments highlighted the uncertainty around his right to belong as well as what he believed to be the divide between white people and others. He referred to situations when it might 'blow up' so, although Edward was prepared to distance himself from other Asian groups, he was fully conscious of the precarity of his situation or place in society. It is enormously difficult to separate the category of race from ethnicity even though there are countless differences within one ethnic community. Racial categorisation is displayed in comments received by Gillian, a third-generation Australian-born Chinese in her 60s who grew up in country Victoria. Like Edward, Gillian differentiated herself from 'overseas Chinese' and expressed indignation at being grouped with them:

> Because of the way you look, they think, 'Oh, you're just one of them. You've just come over from Vietnam or China, and I think that does a lot of damage in that sense. We even now get asked, when we'd go to look at houses up for sale at auction, 'Are you from overseas wanting to buy?' And I said, 'Hang on, we're not one of them. Don't lump us in with them.', thinking we're overseas Chinese, because I think what's happening now with all the publicity is that, 'Oh, all the Chinese are coming over and buying all the land, so our children won't be able to get one, and we're first home owners'.

Implicit in Gillian's refusal to be grouped with overseas Chinese or Vietnamese people was her reinforcement of an othering process. Gillian was disassociating herself from other Asian groups because, in her estimation, these groups were maligned and she was adamant that she was not a member of these groups. The fear of being grouped together was also reflected in comments made by Ben, a second-generation Australian-born Chinese in his 20s. Ben's father came to Australia as a Vietnamese refugee in the 1980s where he met Ben's mother who was originally from China. Ben did not identify as an Australian but as someone who was "globalised, cosmopolitan, Westernised". According to Portes and Rumbaut (2001, p. 148), 'this process of forging a reactive ethnicity in the face of perceived threats, persecution, and exclusion is not uncommon'. The way in which the individual perceives the environment in which they live can have a marked effect on their relationship with that environment. Ben was conscious of the power of certain world events to shape the collective consciousness and, in turn, his sense of belongingness and identity. He expressed a certain unease about his sense of belonging in Australia:

> I've always had this weird paranoia of being in a sense a coloured person, not a white person. There's always a moment where I could be expelled in some sense or some crisis could happen like the Cronulla riots. I belong here but I'm not anchored here. It's also like a contingent type of belonging, a precarious type of belonging where any moment things could turn…. there's always this possibility of being kicked out not in like the physical sense but in the cultural sense.

Ben displayed a high degree of uncertainty about his place in Australia and his sense of belonging was very much contingent upon how others behaved. However, Ben exercised agency to circumvent this when he declared himself to be a global citizen. While both Edward and Gillian grew up in rural Australia at a time when there were few Chinese people within their communities, Ben grew up in Melbourne with its culturally diverse population. It might be feasible to expect that the environmental conditions were more favourable for Ben in terms of cultural acceptance and not feeling like a minority. However, it was precisely this collective visibility that was a source of anxiety expressed by these study participants. It is more difficult to fall under the radar when collective identities are conjured up. Race continues to be an obvious marker of difference that transcends other differences such as culture and nation and 'colour has become the universal calling card of difference' (Martin, 2003, 1.23). This is not dissimilar to 1960s Australia when historical colonialist discourse as embodied in the 'White Australia' policy racialised identity. The role of historical constructions of Australian national identity cannot be ignored and the Australian national imaginary is still very Anglo-Celtic (Dunn et al., 2004). Ian, a third-generation Australian-born Chinese in his 60s, identified as an Australian who happened to have parents of Chinese origin. Ian remarked on the grouping of Asians into one racialised entity particularly at a time when there were fewer Asians because of the White Australia Policy and there may have been anti-Asian sentiment arising from the Japanese being the enemy in the Second World War. Ian noted that misrepresentations were usually instigated by strangers rather than within his social sphere:

> Yeah: people who don't know you, but they're more likely to say you were Japanese and say something awful to you or something, rather than Chinese. They had more an issue with Japanese people in those days than Chinese.

The irony in categorising Chinese with Japanese directly after the Second World War was that the two countries were enemies during war time. Essentialising Asian-looking people in this way highlights the erroneous nature of relying on physical appearance alone to categorise people. As has been demonstrated, one of the outcomes of being seen to be different is a sense of doubt about belonging to the mainstream. Some expressed uncertainty in the public domain about whether their 'race' was a factor in their capacity to fit in. Gary is in his 30s and spoke about the financial hardship that his parents went through to raise four children. His parents were focused on ensuring that their children gained a good education and they would invest in tutors for their children. Consequently, Gary was successful in his educational and work pursuits which he attributed to the work ethic that was ingrained in him. However, speaking on work opportunities and the ability to climb the corporate ladder, Gary observed:

> I think it's about connections, assimilation, and, I don't know, maybe I've resigned myself to the fact that even if you assimilate yourself to the nth degree, you can't change the colour of your skin.

It is difficult to pinpoint whether ethnicity played a role in Gary's work opportunities but the feeling that ethnicity is at the back of people's minds was nonetheless common. Gary remarked on the difficulty of being part of the in-crowd:

> And if you asked me whether or not an ABC can gel in that sort of club: yes, maybe in a superficial way, but delving deeper, I don't think you can ever really 100 per cent get along in one of those clubs. Maybe it's a stigma, because as much as Australia strives to eliminate racism from the country, it's still, I guess to me, an attempt to, or an effort on the part of most people. It's still something that plays in the back of everyone's minds.

Uncertainty in the public domain can be founded. Brenda is a third-generation Australian-born Chinese of mixed descent in her late 30s. Both her parents were the children of immigrants but from different places—China and Europe. Brenda also shared her experiences of racism in the workplace:

I see it in the workplace. I worked for an accounting firm and resumes came in and anyone who had a Chinese name didn't get a look in ... they were racist. They were like 'Oh they're Chinese. We don't want them. They won't fit in.' Oh, it's highly offensive. Yep, discrimination like that still happens. No one will admit to it but it does happen.

As Matthews (2000, p. 31) observes 'Asianness is edified on corporeal difference, implanted racial images and imaginaries... these images and imaginaries involve mechanisms of Othering, marginalisation, racism, and racialisation that press out new alliances, recognitions and affinities.' The pervasiveness of race as a marker of identity is due in part to white privilege and the failure of white people to recognise it as such. According to Martin (2003, 1.23), 'colour is something white people never have to think about because for them it is never a handicap, never a source of prejudice or discrimination, but rather the opposite, a source of privilege.' The power of white privilege is demonstrated in the way in which some of the study participants aspired to be 'white'.

Objectification and Stigma

Jenkins (1994) claims the individual's experience of being categorised may lead to an adjustment in his/her own self-image towards the stigmatising public image. This was evident in the study participants' reluctance to be associated with being Chinese because of its perceived negative connotations. Irene who is a second-generation Australian-born Chinese in her 20s grew up being aware of being physically different. Irene's parents were of Chinese background but born in East Timor. By all accounts, they identified as Chinese and celebrated Chinese festivals. Irene remarked on her sense of shame about her cultural heritage when she was younger:

> When I was younger, I felt like I was uncomfortable in my skin - even though I was Chinese, I wanted to be white. There was a time when I was really embarrassed about my parents. We were waiting in a line for some school function, and this girl was there, and she was Turkish, and she was one of the popular girls, and my dad started to speak to me in Chinese, and I got really embarrassed and frustrated, and I had a little tantrum, because I didn't want my dad to speak to me in Chinese in front of her.

When Harry, a second-generation Australian-born Chinese in his 50s, was younger, he also felt a sense of shame about his Chineseness. Harry said:

> I kind of felt— there was a stage when— and I'm saying very young at primary school— when I kind of thought— you know, when I really didn't like who I was, and didn't like my identity. I often said to myself at that time, 'Why did I have to be born in this family? Why couldn't I be born white?

As school-age children, both Irene and Harry were focused on fitting in and on not being perceived as different or standing out from everyone else. In their minds, Chineseness was imbued with negative connotations and it was difficult to avoid these completely. Chineseness was also perceived as separate from being white, thus reinforcing a sense of otherness. For Portes and Rumbaut (2001, p. 151), 'people whose ethnic, racial, or other social markers place them in a minority status in their group or community are more likely to be self-conscious of those characteristics'.

Experiences of racism serve to compound a sense of otherness. Cathy, a second-generation Australian-born Chinese in her 30s, went through a period when she did not embrace her Chineseness presumably because it was perceived to be a negative trait within her community. Cathy's parents came to Australia in the 1960s but, according to Cathy, did not feel like they belonged in Australia. Their views may have impacted on Cathy. Cathy also grew up in an environment where there were few Asian families and she encountered several occasions where racism was directed at her:

> There was racism not just from the kids but there was racism from the adults as well. I guess I always just felt like I didn't belong because I was made to feel like I didn't belong. It was very clear that I was different. I remember one of my neighbour's kids followed me on his bike all the way home saying really softly under his breath that I had to go back to my own country and then spat on me. Later when I was older, maybe sixteen, my little cousin who is an Australian-born Chinese as well…he was only three and I was walking him down the road and he ran up a little kid's driveway because he saw them playing in the front with balls and he thought it was fun. Their Dad was washing the car, and the little kids ran up to him and they were like "Get lost, you chink and go back to your own country. Get out of our country." I remember watching the Dad just calmly washing the car and I was older then to know a bit more about how you got that from your Dad who's not saying anything.

It is arguably difficult to embrace one's ethnicity when it is perceived to be a negative trait and this may be compounded by lack of agency, something a young person may not have in the face of a perceived hostile environment.

Not only may there be negative self-perceptions, there are also cases of objectification and essentialisation of Chineseness that, while not intended to be negative, have the effect of grouping individuals on the basis of physical appearance alone. One might argue that the likelihood of grouping people together on the basis of phenotype lessens as communities become more culturally diverse. For some of the younger study participants in their 20s, this was not always the case. They still experienced occasions where their physical appearance became a defining feature of their identity. Ann experienced occasions where others were quick to categorise her as stereotypically Chinese:

> It's actually the older people like they will always say "Oh, you Chinese girls, you're always so pretty" or just something like that. It's nice but it's also a bit, you know, uncomfortable. Or they'll say something like "Oh, you're Chinese. I had a nephew who married a Thai girl" or something like along those lines. I think it's not necessarily people my age, it's like people in their 70s or 80s trying to be friendly.

At one level, 'Chinese girls' were being objectified and at another level, Chineseness was also equated with being 'Asian' insofar as it presumably had something in common with being Thai. Ann did not feel that there was any racist intent in the comment. However, underpinning the comment is a normalisation of casual racism and the creation of a dichotomy between the 'in-group' and Asians. Casual racism may refer to 'forms of racism that are defined by ignorance and insensitivity' (Soutphommasane, 2015, p. 149). According to Faye, one of the study participants, while the practice of using the umbrella term of 'Asian' to label Chinese people and other people of Asian appearance may occur in some Western countries, it was not necessarily shared in Asian countries. Faye, a second-generation Australian-born Chinese in her 40s, has a father who is ethnically Chinese and a mother of Anglo-Celtic background. While Faye perceived herself as Asian in Australia, in her travels to Japan and Malaysia, Faye felt she was perceived as a foreigner: "…the Japanese, you know, have no concept of…I mean 'Asia' is a Western concept. I felt I was going to Asia as an Asian person. To them, I was just a foreigner. So that kind of naïve, romantic idea was kicked out of me."

In one sense, Faye was guilty of essentialising Asianness and assumed that being Asian gave her a bona fide claim of acceptance in Asian countries like Malaysia and Japan. What is evident is that the label of Asian has more than one meaning and is a fluid term. Ben is a second-generation Australian-born Chinese in his early 20s whose father came to Australia in the 1980s as a Vietnamese refugee and whose mother came from China. Ben also remarked on the connection between being Asian and being Chinese:

> I'd say a Chinese person would probably consider all Asian people Chinese. A white person would consider all Asian people to be Chinese. I say that for the Chinese people because they tend to always speak Mandarin to me and to think my looks are Asian regardless of whether they know they can speak Mandarin or not.

According to Ben, a 'Chinese person' was someone who originated from China and spoke Mandarin. He felt that Chinese people assumed he was Chinese because of his appearance when, in fact, Ben did not always identify as Chinese. Ben also believed that white people tended to view 'all Asian people' as Chinese. For Ben, being Chinese seemed to be an all-encompassing label both from the perspective of the Chinese person as well as the white person. Ben also felt that racism was a part of Australian culture and this was not just directed at Chinese-looking people but rather the 'non-white' person: "I mean like there is a general racism across the board anyway. Yeah, like to be a non-white person is to be the butt of someone's joke." In effect, Ben's comments reinforced a dichotomy between white and non-white people. Yet as already mentioned, Ben saw himself as a global citizen which was arguably one way Ben used to escape this dichotomised view of Australian culture:

> Like if I was to define myself, I wouldn't say I was Australian; I'd say I was more of that globalised, cosmopolitan, Westernised culture. There's not something specific; the only specific Australian thing about me would probably be my accent. There's nothing really Chinese about me so I might as well adopt any other culture that I know. Sometimes I say I'm Vietnamese and sometimes I say I'm Chinese. Actually, I rarely say I'm Chinese to be honest. In some cases, I say I'm Australian. And when I am overseas, it's a bit odd to say I'm Australian. The reception I get when I say I'm Australian is like a question mark. I just say I'm from Australia.

Ben was able to exercise some control in adapting his identity depending upon the situational context. However, this may also reflect his uncertainty about belonging in Australia based on his idea that he would be perceived as a 'non-white person'. Earlier in this chapter, Ben had remarked, "I belong here but I'm not anchored here…there's always this possibility of being kicked out". This was perhaps indicative of a continued sense of precariousness marked by feelings of being on the outside.

As displayed by some of the older study participants, negative self-perceptions about being Chinese seemed to fade as the participants aged and became more accepting of and comfortable with their life circumstances.over time. However, there may still be a lingering thought in the back of one's mind or a sense of uneasiness around the resurfacing of negative sentiment. The differentiation of groups based on 'race' continues to persist and play on the minds of Australian-born Chinese to varying degrees. One subtle way in which identity is racialised comes in the form of stereotypes. Racialised groups often contend with stereotypes of themselves in comparison to 'white' people who are seen to be more complex and diverse (Song, 2003).

Stereotypes

Dunn et al. (2004) analysed data from a telephone survey of 5056 residents in Queensland and NSW on the extent of racist attitudes. They found that the 'old racisms' of racial hierarchy and separatism are now being eclipsed by "the 'new racisms' of cultural intolerance, denial of Anglo-privilege and narrow constructions of nation" (p. 409). Cultural intolerance is sustained through the perpetuation of stereotypes. One enduring stereotype that Chinese students confront in everyday life is that they excel academically, particularly in the disciplines of Mathematics and the Sciences, or what some label as the "Asian five" subjects. According to Benton and Gomez (2014), a new stereotype of the Chinese is as a 'model minority' that shines at school and work. This stereotype lends itself to another image of Asian immigrants being the 'model minority' which functions to homogenise the image of Asians (Zhou & Xiong, 2005). For Zhou (2004), the model minority stereotype is a negative and only serves to highlight otherness. While Australian-born Chinese may be acculturated to Australian society, they are sometimes subjected to stereotypical designations resulting in undue pressure to live up to external expectations. Frank is in his 20s and is tertiary-educated. According to Frank:

> There was this whole perception of the Asian person being the smartest in the class… small things would happen, like the teacher might ask me to help someone, or we'd all sort of compare our marks, and everyone would be like, 'Oh wow, you always get 90 per cent' or something.

Frank also observed that Asian parents seemed to have greater expectations of achievement for their children:

> I always thought it was an Asian thing for Asian parents to have a strong belief in what their child should do or shouldn't do. It's probably changing a bit more, but I always felt that in school, some of my other friends, they weren't getting that sort of treatment.

Sometimes, stereotypes can work in one's favour. Ben, a second-generation Australian-born Chinese in his 20s, who felt that he did not quite fall into the category of being 'academically gifted' remarked on the advantage of having the stereotype of being smart attributed to him:

> Oh and then there's the positive stereotypes being academically gifted and stuff. It could be somewhat alienating. Some Asian kids who aren't academically gifted, like during primary school and high school, I was pretty average but you were thought of as someone who's smarter than the average person.

Zhou (2014) claims that Asian Americans are presumably on their way to becoming 'white' without ever reaching that point because "new stereotypes can emerge and un- 'whiten' Asian Americans any time and anywhere, no matter how 'successful' and 'assimilated' they have become." (p. 1181).

Another stereotype that persists relates to the perception of international Chinese students as foreigners who are unwilling to assimilate and who speak loudly in Chinese, a stereotype that was also perpetuated by some of the study participants. Emily is a second-generation Australian-born Chinese in her 20s who identifies as Australian and who has also spent time living abroad in both China and Singapore, with her family moving to China for one year when she was eight years old. Emily's family was based in Northern China and Emily did not feel any connection with the local community:

> They're dark-skinned and more of a Northern Chinese people. When we went to the food markets, I'd always have my cheeks pinched by them, and they'd call me fat and white and I hated that so much. I mean, even physically I was clearly out of place, not to mention culturally. The way I had been educated was in English.

Emily also felt a sense of cultural 'separation' from Singapore when she was living there even though over the course of time, she adapted to the 'social environment'. Emily's experiences within the Chinese diaspora demonstrated the cultural diversity of the diaspora and Emily's appreciation of the differences within the group. One might think that Emily would be less likely to profile Chinese people given her experiences. However, Emily also expressed her desire to be disassociated from 'international Chinese students' which in one sense demonstrated her perpetuation of a stereotype of a group within a group:

> They can be sometimes a bit uncouth in the way that they act. They might be a bit exclusionary in the way that they speak Chinese on the bus quite loudly. They're just trying to feel comfortable in the way they act, but they're clearly foreigners. Part of me just still doesn't want to be associated with the foreignness. Sometimes I wonder if the bus driver might look at me funny if I do something silly, or discriminate against me, because of the colour of my skin. I don't really want to be put in the same basket as just a dirty foreigner who doesn't understand the context and doesn't appreciate it. It feels like it's a prejudice of mine against these international Chinese students, but I do want to feel like I belong—that I'm accepted as an Australian here. I mean I think there's a difference between being foreign and trying to adapt to a culture that is clearly differently from one's own, and trying to exclude yourself from that culture, and not being willing to understand the customs and being rude by speaking another language in public.

Racial stereotyping is not the sole preserve of the Western hegemony. It is a phenomenon that is also evident among the Asian diaspora, for example. Paul (2011) interviewed Filipino migrant domestic workers in Singapore and Hong Kong and found that these workers displayed racial stereotyping about their white and Chinese employers. Paul's findings suggest that Filipino domestic workers in Asia engage in both racial distancing from their Chinese employers and racial alignment towards their white/Western employers. What is interesting about Paul's findings is that the racial distancing and racial alignment that occurs are not along biological lines or phenotype but on perceived cultural traits and moral values. According to Paul, these workers were complicit in promoting colonialist stereotypes and racial hierarchies 'that valorize the West and whites as culturally and morally superior to 'Orientals' such as the Chinese and even Filipinos themselves' (p. 1070). In the course of my research, some study participants also made racialised comments highlighting particular behaviour and attributing it to all Chinese as a group. Frank, a second-generation Australian-born Chinese in his 20s, expressed an understanding of Chinese people which was arguably rather limited:

> I feel like Chinese culture is very efficient and very practical, and not as open to change or creativity or imagination as opposed to Western culture, even though a lot of Chinese history goes back years, long before Western culture. Maybe because they have so many people living in the country, a lot of things are standardised, or it's almost like there's a sameness in their culture, and people are coming out the same, and I don't know if it's really true, or people are just saying it, but all Chinese people look the same [laughs], whereas in western culture, you can be different. Uniqueness is encouraged; people like diversity. You can wear whatever you want, but in Chinese culture, I feel like there's a lot of sameness.

Emily also commented on how her Eurasian housemate struggled with his Chinese heritage:

> My housemate George who's half white and half Chinese, in some ways he is quite Chinese in the way that he thinks of family and cooking, and that I identify with him quite a lot. But, he doesn't want to really consider himself as Chinese, and he does look down on Chinese in some respects. I think he has some unresolved issues about his heritage. I think that he's still trying to figure that out. I can understand why if you grow up in a more rural setting, that being Chinese and sticking out wasn't something that he wanted to emphasise, and I think that he can be racist [laughs]. But then I can be incredibly racist too, or at least, you know, discriminating, particularly, as I said, with the foreigners, with the Chinese.

Like Emily, Gary who is a second-generation Australian-born Chinese in his 30s observed that in the grouping of Asian people together, individual identity was lost:

> It's kind of like swimming against the current, because I guess what's adding to the current that you're swimming against is the new wave of immigrants that are coming through. And yes, you've had an entire generation to assimilate with the Australian culture, but you have people that have just come off planes that sort of bring their own culture with them, and appearance wise, you're no different from them. [...] So like when you look at me—the first time you look at me—I'm no different to a 'Yu Ping Wo' that's just come from Beijing, studying at Melbourne University, hanging around Melbourne Central, buying his bubble tea and eating his fish ball noodles from the food court, hanging around his Asian friends. I'm no different from him [...] Yeah, physically—until you get a chance to know me. So that's the sort of current that I'm talking about that I sort of find myself swimming against.

The Racialisation of Identity

Paul (2011) observed that 'migrant domestic workers were active participants in the construction of racialised essentialisations about their white and Chinese employers, cherry-picking group traits to suit their own ends' (pp. 1079–1080). The study participants also displayed occasions where they 'cherry-picked' particular traits as a way of distancing themselves from the Other. The idea of being lumped together with other Asian-looking people and subsequent feelings of annoyance at being unfairly grouped with others based on physical features alone was a recurring theme among the participants. Gillian who is a third-generation Australian-born Chinese in her 60s did not appreciate being associated with negative stereotypes about Asians:

> When they think you're one of the boat people, or because, 'The yellow peril's coming', sort of thing, or, 'We're getting overrun by Chinese', and the thing is I'm not Chinese in that sense. I happen to be Chinese, but I'm an Australian, so that's the way I see it anyway: 'I'm Australian; I'm here; I was born here, and so you can't lump me in with this other group, because I'm not one of them anyway', because you hear the bad side when they're all into drugs, and they think, 'Oh you've come over with the triads' and all that, and it's got nothing to do with that.

Paul (2011) also observed a process of 'identity triangulation' taking place whereby migrant domestic workers were not only essentialising the character of all whites and Chinese, they were also essentialising the Filipino character. Paul posits that these workers were aligning themselves with whites on cultural and moral grounds. Presumably, these workers felt morally superior over their Chinese employers because they believed themselves to be more 'fair, honest and generous' (p. 1083). They also imagined themselves to be more racially aligned to their white employers 'based on an imagined cultural affinity based on open-mindedness, flexibility and fairness' (p. 1083). This was also displayed by some of the participants who expressed indignation at being lumped together with the Other. Some participants expressed dislike about being 'lumped together' with other Asians and there are instances where Australian-born Chinese try to distance themselves from other Chinese people, in particular, newer arrivals. In the US, newer arrivals are sometimes labelled as "FOB" (fresh off boat) as the more 'assimilated' U.S.-born Asian Americans try to distance themselves from them (Zhou & Xiong, 2005). For Gillian, it was important to differentiate herself from other Chinese who she perceived as not belonging and to align herself with the dominant group. In one sense, Gillian was essentialising 'boat people' while, at the same time, demonstrating the layering of Chineseness. In one sense, this may be a defensive measure to raise one's standing in the global racial hierarchy. In another sense, it is a reification of a racial hierarchy that privileges whiteness, where 'whiteness and the West have become associated with modernity, development and progress' (Paul, 2011, p. 1082). Paul (2011) concludes that most 'Asian or African races seeking social uplift are faced with the impossibility of adopting 'whiteness' as a racial classification for themselves and turn to the feasibility of taking on the culture of Western-ness instead' (p. 1084). Hagendoorn (1993) remarks on the way groups perceive other groups in relation to their own value systems and hence, represent these out-groups in a stereotypical way. These stereotypes are based on limited knowledge and can potentially lead to cultural misunderstanding. It may also lead to a perception that one's ethnicity is somehow inferior to the mainstream.

Being the 'Other'

It could be argued that immigrants and their children do not actively seek to construct their ethnic identity in everyday life until the situation demands it. According to Benton and Gomez (2014), studies have shown that new generations of Chinese are ambivalent about their Chineseness and national identity. Most participants did not really think about their ethnicity until it was raised. Growing up in Australia, many study participants came to the realisation that they were Chinese or different from the mainstream at a very young age or once they attended primary school. That realisation usually came about because others had brought it to their attention. Harry, in his 50s, seemed to be treated like a novelty as a young child:

> Probably as a child— yeah, very young, probably even in the café before I even started school, or even when I was at kindergarten, because I was always aware that I was different. I'm quite conscious because, you know, the customers in the café would always call out to me and say, 'Oh, how cute you are, a little Chinese boy', and going to kindergarten, there was one other Chinese girl there in the kindergarten, but I think through kindergarten and primary school, there weren't many Chinese: very few Chinese in the school.

This research contends that public behaviour is a constant reminder of one's ethnicity and this is exemplified by the questions that were usually asked at some stage of the participants' lives, such as 'Where do you come from?' or 'Why do you speak English so well?'. Zhou and Xiong (2005) call this a process of reactive ethnicity. The effect of this line of questioning is reinforcement of the 'othering' process and in some respects, may cast doubt on the participants' authenticity as Australians. Such questions are a reminder of identity denial where an individual is not recognised as a member of an important in-group (Cheryan & Monin, 2005). According to Cheryan and Monin (2005), everyone with an Asian face who lives in America is afflicted by the 'perpetual foreigner syndrome' which means they are figuratively returned to Asia and excluded from America. This is perhaps analogous in Australia where most of the study participants have been asked these questions numerous times. Implicitly, it suggests an otherness and can lead to self-doubt or even feelings of irritation. The focus on visibility negatively impacts on one's sense of belonging and may result in Australian-born Chinese being the perpetual 'other'. Ian, a third-generation Australian-born Chinese in his 60s, highlighted these feelings:

> I suppose as you get older, there is an identity crisis. Who am I? Because people keep on asking, 'Where are you from?' Of course. I mean the first few times, you think it's funny, but then it gets a bit annoying. Yeah, I'd just tell them I was born here, and then they say, 'Oh!', and they try to laugh it off.

Irene, who is of Chinese and East Timorese descent, was also often asked the question "Where do you come from?":

> Oh, all the time, and they always guess really randomly, so I've gotten Maori, Philippino, Vietnamese, and it's hard, because obviously I'm of Asian descent, but I'm a bit darker, so some people do guess Chinese, but they never guess East Timorese, obviously.

One might expect that members of the host society would be the main protagonists. However, for Irene, it was not so much the Anglo-Australians who asked her but the Asian-Australian population:

> A lot of people do ask, 'Oh, what's your background?' A lot of Asian people like to ask me what my background is, I think more than Australians, because Australians already know you're Chinese. The Asians want to know where you fit into it, so if I go to a shop and I see an Asian, a lot of Asians will be like, 'Oh okay, so what's your background?', because they want to know if they're the same.

This suggests that otherness is perceived not just from outside the group but also within the group. Sometimes, the study participants found that there was a refusal to accept that they were anything but the 'other'. Harry found that he was often asked, 'Where do you come from?', and some people were incredulous when he stated that he was from Melbourne:

> Yeah, all the time, particularly from primary school kids: kids sort of coming up to me and asking me where I came from, and I said, 'I was born here, so Melbourne'. 'No, no, you weren't. Where do you come from?' And there was one boy that was just bullying me all day saying he wouldn't believe where I came from.

This sense of otherness transcends borders. When some of the participants ventured abroad, they also found that people in other countries had preconceived ideas about what an Australian should look like. Frank encountered disbelief from others when he told them he was Australian:

> People are judgmental, and sometimes they can't help it. There's been a few times when I've gone overseas, and I've spoken to people, and they've been really surprised at how I sound, and I tell them that I'm Australian, and they go, 'What? You're Chinese; you're not Australian'.

Despite geographical mobility, the tendency to locate people based on phenotype continues to persist globally. As Ian notes:

> But you go to other countries; it's the same. I was in Malaysia, and I walked out of the hotel, and a tourist came up to me and asked me for directions. I mean, they think you're a local. I mean it's just the way you look—you just get used to it.

Gary also remarks that when people ask him where he is from, he eventually concedes that he is Vietnamese out of a sense of resignation. It is sometimes far easier to concede and resign oneself to other people's expectations than to contend with the disbelief of others:

> My initial response would be, 'I'm Australian', and I'd say I'm from Melbourne. When I travel a lot, people look at me and they'll say, 'Well, you don't look Australian'. My family has been in Australia for quite some time. The more and more I get asked about it, the more and more I'll just save myself the explanation. I'll just say, 'I'm Vietnamese'.

Heather, a third-generation Australian-born Chinese, was also asked about where she came from but found it a strange question because of her lack of awareness of being different at the time:

> People would say, 'Where are you from?' And I'd say, 'Here! Like, 'What do you mean, where am I from?' I always used to laugh, 'I'm from here; what do you mean?' I always thought that was such a strange question. I think that was probably a bit of my naivety, not realising how different I looked at times to different people. I used to think, 'Why do people ask me that?'

Gillian worked in a Government office and was told by one client that she (Gillian) was not Australian:

> ...I interviewed people. One was for the pension, and I remember a woman came in and said, 'I'm not talking to you'. And I said, 'Why not?' 'Because you're not Australian'. She picked up her application. I thought, 'What a cheek!' This was when I was like 30 odd. I couldn't believe it, that someone like this has come in and said that in an interview, 'I'm not talking to you because you're not Australian', because I looked Chinese. I may not sound Chinese, so they think I'm Australian, but as soon as they saw me, and I called them in and sat them in the chair— so I went and called the supervisor. He did it, and it was funny, because he's Irish, but he looks Australian, but he's not Australian either. [Laughs] I hate that, and I was a bit indignant, and I said, 'Oh well if that's the way you want it, well okay, I'll go and get someone'. It was quite offensive. I should have just said something to her and said, 'Go away'.

Ethnic identities are contingent upon social context and are shaped by individual self-perceptions and by external definitions imposed by other people. The question of 'Where are you from?' highlights ethnic difference and, at the same time, reinforces identity as a physical ascription. Each participant who has been asked this question comes from different social contexts: Ian, a third-generation Australian-born Chinese in his 60s, expresses his frustration; Irene in her 20s is asked this question by other Asians; Harry in his 60s was asked this question as a school boy; Frank and Gary could not convince others abroad that they were Australian; Heather who has Chinese and Anglo-Celtic parents was perplexed by this question and Gillian experienced racial profiling in the work place. All these instances serve to demonstrate the pervasiveness of phenotype in identity construction over a range of situational contexts and over time.

The Family as a Reinforcer of Difference

The racialisation of Chinese identity and indeed ethnic identity in general is contextually-driven and can also be reinforced by family members. The process of identity construction may be construed as the 'looking-glass self' (Cooley, 1922; Khanna, 2004) based on the imagination of our appearance to others including an imagination of their judgment and consequent self-feeling. This involves one's self-appraisal, the actual appraisal of significant others and one's perception of the other's appraisal or what is termed 'reflected appraisal'. Noels et al. (2010, p. 747) stated that, 'by imagining how we appear to and are judged by others, we develop our own sense of ourselves'. Individuals see themselves as they perceive significant others see them (Alvarez & Helms, 2001; Khanna, 2004). Parent–child relationships can play a key role in shaping ethnic identity among the second generation (Hiller & Chow, 2005) and the extended family can also influence identity construction. Importantly, it is the individual's perception of how they appear to and are judged by significant others including their parents. Intergenerational conflict may be one of the outcomes, particularly among second-generation Australian-born Chinese, when parents reinforce racial distinctions between their culture and that of the mainstream. In this study, parental expectations on marriage and parent–child relationships illustrate the impact on identity construction when parents racialise identity.

Internalising and Normalising Racism Within the Family

The cost of migration is often a deterioration in intergenerational relations (Chung, 2001). In a study examining the differences in intergenerational conflict in relation to gender, ethnicity and acculturation levels of Asian American college students, Chung highlighted the challenges that may be faced. This included language difficulties, cultural adjustment, challenges to established familial roles and gender roles, and parent–child relationships. As children acculturate and become fluent in English, they may become cultural brokers particularly if their parents struggle with the English language. Consequently, the power relations between generations may alter as parents' self-confidence in the wider community may diminish and the children shoulder greater responsibility. Generational differences in values and the rate of acculturation may lead to intergenerational conflict. In terms of dating and marriage, the more protective and restrictive parenting practices were over girls, the more likely intergenerational conflict would occur (Chung, 2001). This situation may be common in other cultures. 'Out-marriage' was also a matter of concern to immigrant parents. Some participants experienced situations where the family discouraged connection with mainstream white society through relationships. This reverse discrimination was manifested in parental desire for their children to form relationships with people of Chinese background in preference to anyone else.

Alice is a second-generation Australian-born Chinese who was born just after the Second World War, one year after her mother was re-united with her father after being separated by distance for fifteen years. Alice's father left his wife and three children behind in China when he migrated to Australia in the 1930s. At that time, he was unable to bring out his wife. According to Alice, her mother's ideals were rooted in China and even after migrating to Australia, Alice felt that her mother never felt at home. Both Alice's parents originated from rural China. Alice's parents wanted to maintain their cultural heritage by stipulating that their daughters were not to go out with Australian boys:

I don't know what they think they were trying to do but they tried to tell us we weren't ever allowed to go out with anybody. We weren't allowed to go to parties. Um, and we shouldn't go out with Australian boys but there were no Chinese boys so what were we supposed to do? I'm not sure. They never specified. Nor did they make any arrangements to find us a Chinese husband.

In a study on second-generation Chinese and Korean Americans, Kibria (2002) noted how members of the second generation were in between two worlds, the immigrant world and the American, and not fully comfortable in either one. In Australia, study participants growing up sometimes felt a sense of marginalisation not just outside the home but also within the home. Ethnic families differ in the ways they project their ethnicity and they exercise varying degrees of control in expressing ethnic identity (Cheng & Kuo, 2000). According to Alice, her mother was too controlling. Alice conflicted with her mother during her teenage years: "I could never relate to her in a friendly way…she just thought we were totally alien. I think she referred to us as foreign devils. She used that word; she used it to describe us as devil girls or foreign devils." In the process of identity construction, it is just as important to look within the family as it is to look outside the family for influences. Preconceived ideas founded on essentialist ways of seeing are just as evident within the family as they are outside. Cathy's initial choice in partners was driven by her parents' attitudes which in turn may have been informed by their own experiences of racism:

My Mum would deny this now, but my parents used to tell me, tell all three of us, that we had to marry a Chinese man and if we didn't, if we married a white man, we would be disowned and that if we married a, um, black man, that they would kill themselves. So, I have on both sides of my family, I've had an Uncle or Auntie disowned by parents. So, I took that very, very seriously. My parents may not have meant it seriously but because that's my family history, I took it extremely seriously so, I might have admired non-Asian boys across the road but I wouldn't have gone near them.

There was also a practical element in choice of partners espoused by first generation immigrants. The weight of expectation regarding marriage partners was important from both a communication and a cultural perspective. Where English was not the first language, some first generation immigrants expected to be able to communicate with their children's partners and, at least, have something in common. Harry, a third-generation Australian-born Chinese in his 50s, felt pressured by his parents to marry a Chinese girl:

I think it's because of communication, because they really wanted to have a Chinese daughter-in law, and I hate to say, pure Chinese grandchildren. My parents, even though they liked all my nephews and nieces, none of the nephews and nieces could speak Chinese, and I think because I married an ethnic Chinese, and our children— my wife is quite traditional, and she forced our two children to speak Chinese, so my parents were very fond of my two children. Lots of favouritism even though they didn't say— and it also caused a huge amount of jealousy from my brothers, and resentment, and to this day, they still don't like my wife. And it is difficult, and I married my wife, not to please my parents, but it just happened that she was Chinese, and I wasn't consciously looking for a Chinese wife.

Resistance to 'out-marriage' continues to persist irrespective of the environmental context. Despite living in a culturally diverse society, Irene, in her 20s, commented on her father's reaction to her having an 'Aussie' boyfriend:

The Family as a Reinforcer of Difference

> I think he always knew that I would probably date an Aussie or a European or someone who's not Asian—I think he always knew it in the back of his mind, but I don't think it hit him until I brought a white boy home. And I think it's not more so about his feelings; I think it's just what's embedded in them, and the shock, and not just that, like having to share that with their family and stuff like that might be embarrassing for him—I don't know.

Experiences of discrimination can also emanate within the family and against the family itself as in the case of Faye's family and her parents' mixed marriage. Attitudes within the home may not always be consciously conveyed. Sometimes, essentialist ideas may be seen to be natural or part of the norm. While ethnic identities may be socially and politically constructed, they are commonly experienced and expressed as natural (Portes & Rumbaut, 2001, p. 161). Faye, a second-generation Australian-born Chinese in her 40s, has a father who is ethnically Chinese and a mother of Anglo-Celtic background. Some of the comments that her mother used to make were perplexing to Faye:

> I wonder because my Mum was white whether that was a thing for me looking back, you know ... Mum used to say funny things to me. I remember Mum saying things to the effect of 'There's nothing wrong with being Chinese.' And I look back and think 'But why do you say that? Why are you telling me there's nothing wrong with being Chinese?'

It is possible that Faye's mother was pre-empting any potential stigma around being Chinese. But in doing so, there is the presumption that others see Chineseness as a negative and this may have had a bearing on how Faye perceived herself. The experiences of discrimination encountered by Faye's mother when she married a Chinese man may, in part, explain why she expressed her views about being Chinese in that way:

> There was a lot of conflict over my parents' marriage and my mother's parents didn't come to the wedding. She said also there were people who stopped talking to her after she got married or when she got engaged. So it was quite a controversial thing back then ... I think it would have been like '64 or something like that, around that time.

It was only later that Faye's mother found out that her father wanted to attend her wedding:

> And she found out almost close to when her father was dying that he was really torn about the conflict and that, although he and his wife agreed they wouldn't go to the wedding, he wanted to honour that promise but he also wanted to go to the wedding. Apparently, he stood outside the church. It's just the saddest story while they were getting married.

Not only did Faye's mother have little support from her parents at the time of her wedding, she also encountered misunderstandings from the public. When Faye was a baby, her mother was with her in a country hotel dining room having breakfast when another hotel guest approached her:

> She remembers another lady looking at me and saying something like 'Where did you get her from?' And I suppose it's interesting, you know, your child should be racially the same as you, the ethnicity should be the same. And Mum took it to be a reference to orphans from the Vietnam War and she kind of says 'Oh, she's mine' and ended the conversation there.

Faye's father was also subjected to discrimination by being objectified as a Chinaman:

He can remember being here as a very young man and people were doing, you know that touch a Chinaman for luck, like strangers going up and like touching his shoulder and walking off....Yeah and I said to him, "Why were they doing that?" And he said, "Oh you know there's that phrase, 'Touch a Chinaman for luck'." You know, it's never happened to me - it would really upset me if it did.

Faye's experiences perhaps uniquely reflect the culture of White Australia at the time and how it weaved itself into her own family as well as blurring the distinction between the public and the private sphere. The role of the family is traditionally one of support but in this instance, the extended family did not provide that support which was due in part to public sentiments at the time.

Being Half and Half

Sometimes, participants experienced confusion and lack of support in the home environment in terms of their identity. Heather, a third-generation Australian-born Chinese in her 40s, has a father of Anglo-Celtic background and a Chinese mother who was born in Australia. She felt little support from her parents when she was teased at school because of her Asian features. Her mother would tell her daughter to 'toughen up' because she had also encountered racist name-calling in her youth. In response to the name-calling, Heather's mother would chase the protagonists and 'get them back' and it is what she expected her daughter to do as well. Heather's father would call her a 'half-caste' and not think anything of it. Heather, however, felt like she didn't belong anywhere because she was neither 'full Chinese' nor fully Australian. As a result of her negative school experiences and growing up part-Chinese, Heather rejected her Chineseness and seemed to struggle with the label of 'half-caste' bestowed by her father:

> I hated it, because that was my sole source of ostracisement. You know, it was like any time anyone looked at me, I was different, and I was laughed at, and I was made fun of, and it was all because I was what Dad used to say, a 'half-caste', so I hated that I was a half-caste. I wished anything that I could have just been Australian, and it wasn't until I grew up that I even accepted the fact I was half Chinese. I just— you know, people would say, 'Oh, there's something in you'. And I'd go, 'No'. I don't even want to acknowledge that because I had such bad experiences growing up, and I would run from anything Asian—run in the opposite direction—because it had such a negative connotation for me growing up.

Heather's school experiences were largely negative as she encountered relentless bullying receiving little support from the teachers as well as little support from home. Heather's mother would tell her to just put up with the bullying as it was far worse when she was growing up. Asked about her identity in her formative years in 1970s Australia, Heather said:

> It was a confusing place to be, really, because I didn't feel like I belonged either way. My Dad used to always call me a half-caste; he didn't mean it in a derogatory way. I think— you know when I tell people these days that Dad used to call me a half-caste, people get kind of offended almost on my behalf, and I think, 'What? That was just what I was'. That's how he

used to say', and you know, Mum never used to say anything. But yeah, I never really felt like I fitted, because I wasn't Australian to fit in with the Australians, and I wasn't Chinese to fit in with the Chinese, so I kind of just floated around feeling a little bit unfamiliar wherever I was.

Heather had no control over her physical appearance and felt in-between cultures, 'neither truly Western nor authentically Asian' (Ang, 2001, p. 194). It troubled Heather that her parents were seemingly unaware of the ramifications of their actions on her sense of well-being. It could be argued that parents may not always express empathy because they interpret their actions from the perspective of their own position rather than that of their children. Hence, they may be unwitting protagonists in promoting negative self-images among their children.

Under circumstances where participants questioned their sense of belonging to Australia, there was also an acknowledgment that they did not feel that they could fully embrace a Chinese identity. Some participants said they were 'quarter Chinese' or 'half Chinese' but not 'fully Chinese' which begs the question of which part. Faye, a second-generation Australian-born Chinese in her 40s with Anglo-Celtic and Chinese heritage, was told by her mother that she was 'half Chinese' and Faye also realised that she 'felt really not white':

> Mum raised me with this term 'you're half-Chinese' – knowing I was half-Chinese and then there was this joke – which half, left or right? – but not knowing what that meant or how I fitted in. I think I was very conscious of the media images so, you know, the Target catalogue, reading whatever young women's magazines I would have been reading. You know, Claudia Schiffer, with her blonde hair and whatever. You know, being very conscious that I wasn't, but where do I fit in to this sense of there not being a place for me in whatever that cultural representation.

Rather than claiming multiple identities, the notion of having a fractional identity implies that one is not quite right, neither fully Australian nor fully Chinese. Apart from homogenising identity, one's sense of belonging may be affected. Some of the participants also expressed a sense of fraud in proclaiming to be Chinese. Frank, a second-generation Australian-born Chinese in his 20s, expressed nonchalance about his Chinese identity: "Being Chinese is someone who's grown up for most of their life in China. If I said I'm Chinese, I feel like I'm lying. [Laughs] But I see myself as maybe a quarter Chinese". Ethnic identity construction may be founded on perceived truths based on lack of experience. In Heather and Faye's experience, their parents' ideas about being 'half-caste' or 'half Chinese' were a reflection of the environmental context. In Frank's case, both his parents grew up in Malaysia so their first-hand experience of life in mainland China was possibly limited.

Fostering Chineseness

The second generation are placed in a position where they are experiencing 'hybrid in-betweenness': 'neither truly Western nor authentically Asian; embedded in the West yet always partially disengaged from it' (Ang, 2001, p. 194). This can sometimes result in a sense of marginality where belongingness is called into question. The first generation can sometimes unwittingly exacerbate or compound the sense of alienation that their children may experience by instilling their traditional practices on to their children and failing to understand the host culture. Phenotype is an obvious marker of difference between the mainstream and the minority group. However, physical difference extends beyond phenotype, race, ethnicity and other immutable characteristics. For the second-generation, whilst phenotypical differences were hard to avoid, external differences such as dress could at least be manipulated by the individual. This was not to be the case for some of the respondents in this study whose parents insisted on dressing their children in what they perceived to be the Chinese way. Alice remembers how her mother would give her haircuts that were not deemed acceptable:

> I remember going to school with a haircut; I remember our mother decided to cut our hair and she used to cut our hair in the same way, probably the same way she would cut someone's hair in China which is straight across the top near your fringe and straight around like that which is not very cool … we didn't want a haircut like that but my mother just didn't understand what we were on about. She decided well you're going to get a haircut like that and that's how I'm going to cut it and if you don't like it, too bad. So, all three of us went to school with this haircut and it was pretty gross I thought and we just copped shit at school. We got teased because of the way we looked.

Such attitudes and practices still prevail among some. Ann is a second generation Australian-born Chinese in her early 20s. Ann's father is tertiary-educated and, as part of the Australian Government's amnesty following the Tiananmen Square incident in 1989, permitted to stay back in Australia. Ann's mother came to Australia two years later. Ann's grandparents also live with the family and it is fair to say would have had some role in Ann's upbringing. Ann remarked on how her mode of dress as a primary school age child highlighted what she perceived to be her difference from other children:

> Like Chinese children, their parents always layer them up in so many layers of clothes and like at school, you know, the teacher would always be like 'oh, why are you wearing so much? Like take off your jumper.' You'd come home with sort of like an armful of discarded long-sleeve garments, like your grandparents made you wear and I think that was a bit embarrassing.

Family relationships play a fundamental role in shaping ethnic identity construction. Underpinning resistance to 'out-marriage' is discrimination on the part of some parents against non-Chinese people has the effect of reinforcing division and perpetuating an essentialist racial hierarchy. Families can also normalise racist behaviour by using terms like 'half-caste' without realising the detrimental effects this may have on recipients of such labels. And by not being cognisant of differences between the traditional Chinese cultural practices of the first generation and the cultural practices of the host community, parents may inadvertently exacerbate the sense of alienation felt by some second generation Australian-born Chinese. However, experiences of discrimination do not necessarily lead to 'depressive symptoms and greater parent–child conflict' (Rumbaut, 1994). As the following section demonstrates, there is always the capacity to adapt to a perceived negative situation.

Embracing Chineseness

While Heather did not feel like she fitted in when she was growing up, some of the study participants took measures to assimilate to mainstream society. Gans (1979) claims that the main sociological approach to ethnicity has long been one based on 'straight-line theory', in which ethnic groups are absorbed into the host society. Similarly, classic assimilation theory assumes that there exists a unified core of society to which immigrants are expected to assimilate and that, over time, assimilation will occur across generations regardless of national origins, socio-economic status and phenotype (Zhou, 1997). Both theories fallaciously assume homogeneity in ethnic groups and in the host society. In the process of migration, adaptation to the new environment will be an inevitable outcome. The question is to what extent this adaptation will take place. The second generation are generally in a unique position of exposure both to their parents' cultural background as well as to that of the host society. This places them in a different position to that of their parents in terms of adaptation and possibly assimilation to the environment. The assumption that ethnic groups will completely discard their old ways of life in favour of mainstream integration is a classic but flawed view of the assimilation process that continues to persist (Portes et al., 2005).

A recurring theme among study participants growing up in Australia was the desire to fit in by assimilating with the mainstream. While participants could not change their physical appearance, they could enact lifestyle choices that were more in line with the host society. Whether it included a desire to abandon the old ways of life is a separate issue. In contrast, first-generation immigrant parents seemed more inclined to embrace their own cultural customs and traditions rather than adopt those of the host culture. This often led to a source of cultural conflict between the first and second generation. Being able to fit in was often more important than family harmony and it was only later in life that some study participants realised that the two ways of life could co-exist. Harry is a third-generation Australian-born Chinese and grew up in 1960s Australia. Harry noted:

> I think I probably saw myself as Australian, but not being accepted as an Australian; like I did things— like I'd follow the footy, and I'd watch all the TV shows and do things most white Australian kids did, but I always kind of felt that what I was doing— you know, I was just following what everyone did.

The desire to do what everyone else is doing is associated with belonging, to assimilate to the mainstream out of necessity. Edward who is a second-generation Australian-born Chinese and grew up in a rural town in the 1960s stated: "Well, that's the only way to— we just had to fit in with everyone else. I mean we weren't going to get people to change to fit in with us, so we just had to fit in with them". Having a Chinese background is almost peripheral for Edward:

> I am who I am, I guess. I haven't really tried to change. I mean I do sort of— I'm not, you know, really into finding my Chinese roots. You know, I was born in Australia, and as far as I'm concerned, I'm Australian. I might have a Chinese background and look Chinese, but I was born here, so this is my country. China is this other country that I have an interest

in— not a deep interest, but you know, I have an interest in because of my background, I suppose.

Edward goes further to say that his children see themselves as Australians: "I think they see themselves as Australians, because my daughter, she didn't learn Chinese. She's very Westernised, I suppose. My son is very Westernised as well". It seems that Edward is much more interested in fitting in with the mainstream:

> I guess it really depends on the person. Gillian and I come from very similar backgrounds. We're not adept at pushing our Chinese-ness all the time; we just accept who we are, and we live in Australia; it's a different society here; you fit in with the way people live here.

The desire to fit in or the reality of assimilation is much more complex given the lack of homogeneity of both the mainstream and the immigrant population. According to Portes and Rumbaut (2001), race, for example, is an important criterion of social acceptance in the USA and can override the influence of class, religion or language. Phenotypical similarity with members of American mainstream society increases one's likelihood of being able to choose to adapt to the mainstream. Accordingly, Irish and Polish immigrants and their children are thus more likely to be able to choose their ethnicity and to identify with the mainstream than Asian, Hispanic/Latin or black immigrants. For Edward, his primary focus was to fit in with the dominant culture and it would seem from his account that he was not too concerned about focusing on his Chinese identity. In addition, there was almost a sense of resignation when Edward stated 'we just had to fit in with everyone else'. However, Edward was also aware that his physical appearance was a hindrance to his ability to fit in completely when he expressed his 'discomfort' with negative commentary on Asian immigration and how it would reflect on him.

Segmented assimilation theorists recognise characteristics such as race and offer an alternative approach to classic assimilation theorists who posit the notion of a unified white middle-class core to which one aspires. For segmented assimilation theorists, the central question is to what segment of society assimilation will take place and not whether assimilation to a 'core' society will take place (Portes et al., 2005). For some study participants, biology does not really matter. There seemed to be little doubt that participants, like Harry and Edward, strove to assimilate with mainstream 'Australian' culture. However, there were other participants who embraced their Chineseness or they acknowledged that they may have looked like a 'foreigner' but did not feel like one. This was largely due to their sense of agency which was attributable to the support they felt from their family and friends. Brenda, a third-generation Australian-born Chinese in her 30s of mixed heritage, described herself in cultural terms:

> An ethnic Australian - I suppose that's the best way of putting it. I don't identify fully as Chinese and I don't identify as fully ethnic but I do have an understanding of other cultures. I guess I have a cultural sensitivity so I think, yeah I think that's the best way of putting it. I'm not Chinese. Chinese is part of the quilt, you know.

Intergenerational relationships can have a positive influence on identity development. Family structure may affect the social identity and self-esteem of children in a

The Family as a Reinforcer of Difference

new cultural environment (Cheng & Kuo, 2000). Accordingly, parents may play an active role in shaping children's racial concepts and ethnic consciousness through the teaching of ethnic language and cultural transmission. Caitlin is a second-generation Australian-born Chinese in her 40s. Her great-grandfather came to Australia in the late nineteenth century during the Gold Rush period and returned to China after that period. Her father came to Australia in the 1950s as an overseas student. Caitlin grew up in a relatively mono-cultural small city and her parents were active members of a close-knit Chinese community. While acknowledging her strict upbringing, Caitlin has embraced the values transmitted by her parents and appreciates the sacrifices they made for the family:

> My mum is very traditional, and she handed that down to me, so I'm very traditional, even though I'm very Western, but I like my culture ... my mum raised me very traditional Chinese. You weren't allowed to go out; you weren't allowed to have friends over. Well I didn't mind, because at that time, I consider us poor, because you come from the market garden, and it's a hard life, and you can see your parents working hard. You had a good family life, and that was it. I like being Chinese. Here, there's hardly any Chinese people, so your features stand out. That makes me unique, right? I like that. Whereas if you go to Melbourne or Sydney, there's so many people; everyone's got tunnel vision, and no-one sees you; no-one knows who you are, and you're just another number in the system. So, for me, being Chinese feels unique.

It is difficult to say why Caitlin has embraced her parents' ethnic identity when other participants in this research resented their 'traditional' upbringing. It may simply be her feelings of acceptance at home but also in the wider community. Caitlin remarked on her positive experiences in secondary school:

> I remember when I was in grade 7, we were doing Asian Studies or something, and the teacher said, 'Does anyone here know anyone that's Asian?' And no-one put up their hand. I'm sitting right there; I'm sitting next to them; I'm their friend, and no-one put up their hand ... They don't see me as Asian. They just see me as 'my friend', you know. So seeing that sort of like—that's okay.

In this instance, phenotype played no role in how Caitlin's classmates perceived her. Significant others may also extend to grandparents and other family or community members. Those of the third generation may demonstrate stronger ethnic identification than the previous generation through symbols like festivals and food (Gans, 1979; Khanna, 2004). Holly is a third-generation Australian-born Chinese in her 30s. Her father is Anglo-Celtic in origin. Holly's mother was emotionally disconnected from her own mother. However, Holly has embraced her grandmother's idiosyncratic Chinese behaviour, the very behaviour that her mother rejected:

> I love the way that we do family; I love the importance of food; I even love the emotional retardation. Like I can't say, 'I love you', or hug you, but you know, I'll make you a cup of tea, and make your favourite food. And it's very deep, more than words, and you know, it's funny—it's hilarious—like you know, the things people say and do, and it's funny being a Chinese Australian.

The difference between Holly and her mother in terms of their relationship with Holly's grandmother is that Holly had other avenues for parental warmth whereas her mother did not or they were limited. Identity construction may indeed be affected by relationships within the family home but it is also affected by the broader social environment constructed by the individual.

In a study examining how Chinese people in the Netherlands account for their ethnic identity, three different ways of talking about ethnic identity were discussed: 'being', 'feeling' and 'doing' Chinese (Verkuyten & de Wolf, 2002). In these discussions, 'being' Chinese involves biological references stressing that one is Chinese by birth and by their Chinese appearance and is reinforced by their everyday experiences Albert is a fourth-generation Australian-born Chinese in his 60s who has lived in Darwin his whole life. Albert grew up in an environment where he felt the Chinese were in the majority and there were few occasions growing up where his ethnicity was raised:

> In Bendigo or down the Southern States the Chinese were the minority. Up in Darwin we were a majority. Being a minority down in Bendigo way and that, they tried to anglicise themselves. They anglicised their names. They married into Australia. They had more pressure to. I didn't even know that I was Chinese until I was like 17 years old and I went over to Singapore. I went over to Singapore on the way to Hong Kong and I just couldn't believe there was so many bloody Chinamen in the world. I saw myself as an Australian. Like all my friends. Like all my peers, yeah, I was me. The point being that I was actually a foreigner living, you know I looked like a foreigner living in Australia but I never felt like a foreigner if you get what I mean. So, when I went to Singapore, it was alright like I went in the shop, sure enough as soon as I opened my mouth they ripped me up.

In this instance, Albert was 'being' Chinese but 'feeling' Australian and he was not bound to his ethnicity by appearance alone. This is also reflected in his comments regarding membership of the local Chinese Community Association:

> The true Chinese to me, let me put it this way, [the Chinese Community Association] means Chinese people and in that Constitution, I think it says that members are to be Chinese. Well I haven't checked but I think it was an assumed thing right. Then we had some people who really objected because they're actually married to a Chinese and they actually consider themselves to be more Chinese than actually Caucasian. So, they complained. They said I actually consider myself to be Chinese. So, this is going back to your question, if you consider yourself to be Chinese and you believe in the Chinese culture and like the Chinese social aspects of life then we accept them as a member. Yes, it's your own perception and it's all in the culture and all in the family structure and it's all in the [way] you can consider yourself Chinese.

One can observe in this instance a case of 'feeling' Chinese and that physical appearance is not necessarily the main factor for group membership. 'Feeling' Chinese is based on private inner feelings in early socialization that are acceptable explanations for one's sense of ethnic identity (Verkuyten & de Wolf, 2002). For the non-Chinese partners who became members of the Chinese Community Association, they are 'doing' Chinese by their active participation in the Association. Albert also demonstrates how his Chinese identity was a reflection of his environment from the way in which Chinese food is adapted: 'it's called Darwin Chinese food and a lot of it is Bully Beef because back in those days you couldn't get fresh meat. There was Bully Beef with cabbage, Bully Beef with potatoes and tomatoes and Bully Beef. It was nice.' Albert grew up in Darwin and did not feel like he was an outsider. On the contrary, he did not see himself as different from his peers and even on the odd occasion growing up where he experienced exclusion, he was resourceful and confident enough to adapt the situation to his advantage: 'we couldn't play sport with the white people so we formed our own Chinese Recreation Club. We just got on with things, got on with it. There were no issues.' If he couldn't be a part of the sports team, he set up his own sports team. Under these circumstances, Albert had agency and his self-perception was not compromised. This confidence perhaps stems from the fact that being Chinese was like wearing a badge of honour:

> I had a lot of school friends who envied me for being Chinese because of the way our family got on. The parties we used to have and the culture you know they loved it. There was no racism, no nothing in Darwin back in those days. Darwin is made up of a certain type of people. A lot of my friends, their parents came to Darwin for a week. I'm talking about in the 60s. Come up for a holiday, visit someone and they loved it so much they stayed. That's how Darwin grew. It attracted a certain type of people. People who loved the fishing, who loved the weather, who loved the simple way, the big country town type way of life and the parties.

The importance of environment is highlighted by what Albert perceived to be a change in behaviour when he made a visit to Southern NSW. The discriminatory behaviour he experienced there was not something he was familiar with in Darwin:

> I went down to Jindabyne going to the snow. I was in a pub and there was this one person it was obvious they were going as they were saying goodbye and everything and the chair became vacant. I said excuse me mate, no one sitting here? Like I knew that no one was sitting there because he just left. And they said "Ahhhhhh, hang on". And he looked around to see if anyone else wanted the chair. And to me, I never, like if somebody had done that to me in Darwin I probably would have had a go at him. But I thought that it's different down here. I felt a little bit of racism down here. Maybe I was wrong but it was the first time I ever felt it.

Earlier, ethnic identity was referenced in terms of 'being' Chinese based on biological factors. This account is also flawed when we consider Isabelle's experience growing up. Isabelle is a second-generation Australian-born Chinese in her 60s who grew up in an environment very similar to other participants. Compared to her counterparts, Isabelle's physical appearance as a person of Chinese background went unobserved initially:

> They didn't think of me as being Chinese, which is quite interesting. And I experienced this at ballet too. I was doing a performance, or practising for a performance, one year, and I had to do a Chinese dance. Well it was actually a Japanese dance, because I had to wear these thongs, but when it came to the dress rehearsal, one of the girls at ballet said, 'Gosh, you look really Chinese. I never thought of you as being Chinese before'. I don't even know what it was, but I think I had to wear a kimono, so it was Japanese. And she suddenly said, 'Oh gosh, I didn't realise you were oriental!' [Laughs].

Isabelle felt quite acculturated with the local environment and did not express any experiences of conflict with her Chinese heritage.

Importance of Filial and Social Support

Assumptions about ethnicity based on physical appearance and experiences of racism and discrimination can have a detrimental impact on ethnic identity construction in circumstances where the individual is in the minority with few support networks and little sense of agency. When an individual has a sense of agency, experiences of racism and discrimination are likely to have less impact on their sense of identity. As we have seen from Albert, population mix and other environmental factors were key to the development of his sense of identity. Similarly, David, who is a second-generation Australian-born Chinese in his early 20s, has grown up in an environment where both his family and friends have been very supportive. David's father was quick to assert his rights when he felt that the family name was being dishonoured by teaching staff at his son's school and the school promptly responded in an appropriate manner:

> I have the surname Lu, and one teacher thought it was funny to connect Lu with the toilet loo. And one day my dad blew a fuse, went to the school, and it was a big deal. That was very offensive to hear, because the family name is very important for Chinese—not just for Chinese; I think for all cultures, the family name means a lot, especially as it's passed down through generations. I think that was more that the teacher was very naïve, rather than them being prejudiced towards Chinese. I think they were pretty kind of caught off guard that it happened. I think a lot of the time Chinese families seem to be quite passive. They kind of just came in and said to them, 'That's very disrespectful; my son's very upset; I'm very upset... my family name; you've trashed it. I'm paying 17,000 to 18,000 dollars to send my child to your school. A bit of respect, a bit of dignity'. And I think after that, I never had any issue with the school with that issue. I don't know if it was because of my Dad, or just the school kind of figured out, 'Well we shouldn't do this'.

For first-generation immigrants of ethnic minority groups, this type of assertive behaviour may be atypical but irrespective of this, it was a demonstration of strength and pride in one's culture. The children of immigrants who demonstrate 'power' are arguably more likely to be confident in their own ethnic background. In the early years, immigrant parents who were less likely to step outside their ethnic community and continue to maintain traditional parental expectations may inadvertently cause intergenerational conflict with their children who have desire to adopt the values of the host society (Thai, 1999). Denise was at odds with her parents' values particularly her mother's views:

> My father was probably more integrated into Australian society. He had a better command of English. I mean he was here for a lot longer. My mother was well, she was what 35 to 36 when she came out here so, it was very hard for her I would think for her to assimilate in the same way. So, her contacts were with other Chinese people. Whereas my father because of his business associations was much more part of the wider community. I think that to a large extent, it's a bit like a time warp. Their attitudes and culture is frozen at the point that they left China and they don't realise that China has changed as well until they go back and think, oh, that wasn't how I remember it.

David, on the other hand, acknowledges his parents' values about education and even embraces them:

> There were some cultural differences, like we valued education maybe a bit more than perhaps our neighbours did, for example, so sometimes we would stay in and not go out and play with the next-door neighbours — sometimes their parents didn't get that, or sometimes they were a little bit like, 'Oh, maybe you're pushing your child too hard', and for us we'd see them outside playing, and 'Why can't we join them?' Certainly, those kinds of issues existed, but definitely the whole kind of, did I feel like I was being racially picked on? I certainly did experience that, but wasn't terrible.

David had the firm backing of both his family and his friends and it can be argued that this has had a positive impact on his sense of ethnic identity. Even with encounters of racism, David does not have to face these encounters alone because of the strong support network he has which highlights the role of others in framing one's identity:

> You always get some kind of racist, derogatory terms. You know, 'yellow', 'squinty eyes'; you definitely get that stuff, but I personally didn't have a lot of major issues with it. A lot of people just took me as kind of one of them. I play AFL football, and one guy [on the other team] was like, 'Yeah, I don't think Asians belong here'. My team mates came in and they kind of took him out. And then in athletics one time, some guy said to me, 'Asians just can't run as fast'. I didn't really care, because I ended up beating him by about four minutes or something. So, these incidents do happen, but I just don't take it to heart. I usually have the support of my friends and family and stuff, so I never felt alone about it [racism]. My mates, most of them were predominantly Caucasian, so they'd stand up for me, so it was never me against them; it was a whole range of people looking out for me as well. I think it's very important, just knowing that you've got some people behind you. I think that if you didn't have many friends here, and you were getting picked on and stuff, I think the response would be very different, and I think what I'd be telling you would be very different as well.

While Brenda shared experiences of racism in the workplace earlier, David has had many job opportunities:

> I mean I've seen research that said like, 'If you've got a Chinese surname, you have to do 20 per cent more applications to get a job', and stuff. I read this article in *The Age* a few months ago. I've certainly read that stuff, and there's a few other kinds of racial profiling. I haven't had that issue before. I mean I got into one of the most lucrative investment banking internships in Australia a year and a half ago, and my race— the race wasn't an issue. You know, I've managed to play cricket and stuff, and I haven't copped flack. I've been able to play for some of the best local teams in the state, and it hasn't been an issue. I've played football and it hasn't been an issue, so I really don't know— maybe other people have, but I've never really had an issue with being Chinese. I've had a lot of doors opened; I've had a lot of job opportunities come up; a lot of study opportunities come up as well—you know, scholarship opportunities and stuff.

It is difficult to draw any conclusions about workplace culture in general based on these two accounts. What is important to recognise though is that how one relates to these encounters varies considerably depending upon a range of contextual factors. In David's case, essentialised constructions of Chineseness have had little bearing on his sense of well-being and indeed in his everyday life.

Discussion

This chapter has demonstrated that the construction of Chineseness based on phenotype has a pervasive influence on the way in which Australian-born Chinese see themselves. As school-age children, encounters with bullying and name-calling were commonplace and as adults, some of the study participants were quick to disassociate themselves from other Chinese for fear of being seen as one of those Chinese buying up the real estate, a 'boat person' or one of those 'international Chinese students'. This fear is founded on the racialisation of identity and the resultant stigma associated with being Chinese, with the perpetuation of negative stereotypes, and the possibility of being labeled a 'perpetual foreigner'. Depending on the social and political context, these fears traverse time especially if they are reinforced within the family. However, it would appear that family relationships built on mutual respect have the capacity to override any negative impacts associated with the racialisation of identity and that being Chinese is embraced rather than rejected. From a generational perspective, third and later generations seem to embrace their brand of Chineseness more readily.

Chineseness as an identity is constructed based on individual lived experiences. At the same time, it is also driven by the public image or how others see us. Whether the public image is an accurate portrayal of Chineseness is not the issue. Rather, the public image has a powerful influence on one's identity construction and is difficult to escape. Werbner and Modood (1997, p. 226) assert that while social constructionists assume the fluidity of culture and identity, they may have gone too far "in denying the ontological grounds of experience as a source of cultural meaning". In this sense, ethnicity is not only shaped by the self, it is also shaped by our experiences including how others see us.

In the case of Chineseness, historical antecedents have played a significant role in the public perception of Chineseness. The passing of the Immigration Restriction Act 1901 at the turn of the twentieth century instantly presented Chineseness as a negative construct and highlighted the sense of otherness. For multi-generational Australian-born Chinese growing up in Australia during the 1960s and 1970s, this sense of otherness was particularly evident in the schoolyard. The participants in this study often experienced name-calling on the basis of their ethnicity and despite attempts to fit in with the mainstream, the precariousness of their identity was often highlighted as they were growing up in a relatively mono-cultural white Australia.

Despite the passage of time and the growing cultural diversity of the population, the precariousness of identity was still an issue for Australian-born Chinese. Key media events which focus on the issue of race had the effect, in some instances, of the study participants feeling a sense of unease when faced with the risk of being associated with particular ethnic groups. For example, when prominent individuals such as Geoffrey Blainey and Pauline Hanson expressed negative views about particular ethnic groups of Asian origins, some study participants expressed a sense of threat to their place in Australian society. This is contrary to the classic assimilationist view that assumes that immigrants aspire to or that society expected that they would aim

Discussion 81

for full assimilation to mainstream society and would eventually achieve this state of being over the course of time. The reality may be more closely aligned to the theory behind segmented assimilation where immigrant descendants assimilate seclectively with respent to some features of host society, not all.

The role of race or phenotype in identity construction is immutable. 'Ways of looking' become 'ways of being' (Yue, 2000, p. 178). Even in a globalised world, race, by default, has become one of the main identifiers. Racial differentiation illustrates how one ethnic group differs from another, thus resulting in the creation of racial hierarchies. The perpetuation of difference based on phenotype was compounded by Modern European society when it appropriated whiteness, racialised the concept and made it a part of their identity. Historical colonialist discourse only served to highlight racial difference and it is the legacy of such discourse that continues to influence ethnic identity construction among Australian-born Chinese.

Phenotype is manifested in several ways: the perpetuation of stereotypes both by the individual and by society; the stigma associated with race; the role of the family and of society in terms of lack of support and discriminatory practices; as well as the implication of difference as displayed in the questions of 'Where do you come from?' and 'Why do you speak English so well?'. The common theme is one founded on visualism. Some of the stereotypes that are abound relate to the idea of Chinese being the 'model minority'. Coupled with this is the stereotype of the Chinese student being smart and of the Tiger Mother pushing their children to succeed academically. These stereotypes only serve to alienate people of Chinese appearance from the mainstream and can sometimes place undue pressure on Australian-born Chinese to live up to expectations. Similarly, questions often asked of study participants, such as, 'Where do you come from?', can serve to highlight otherness. In the process of trying to fit in or to belong, some of the study participants came to accept negative constructions of Chineseness and actively sought to disassociate themselves from various Asian ethnic groups.

It is not only society which is responsible for the imposition of otherness. The perpetuation of difference may also be affirmed from within the family structure. Some study participants observed that their parents would exhibit discriminatory views towards people of non-Chinese origin when it came to relationship choices. Underlying these views is the idea around the purity of the Chinese race and the experience of racism and discrimination.

Ethnic identity construction for Australian-born Chinese can be a difficult process. Obstacles such as 'groupism', classic assimilation theory which views 'core' society as a predominantly white Western society, and factors such as race and stereotyping all serve to shape the process of ethnic identity construction. As has been demonstrated in this chapter, Australian-born Chinese address these obstacles in varying ways throughout their life course depending upon their social context, social capital and family relationships. The stronger the family relationship, the more likely the participants were to demonstrate agency in adapting their identity formation based on their experiences, both positive and negative to arrive at a hybridised identity that embraces their Chineseness rather than rejects it. Hybridity is about finding a voice without seeking cultural supremacy or sovereignty (Bhabha, 1996).

References

Ali, L., & Sonn, C. C. (2010). Constructing identity as a second-generation Cypriot Turkish in Australia: The multi-hyphenated other. *Culture & Psychology, 16*(3), 416–436. https://doi.org/10.1177/1354067X10361398

Alonso, A. M. (1994). The politics of space, time and substance: State formation, nationalism and ethnicity. *Annual Review of Anthropology, 23*, 379–405. Retrieved from http://www.jstor.org.ezproxy.lib.monash.edu.au/stable/2156019

Alvarez, A. N., & Helms, J. E. (2001). Racial identity and reflected appraisals as influences on Asian Americans' racial adjustment. *Cultural Diversity & Ethnic Minority Psychology, 7*(3), 217–231. https://doi.org/10.1037//1099-9809.7.3.217

Ang, I. (1994b). The differential politics of Chineseness. *Southeast Asian Journal of Social Science, 22*(1), 72–79. Retrieved from http://www.jstor.org.ezproxy.lib.monash.edu.au/stable/24491920

Ang, I. (1994b). On not speaking Chinese: Postmodern ethnicity and the politics of diaspora. *New Formations, 24*, 1–18.

Ang, I. (2001). *On not speaking Chinese: Living between Asia and the West*. Routledge.

Asghari-Ford, M., & Hossain, S. Z. (2017). Identity construction of second-generation Iranians in Australia: Influences and perspectives. *Social Identities: Journal for the Study of Race, Nation and Culture, 23*(2), 126–145. https://doi.org/10.1080/13504630.2016.1207515

Bailey, B. (2000). Language and negotiation of ethnic/racial identity among Dominican Americans. *Language in Society, 29*(4), 555–582. https://doi-org.ezproxy.lib.monash.edu.au/https://doi.org/10.1017/S0047404500004036

Barth, F. (Ed.). (1969). *Ethnic groups and boundaries: The social organization of culture difference*. Little, Brown and Company.

Benton, G., & Gomez, E. T. (2014). Belonging to the nation: Generational change, identity and the Chinese diaspora. *Ethnic and Racial Studies, 37*(7), 1157–1171. https://doi-org.ezproxy.lib.monash.edu.au/https://doi.org/10.1080/01419870.2014.890236

Bhabha, H. K. (1996). Culture's in-between. In S. Hall & P. du Gay (Eds.), *Questions of cultural identity* (pp. 53–60). Sage Publications Ltd.

Boese, M., & Phillips, M. (2017). 'Half of myself belongs to this town': Conditional belongings of temporary migrants in regional Australia. *Migration, Mobility & Displacement, 3*(1), 51–69. http://dx.doi.org.ezproxy.lib.monash.edu.au/https://doi.org/10.18357/mmd31201717073

Boese, M., & Phillips, M. (2011). Multiculturalism and social inclusion in Australia. *Journal of Intercultural Studies, 32*(2), 189–197. https://doi.org/10.1080/07256868.2011.547176

Bonnett, A. (1998). Who was white? The disappearance of non-European white identities and the formation of European racial whiteness. *Ethnic and Racial Studies, 21*(6), 1029–1055. https://doi.org/10.1080/014198798085656 51

Brubaker, R. (2004a). *Ethnicity without groups*. Cambridge, Mass.: Harvard University Press.

Brubaker, R. (2004b). In the name of the nation: Reflections on nationalism and patriotism. *Citizenship Studies, 8*(2), 115–128. https://doi.org/10.1080/1362102042000214705

Cheng, S. H., & Kuo, W. H. (2000). Family socialization of ethnic identity among Chinese American pre-adolescents. *Journal of Comparative Family Studies, 31*(4), 463–484. Retrieved from https://search.proquest.com/docview/60093440?accountid=12528

Cheryan, S., & Monin, B. (2005). Where are you really from?: Asian Americans and identity denial. *Journal of Personality and Social Psychology, 89*(5), 717. https://doi.org/10.1037/0022-3514.89.5.717

Chow, R. (1998). Introduction: On Chineseness as a theoretical problem. *Boundary 2, 25*(3), 1–24. Retrieved from http://www.jstor.org/stable/303586

Chung, R. H. G. (2001). Gender, ethnicity, and acculturation in intergenerational conflict of Asian American college Students. *Cultural Diversity & Ethnic Minority Psychology, 7*(4), 376–386. https://doi.org/10.1037//1099-9809.7.4.376

Cooley, C. H. (1922). *Human nature and the social order*. Charles Scribner's Sons.

References

Dunn, K. M., Forrest, J., Burnley, I., & McDonald, A. (2004). Constructing racism in Australia. *Australian Journal of Social Issues, 39*(4), 409–430. https://doi-org.ezproxy.lib.monash.edu.au/https://doi.org/10.1002/j.1839-4655.2004.tb01191.x

Gans, H. J. (1979). Symbolic ethnicity: The future of ethnic groups and cultures in America. *Ethnic and Racial Studies, 2*(1), 1–20. https://doi.org/10.1080/01419870.1979.9993248

Goffman, E. (1959). *The presentation of self in everyday life*. Anchor Books.

Hagendoorn, L. (1993). Ethnic categorization and outgroup exclusion: Cultural values and social stereotypes in the construction of ethnic hierarchies. *Ethnic and Racial Studies, 16*(1), 26–51. https://doi.org/10.1080/01419870.1993.9993771

Hiller, H. H., & Chow, V. (2005). Ethnic identity and segmented assimilation among second-generation Chinese youth. *Sociological Studies of Children and Youth, 10*, 75–99. https://doi.org/10.1016/S1537-4661(04)10005-6

Howard, S., & Gill, J. (2001). It's like we're a normal way and everyone else is different': Australian children's constructions of citizenship and national identity. *Educational Studies, 27*(1), 87–103. https://doi.org/10.1080/03055690020002152

Jenkins, R. (1994). Rethinking ethnicity: Identity, categorization and power. *Ethnic and Racial Studies, 17*(2), 197–223. https://doi.org/10.1080/01419870.1994.9993821

Khanna, N. (2004). The role of reflected appraisals in racial identity: The case of multiracial Asians. *Social Psychology Quarterly, 67*(2), 115–131. Retrieved from http://www.jstor.org/stable/3649082

Kibria, N. (2000). Race, ethnic options, and ethnic binds: Identity negotiations of second-generation Chinese and Korean Americans. *Sociological Perspectives, 43*(1), 77–95. https://doi.org/10.2307/1389783

Kibria, N. (2002). *Becoming Asian American: Second-generation Chinese and Korean American identities*. The John Hopkins University Press.

Lee, J., & Bean, F. D. (2004). America's changing color lines: Immigration, race/ethnicity, and multiracial identification. *Annual Review of Sociology, 30*, 221–242. https://doi.org/10.1146/annurev.soc.30.012703.110519

Levine, H. B. (1999). Reconstructing ethnicity. *Journal of the Royal Anthropological Institute, 5*(2), 165–180. Retrieved from http://www.jstor.org/stable/2660691

Lo, J. (2000). Beyond happy hybridity: Performing Asian-Australian identities. In I. Ang, S. Chalmers, L. Law, & M. Thomas (Eds.), *Alter/asians: Asian-Australian identities in art, media and popular culture*. Annandale: Pluto Press Australia Ltd.

Martin, J. (2003). The global hierarchy of race: As the only racial group that never suffers systemic racism, whites are in denial about its impact. *The Guardian*, 20 Sep 2003, 1.23.

Matthews, J. (2000). Violent visions and speechless days: Corporeality and the politics of image. In I. Ang, S. Chalmers, L. Law, & M. Thomas (Eds.), *Alter/asians: Asian-Australian identities in art, media and popular culture*. Annandale: Pluto Press Australia Ltd.

Min, P. G., & Kim, R. (2000). Formation of ethnic and racial identities: Narratives by young Asian-American professionals. *Ethnic and Racial Studies, 23*(4), 735–760. https://doi.org/10.1080/01419870050033702

Noels, K. A., Leavitt, P. A., & Clement, R. (2010). To see ourselves as others see us': On the implications of reflected appraisals for ethnic identity and discrimination. *Journal of Social Issues, 66*(4), 740–758. https://doi.org/10.1111/j.1540-4560.2010.01673.x

Paul, A. M. (2011). The 'other' looks back: Racial distancing and racial alignment in migrant domestic workers' stereotypes about white and Chinese employers. *Ethnic and Racial Studies, 34*(6), 1068–1087. https://doi.org/10.1080/01419870.2010.528783

Portes, A., Fernandez-Kelly, P., & Haller, W. (2005). Segmented assimilation on the ground: The new second generation in early adulthood. *Ethnic and Racial Studies, 28*(6), 1000–1040. https://doi.org/10.1080/01419870500224117

Portes, A., & Rumbaut, R. G. (2001). *Legacies: The story of the immigrant second generation*. University of California Press.

Rosenthal, D. A., & Feldman, S. S. (1990). The acculturation of Chinese immigrants: Perceived effects on family functioning of length of residence in two cultural contexts. *The Journal of Genetic Psychology, 151*(4), 495–514. https://doi.org/10.1080/00221325.1990.9914635

Rumbaut, R. G. (1994). The crucible within: Ethnic identity, self-esteem, and segmented assimilation among children of immigrants. *International Migration Review, 28*(4), 748–794. Retrieved from http://www.jstor.org/stable/2547157

Song, M. (2003). *Choosing ethnic identity*. Polity Press.

Soutphommasane, T. (Ed.). (2015). *I'm Not Racist But... 40 Years of the racial discrimination act*. New South Books.

Thai, H. C. (1999). "Splitting things in half is so white!": Conceptions of family life and friendship and the formation of ethnic identity among second generation Vietnamese Americans. Paper presented at the American Sociological Association. *Amerasia Journal, 25*(1), 53–88.

Verkuyten, M., & De Wolf, A. (2002). Being, feeling and doing: Discourses and ethnic self- definitions among minority group members. *Culture & Psychology, 8*(4), 371–399. Retrieved from https://search.proquest.com/docview/60454240?accountid=12528

Werbner, P., & Modood, T. (Eds.). (1997). *Debating cultural hybridity: Multi-cultural identities and the politics of anti-racism*. Zed Books.

Yeh, D. (2000). Ethnicities on the move: 'British-Chinese' art–identity, subjectivity, politics and beyond. *Critical Quarterly, 42*(2), 65–91.

Yeh, D. (2014). Contesting the 'model minority': Racialization, youth culture and 'British Chinese'/ 'Oriental' nights. *Ethnic and Racial Studies, 37*(7), 1197–1210. https://doi.org/10.1080/01419870.2014.859288

Yue, M.-B. (2000). On not looking German: Ethnicity, diaspora and the politics of vision. *European Journal of Cultural Studies, 3*(2), 173–194.

Zhou, M. (2004). Are Asian Americans becoming "white?". *Contexts, 3*(1), 29–37. Retrieved from http://www.jstor.org/stable/41800832

Zhou, M. (1997). Segmented assimilation: Issues, controversies, and recent research on the new second generation. *International Migration Review, 31*(4), 975–1008.

Zhou, M. (2014). Segmented assimilation and socio-economic integration of Chinese immigrant children in the USA. *Ethnic and Racial Studies, 37*(7), 1172–1183. https://doi.org/10.1080/01419870.2014.874566

Zhou, M., & Xiong, Y. S. (2005). The multifaceted American experiences of the children of Asian immigrants: Lessons for segmented assimilation. *Ethnic and Racial Studies, 28*(6), 1119–1152. https://doi.org/10.1080/01419870500224455

Chapter 4
Language and Ethnic Identity

Ethnic language is often seen as an important signifier of an ethnic group's identity (Luke & Luke, 2000; Smolicz et al., 2001; Phinney et al., 2001). Ethnic language maintenance in immigrant families may also contribute to the successful intergenerational transmission of cultural practices and values. In language-centred cultures, language may be a symbol of ethnic identity as well as a measure of authenticity within the group (Smolicz, 1992). Brubaker (2013) contends that language is a basic forms of social, cultural and political identification. Accordingly, it is central to most ethnic and national identifications and is often used as a marker or symbol of such identifications. Yet, language is not primordial or fixed and can change depending upon circumstances. The extent of language retention among immigrant groups is also widely varied (Portes & Hao, 1998).

This chapter examines the role of ethnic language as a marker of ethnic identity for Australian-born Chinese. It also considers the factors that impinge on language loss or retention including the family context and societal expectations and the consequent impact of that language loss or retention. This research suggests that ethnic language is perceived as an important signifier of ethnic identity for the first and second generation but becomes less important as a marker of ethnic identity by the third and fourth generation. The notion that ethnic language maintenance contributes to the successful transmission of cultural practices and values is juxtaposed against the idea that ethnic language is primarily a medium of communication between the first and second generation and its role is only functional in nature. The Australian-born Chinese develop their ethnic identity in a myriad of ways depending upon individual experiences both within and outside the home and with or without ethnic language maintenance. By and large, language as a symbol of ethnic identity is not in dispute. However, its importance and functionality as a marker of identity seems to diminish over time and space and across generations.

Language as a Marker of Identity

"You'd Be Less Chinese If You Didn't Speak the Language"

The importance of language as central to most ethnic and national identifications is indisputable. It is a way of construing sameness and difference and naming social groups (Brubaker, 2013). Language can define one's connection with the homeland and can also define one's connection to the host society. Speaking Chinese can be a marker of Chinese identity while, at the same time, it can also be a marker of difference from the host society. Alice is a second-generation Australian-born Chinese in her 60s who grew up in Hobart. Hobart was largely a mono-cultural environment in the first few decades after the Second World War and Alice and her siblings were the only Chinese family in her primary school. Alice's attitudes towards retention of her parental language evolved over her life course beginning with one of rejection of her parental language towards one of acceptance and acknowledgment of its value. Alice's attitudes exemplify the central role that language plays in identity development for many Australian-born Chinese. For Alice, speaking Chinese was a representation of being Chinese and Alice wanted to be Australian:

> Being Chinese would be like speaking Chinese and sounding Chinese right. So, sounding strange, not sounding like Australians. You wanted to dress like Australians and you didn't want to look like a Chinese person because that wasn't cool really. And all the things that Chinese people want to do, like my parents wanted to do, really didn't fit in with what we wanted to do at school and growing up.

Alice was intent on assimilating to mainstream culture and one way to do this was by rejecting spoken Chinese. Whether intentional or otherwise, it also had the effect of creating a communication barrier between Alice and her mother:

> I think I've always spoken Chinese to my mother but as time went on, it became more difficult to speak to her in Chinese. And, therefore, I didn't communicate very well with her. We tended to speak English as we got a little bit older. I'd say there were a lot of arguments between us, the three sisters who were born in Australia, and our parents. There were a lot of discussions but difficult to communicate exactly what you wanted to say.

As an adult, Alice continued to maintain her identity as an Australian but, at the same time, qualified this by seeing herself as part Chinese. Over time, Alice has come to appreciate her cultural heritage and lack of proficiency in her parents' language has not diminished Alice's identity as Chinese:

> Being Australian is a composite of being Chinese and being brought up in Australia. I belong in Australia but, I'm not like all Australians. I really don't think I would have liked being brought up as an Aussie, garden variety Australian family. That, I think, is the ultimate in cultural loss really.

Alice's comments demonstrated a revision of what she perceived being 'Australian' was in her formative years. Where Chineseness was once viewed as a negative and separate from an 'Australian' identity, it had become a positive trait that differentiated

Language as a Marker of Identity 87

her from the 'garden variety Australian' and expanded her idea of what an 'Australian' was. Where Alice once aspired to fit in with other Australians, she was decidedly patronising towards 'white' Australians. This was perhaps more a reflection of her being comfortable in her own skin as opposed to denigrating someone else. On the other hand, it was an essentialisation of another identity.

Coupled with Alice's acceptance of her Chinese identity was her acceptance of the Chinese language in terms of its functional value. Alice perceived that an inability to converse with her business colleagues abroad would make her less Chinese. During her working life, Alice travelled to China for business and recognised the value of being able to converse in Chinese. Alice remarked on the inability to relate to business colleagues in China without that language ability:

> You'd be less Chinese if you didn't speak the language. You would really miss out on a lot. You really wouldn't understand; you wouldn't pick up a lot of the subtleties, I think, and the attitudes if you couldn't speak at all. I mean, having comprehension of the language helps a little bit but probably you need to speak quite well to fit in.

For Alice, the ability to speak Chinese had a functional value insofar as she would have been able to communicate with her mother on better terms and it would aid her in doing business in China. However, according to Alice, it is not language alone that was a measure of one's cultural belonging:

> I think it's about language but not only about language - it's accent or the way you speak because Australians have a particular way of speaking or expressing themselves. And if you're born in Australia, that's how you speak. So that's what makes you Australian. If you speak and talk like an Australian, and you have attitudes and ideas in common with Australians, that would make you Australian. But you are also aware and conscious of your Chinese heritage and Chinese ideas as well. So, you might not be as extreme in one area as some other Australians may be. For example, a lot of Australians just go out and get drunk every night and drink a lot. Well, there would be a lot of Asians who wouldn't do that. They would think it was not very good.

"It Doesn't Matter What Language You Speak"

The importance of language as a measure of cultural belonging was also evident over time among second-generation Australian-born Chinese born in the 1990s. Cameron is in his 20s and is a second-generation Australian-born Chinese. Both his parents were born in South Africa, spoke Afrikaans and English, and were acculturated in a non-Chinese speaking environment. Cameron had noticed the language barrier that existed in his interactions with his Chinese-speaking relatives but considered 'blood relations' more important in connecting him to his extended family than language proficiency:

> You do feel a bit of a stranger. Even though you've got the same colour skin, they are your family. We were staying with my great uncle, and they do welcome you with open arms and take you out for lunch, take you out for dinner—very hospitable, but because of the language barrier, it's very difficult to hold the connection. The fact that we share the same family name and blood relations [counts].

There is a conception that being Chinese is 'a matter of blood or shared descent from a common ancestor' (Kibria, 2002, p. 46). Cameron is irritated by the 'perception that if you can't speak the language, you're not one of them', a perception that he refuted even though he felt a lot of people think:

> When you do go there [Hong Kong], if you can't speak the language, they will not see you as a Chinese person; they will see you as something odd—you know, they'll see you as a banana—yellow on the outside and white on the inside.

Cameron felt that language loss also impacted on his ability to form relationships with Chinese women. Although Cameron has acknowledged that language proficiency was not the only measure of cultural belonging, he felt that it had an influence on his life:

> If you are Chinese and you can speak it, generally you would either pick a Chinese partner if they can speak the same language, and communication-wise, I've had a few Chinese girlfriends, or Chinese people that I've met, and the reason why I've been rejected is because you couldn't speak the language—the communication is a bit of a problem.

Authenticity as a Chinese person without being able to speak Chinese was also called into question by Caitlin, a second-generation Australian-born Chinese in her 40s. Caitlin has embraced her parents' cultural heritage and owns a Chinese restaurant with her Chinese husband. For Caitlin, not being able to speak Chinese was a sign of being a 'fake' Chinese. Referring to a popular Australian-born Chinese chef:

> I think she is the most fake Chinese. To be on TV, to represent Chinese cooking and stuff—no disrespect, right? But not to be able to speak the language itself, I think is like— that's a fake Chinese. To be a real Chinese, you should know all about your own culture, or at least speak it.

Although Caitlin was quick to label someone who does not speak Chinese as a 'fake Chinese', she also drew on Chinese cultural practices and festivals being more important signifiers of being Chinese. The diversity of languages spoken for different Chinese groups in Caitlin's community had meant that language on its own was no longer a defining feature of being Chinese. The increased diversity of the Chinese community meant that communication barriers were created as there was no commonality in the Chinese languages spoken. What eventually brought the different groups together was their participation in a common event rather than the languages spoken:

> The Chinese community has grown, but that's another problem that we have, because our clubs are all separate based on language, because our club—the CCAT—we're all the older-generation Chinese that have been here for 40-50 years. So, we're the Taishan-speaking group, and then you've got another group that's the Chinese Cultural Society, and they're the Mandarin speakers. A couple of them came into our group, but you can't talk. I mean you want to, but you can't. They can't talk to you; you can't talk to them. So, they pulled away and formed their own group. Most of them are overseas students and things. This Chinese community festival pulls all these groups together because our one aim is to have one big one under our umbrella—everybody, because they want to be involved too. They're Chinese. Chinese is Chinese; it doesn't matter what language you speak.

Over the course of the interview, Caitlin conceded that a 'fake Chinese' was someone who may look Chinese but neither engages in Chinese cultural activities nor has any idea about Chinese culture and traditions. Cameron added that language was not the only marker of identity. Rather, the focus should also be on where you are born:

> There's a perception pretty much in a lot of places—Hong Kong and Australia— there's a perception that if you can't speak the language, you're not one of them. [However] they also have ties to where you physically are born. If you're born in Australia, you should be an Australian; if you were born in China, you're a Chinese person.

Although ethnic language continues to be a marker of ethnic identity, language on its own is not the sole marker of Chinese identity given factors such as blood relations, cultural practices, traditions and birth place. Some of the participants in this study felt that language was an important measure of ethnic identity while others did not. Some study participants believed being Chinese was not necessarily dependent upon Chinese language skills. Cathy, a second-generation Australian-born Chinese in her late 30s grew up in Melbourne in suburbs where there were few ethnic Chinese around during her primary school years. Cathy did not feel that an ethnic Chinese was less Chinese if they did not speak Chinese:

> I don't think they're less Chinese because I'm sort of in that boat. But I can understand if they feel less Chinese because it's not necessarily about the way that they feel themselves. It's about the way other Chinese people treat them but that's been my experience.

"You're Chinese in Your Heart"

As Luke and Luke (2000) observe, language loss may strengthen the determination to retain cultural values and practices as a way of maintaining cultural identity. Doris is a fourth-generation Australian-born Chinese in her 50s. Doris had an unconventional upbringing as her father was a travelling showman following the agricultural show route and the family of fifteen children lived an itinerant lifestyle around Australia attending the local schools when the show was in town. Doris' mother was of Irish Catholic heritage but Doris does not really acknowledge this part of her ethnicity focusing primarily on her Chinese heritage in her ethnic identity formation. Doris' mother lost her own mother just after she was born and was raised by her 'alcoholic railway Irish father' before being placed in foster care. Doris purportedly did not have the opportunity to embrace her Irish heritage given that she was placed in foster care by a father incapable of looking after her. Doris lives in the Goldfields region of Victoria, a region that is rich in Chinese history and where the Chinese community has an established place in the wider community. Chinese festivals are celebrated by the wider community and in terms of social positioning, the Chinese community seems to hold a strong position. Doris' association with various Chinese groups has only served to strengthen her Chineseness and this is carried on by her children and grandchildren.

Doris has no knowledge of any Chinese language but this does not diminish her identity as a Chinese person. Doris cannot speak Chinese but immerses herself in Chinese cultural festivals, participates in Chinese community organisations, visits a Chinese doctor and a Chinese acupuncturist and her grandchildren refer to her as 'Por por' ('Grandmother' in Cantonese). Doris is the only one of her siblings to engage in Chinese cultural practices. For Doris, these actions reinforced her sense of Chineseness and she actively encouraged her children and grandchildren to continue to embrace Chinese cultural practices. To Doris, active participation was an acknowledgment of her Chinese heritage and indeed her Chineseness and that of her grandchildren even though they have Anglo-Celtic features. Doris says:

> I was associated with every Chinese group in my town because I am Chinese. I'm born Chinese; I'm not married Chinese; I'm born and my children, my son especially, he's twenty-five this year next month and I've asked him to do my 'passing over' because I know he's the one that will acknowledge my past and always remember the culture we had in our community, in our own Chinese descendants of what my father did, his Poppy or Goong Goong (Grandfather), and then my grandchildren will know. Now Daisy is only seven. She calls me Por Por. She knows [about] her 'Dai Goong Goong'. Daisy is going to learn Mandarin because that's the new language and Daisy is a Blossom Dancer at the Chinese Association and has been for four years.

In this instance, it was Doris' practices that defined her. Doris' extended family carried on some Chinese traditions and in doing so, she felt that the family's Chinese heritage would continue to be passed on. For Doris, being Chinese comes from within:

> Uncle said last night – he said, "You're Chinese in your heart." I said that's all I wanted to be. And that says it all because you can have it in your looks, you can have it in your family but if you haven't got it in your heart and you're not walking with it and talking with it, it shall disappear.

Similarly, Albert, a fourth-generation Australian-born Chinese who lives in Darwin and is actively involved in the local Chinese community association, believes that one's identity is based on self-perception—if one perceives themselves to be Chinese, then they are Chinese. There is a mixing of cultures rather than a separateness (Pieterse, 1994). Doris' grandchild has blonde hair and blue eyes but Doris perceived her to be Chinese. Albert spoke a rudimentary level of a Chinese dialect and identified as a 'Chinese born in Australia'. His mother-in-law spoke 'Chinglish'. Albert differentiated between different Chinese groups—a 'proper Chinaman' can speak Chinese and is invariably a China-born Chinese (CBC) as distinct from an Australian-born Chinese (ABC). In the local Chinese community association, the constitution stated that members must be Chinese. Caucasian spouses of Chinese people who follow the Chinese culture and embrace Chinese traditions are accepted as members. In this sense, ethnic language is peripheral to being Chinese:

> We spoke enough Chinese and like I said it wasn't a big deal. For example, my mother-in-law she speaks 'Chinglish'. You know what Chinglish is? Chinese English right. They'll be talking Chinese and a few English words come into it or the other way around. But we didn't have to speak Chinese. Only with our grandparents. Obviously, [we are] less Chinese than a person that can speak the language. That's a proper Chinaman and we have an expression

Language as a Marker of Identity

CBC – Chinese-born Chinese. Speaking Chinese obviously helps but if they don't speak Chinese, they are probably bloody ABC.

On the face of it, Albert's comments could be interpreted as derogatory towards Australian-born Chinese. However, given that Albert is fourth-generation, it could be argued that his use of the term 'bloody' is a part of the Australian lexicon and therefore used to emphasise more than anything else.

For fourth-generation Australian-born Chinese like Albert and Doris, knowledge of a Chinese language is incidental to their identity as Chinese. For Albert, there was a differentiation between Chinese who speak Chinese and those who do not. Yet, Albert still considered himself Chinese despite his rudimentary use of the Chinese language. For second-generation Australian-born Chinese like Alice, knowledge of a Chinese language is functionally important insofar as it would have facilitated communication with her mother and other Chinese people. From this perspective, there is the potential for inter-generational cultural transmission. However, given the diversity in Chinese languages or dialects, language is arguably no longer a central tool for cultural transmission as Caitlin's experiences in her Chinese community association would attest.

Social context plays a key role in the extent to which ethnic heritage is embraced. In other words, how the Australian-born Chinese perceived their identity was largely influenced by the situation they were in and who they considered to be significant others. Ethnic language retention was not always central to one's identity when other factors like environmental or social context are deemed more important. Holly is a third-generation Australian-born Chinese of mixed descent in her 30s who grew up surrounded by many members of her extended family. She spent a significant amount of time with her Chinese grandmother who Holly felt was the epitome of Chineseness. Holly compared herself to her cousins who grew up in Austria without any extended Chinese family members around. Despite her cousins' ability to speak Mandarin and having lived and worked in China for ten years or more, Holly felt that her cousins were less Chinese than her because they did not experience intimate relationships with their Chinese relatives:

> My cousins, who are half Chinese Australian and half Austrian, so they're as genetically Chinese. They both speak Chinese and I'm pretty sure they speak Mandarin. They're now both living there [in China], so they're now more versed in modern Chinese culture. But in terms of a kind of an assimilation and an orientation at a basic level, I would say they'd be less Chinese, even though they have the language over me, and we're genetically as Chinese. Because they haven't been raised with their Chinese family, you know, there's a lot of things that they can't be. The joint experience of a Chinese grandmother, like you talk to any person - it doesn't matter what sort of Chinese or how long their family have been in a non-Chinese country - everybody has this kind of universal experience of the Chinese grandmother, and it's something that's quite unifying, which you know, [they] don't really have, because they've only met her a couple of times. You know, their idea of grandmother is a sort of round Austrian woman who makes cakes and torte and things like that. And they live in the mountains and yodel— they don't actually yodel, but that's their idea of grandmother.

The content of ethnic identity or what it is that people within a boundary share varies along three dimensions: interests, institutions and culture (Cornell, 1996).

Communities of interest are dynamic and can vary in terms of economic or political circumstances. Communities of culture and institutional communities are more stable. For Holly, her Austrian-born cousins do not fit into her idea of Chinese identity because they did not share the same Chinese upbringing. This is not to say that Holly's cousins are less Chinese than her. Rather, their ethnic identity may be founded on different interests and cultural experiences. Both Holly's cousins resided in China for many years and were immersed in Chinese culture in terms of speaking Mandarin, socialising with the local community and partnering with Asian women. However, Holly perceived that their childhood experiences revolved around an Austrian upbringing and, therefore, her cousins did not have her brand of Chineseness. Arguably, Holly's cousins have a more 'authentic' experience of Chineseness having embraced Chinese culture in the 'homeland'. As Cornell (1996) observes, the ties that bind members to each other are diverse and the combinations vary. Holly defined her Chineseness around a Chinese upbringing which was shared by other members of the Chinese community in a specific situational context (Eriksen, 2010) where Chinese people were a visible minority. Even if Holly's cousins constructed their ethnic identity as Chinese, based on their lived experiences as adults surrounded by Chinese culture and institutions, in Holly's mind, they were not as Chinese as she was. For Holly, knowledge of Mandarin was incidental to her perception of being Chinese. This attests to the subjective and individual way in which ethnic identity is constructed.

Ethnic language retention can facilitate family communication particularly among the first and second generation and has the potential to foster cultural heritage maintenance. However, ethnicity can also be preserved through other core values such as religion (Smolicz, 1980; Smolicz & Secombe, 2003) and in Doris' case, through cultural activities. According to Ommundsen (2003), diaspora is not homogeneous but imagined differently depending on personal preferences and one's circumstances. Souchou (2009) conducted a survey of Malaysian Chinese students' perceptions of themselves in terms of Chineseness and found that their perceptions of what constitutes Chineseness were based on three criteria: ancestry, descent and blood; participation in Chinese activities like temple worshipping, eating Chinese food and lion dance; or identity is a matter of governmental definition. Thus, being Chinese is unimpeded by Chinese speaking ability or lack thereof. One of the potential reasons why language does not necessarily play a central role in the identity construction of Australian-born Chinese may have something to do with familial relationships and the potential for conflict when two cultures collide and this is examined in the following section.

Family Dynamics and Language Use

Data from the 2016 Census demonstrate that 72.7% of people spoke only English at home. However, this figure has slightly dropped from the 2011 Census, where 76.8% of people spoke only English at home. Today, despite increased migration and policies promoting LOTE programs in schools, the de facto national language is still English. English is also the *lingua franca* in many work settings globally. The immigrant second generation in general is inclined towards loss of their parental language, given that they speak English at school and parental languages at home, if at all, and complete loss is arguably inevitable in ensuing generations. As Portes and Rumbaut (2001) observe, by the third generation, foreign language proficiency is lost because it is neither supported inside or outside the home.

"We Would Reply in English to Our Parents"

Alice's parents emigrated to Australia from mainland China prior to the abolition of the 'White Australia' policy. Most immigrants from China up until that period originated from Guangdong Province in China's South, were generally poorly educated, and from rural areas. Lack of education was due, in part, to the advent of Japanese occupation and the subsequent war leading to the inability to continue with education during that period. Alice's father migrated to Australia in 1933 without his wife and two children at the time. It was not until 1948 that Alice's parents were reunited in Australia and they subsequently had four more children, one of whom was Alice who is in her 60s. Kibria (2002) studied second-generation Chinese and Korean Americans and found that they were between two worlds, not fully comfortable in either one. Alice's parents had settled in Hobart, a community which was largely white and Anglo-Celtic. With the White Australia Policy in force, cultural diversity in Hobart was at a minimum. In this environment, Alice's mother never felt a sense of belonging to Australia and her mistrust of the community at large manifested in her strict adherence to her cultural roots through food and customs, her mixing only with other Chinese people, her failure to mix with the wider, mainstream community except in her interactions with customers in their small business and her failure to learn the English language:

> It got difficult at times because my mother had attitudes that were totally different to the attitudes of Australians. And there was always a lot of disagreement about points of view about various things. And you really couldn't have a discussion with her about it because the English, my level of Chinese was not as good as my level of English. So, it was very difficult to say what I wanted to say to her.

Alice described her mother as Chinese and like 'a fish out of water' unable to adjust to life in Australia. These factors had an enormous impact on Alice's relationship with her mother as she perceived that their ideals were a total 'mismatch'. Alice's mother insisted that her daughters dress and behave in accordance with her wishes and she expected her children to converse to her in her native tongue. In one sense, this was one way Alice's mother could exercise control over her children and, at the same time, transfer her cultural values to her children. However, Alice's mother's expectation of filial piety backfired as her Australian-born children made every attempt to assimilate to mainstream culture against their mother's wishes. This meant a rejection of their mother's cultural expectations and anything that represented their Chinese background. To a lesser extent, Alice was also rebelling against her father but as he was less vocal and involved than his wife in the disciplining of his children, Alice's mother was the focus of family conflict. Alice, as a school girl, wanted to look and sound like everyone else in her school and speaking Chinese was not part of this process. In this sense, speaking Chinese was a representation of being Chinese as perceived by both Alice and her mother:

> There are a lot of people who would speak Cantonese [in China] and it's a connection to your childhood because when you hear Cantonese, you hear the language that was spoken as you were growing up. So, I suppose that's Chinese. You know, you were brought up in a household where Cantonese was spoken and Taishan so that makes you part Chinese, I think.

Alice expressed regret at the partial loss of her parents' language because of the breakdown in communication and understanding that resulted. From this perspective, language is a tool that acts as a bridge between cultures and without that tool, there is likely to be a disconnect between cultures. In hindsight, Alice was aware of the language barrier but had reached the point where her poor relationship with her mother could not be easily resolved. The relationship between Alice and her mother suffered because of the language barrier but it was not the only cause of their relationship problems. Despite the language barrier, the chasm between their cultural values was too great during Alice's teenage years and would likely have existed even if Alice had retained fluency in her parents' language:

> The language breakdown and social breakdown in, I suppose, differences in cultural attitudes because you're brought up in Australia, you're going to school and you spoke English and you everything you read was in English and you were adopting the culture of that country whereas mother was at home. She didn't speak English and she wasn't able to adjust. I don't think she was able to, I don't think she could, I don't know why. She was only 33 when she came out to Australia and I'm thinking that all through the time I was growing up, I couldn't understand why she didn't learn English properly. She never did. She was still in China. I think coming to Australia then having children born in Australia was just a divide that could never be bridged.

In a study involving 184 Chinese American and 80 European American high school students, Wu and Chao (2005) found that a primary source of conflict centred on parental beliefs and practices, notably the mismatch between adolescents' ideals and perceptions of parental warmth. While family values form the basis of an individual's cultural map, the interpretation of these values is heavily influenced by the dominant culture via media, schools and peers. According to Wu and Chao, psychological problems arise from difficulties in reconciling parents' values with mainstream values. In terms of language retention, some study participants like Alice refused to retain their parents' parental language despite parental desire for them to do so because parental language represented difference. Alan, a second-generation Australian-born Chinese in his 30s, was aware of being different in primary school and his earlier negative experiences influenced his desire to learn the Chinese language:

> I think in primary school, I felt it a bit more – the differences – only because you occasionally heard, you still heard the racial slurs and that kind of reminded you of the difference. Unless you have got a teacher who really values that kind of diversity, the only things you associate with being different, with being Chinese, is negative. I think that was definitely a factor in the fact that we didn't want to learn the language. And so, when our parents wanted to speak to us in Cantonese or Mandarin, we would reply in English. And I think that tends to be a common theme that I have heard around with a lot of my friends who tend to think this as well.

Both Alice and Alan are second-generation Australian-born Chinese separated by over thirty years yet their desire to assimilate was a common objective. The theme of culture clashes with parents is an important one in childhood memories of participants (Kibria, 2002). These culture clashes were particularly evident in families where communication problems were brought on by a lack of proficiency in the parental language. For these participants, their authenticity as 'real Chinese' was challenged when they made 'homeland' trips and their lack of fluency in the Chinese language highlighted their difference. David, a second-generation Australian-born Chinese in his 20s, comments on the necessity of parental language retention in his communication with family members in Australia and in China:

> Just in my relationship with my parents, even with my grandparents and my uncle, and most of my family in China as well, most of them don't speak English. If you can't speak Chinese to them, well we don't really have much to talk about. It's pretty much a necessity. I think that's the best way to put it. It's a tool, of course, but it's a necessity. That is the only way I can communicate with them, and that's my way to be able to talk to them and understand them.

The functional element of parental language retention is often undermined by the desire to assimilate to the host culture and this seems to be evident over time and across second-generation Australian-born Chinese irrespective of age. Growing up, David was not interested in learning Chinese because his focus was on fitting in and making friends:

> Mum and Dad sent us to Chinese school, and that was very big for them. They wanted us to learn Chinese. We didn't want to learn Chinese, one, because we didn't value it, and two, we felt learning Chinese would make it more difficult for us to fit in. Well, we just didn't care about it enough to learn about it, and I think we wanted to fit in with everybody, so we wanted to do what 'everybody [else was doing] - playing football on Saturday. So why don't we play football [on] Saturday with them?' kind of thing. So, it was probably more when I was a child more than anything, because you want to fit in.

"Chinese Is What Keeps Me Really Connected with My Parents"

It is only with the benefit of hindsight that some second-generation study participants realise the value of maintaining their parents' language. David talked about the quality of family relationships when one could communicate:

There's a limit to my ability to be able to relate to them and understand their stories and what their history is, and just relate to my family a bit more. My brother doesn't speak Chinese so my Dad's relationship with my brother is very superficial. He's asking me all the time, 'What's your brother up to? How does he feel about stuff?' And because I can speak Chinese, we have a far stronger relationship; it's a lot deeper and a lot more kind of meaningful. I think for our family, the Chinese [language] is what keeps me really connected with my parents, and they can understand what I'm saying as well. And without [speaking] the Cantonese, I think our relationship would be far less deep and meaningful.

The type of role that children of immigrants adopt with their parents can influence the formation of racial and ethnic identities, the different languages spoken and affiliation with different social networks (Chung, 2013). For example, Caitlin was a 'cultural broker' who supported her family through care-giving and household responsibilities. Caitlin who is in her 40s grew up in the same town as Alice but her relationship with her parents was somewhat different to that of Alice. The environmental circumstances during Caitlin's formative years were also different. While both Caitlin and Alice are second-generation Australian-born Chinese, Caitlin's relationship with her parents was a lot more supportive and filial piety was evident. Caitlin acknowledged that her parents were 'traditional' and that this traditional upbringing has been carried on by Caitlin:

My parents have been here for that long. My parents are 80 and they don't speak very good English—they still have broken English. I still have to translate everything for them. So, my mum is very traditional and she handed that down to me.

Caitlin continued to act as a dutiful daughter and she was a translator for her parents; she practiced Chinese customs, she married a Chinese person who owned a Chinese restaurant and she passed on Chinese traditions to her own daughter. Where Alice experienced conflict between her home life and her school life, Caitlin did not seem to feel the same conflict insofar as she seemed to blend in with her school peers. The environmental conditions that both Alice and Caitlin experienced were different—by the 1970s, the White Australia Policy had been abolished and Asian immigration patterns had changed. Caitlin's family socialised with the small Chinese community in the area and although Caitlin was the only Chinese person in her primary school class, she did not experience any racial problems. Even in secondary school, Caitlin felt a sense of acceptance. There was the odd occasion when Caitlin experienced racial taunting but by her accounts, those occasions were rare:

I mean you get the odd— 'Ching Chong' and 'Slanty Eyes' and all those sort of comments, but it's just a one-off. When you're younger, you do get a little bit upset. But now it's like as you make friends and people get to know you, it all falls away.

It would seem that Caitlin was well-integrated in her school community to the extent that her ethnicity was incidental. A common observation among many Australian-Chinese was that they were generally not focused on their ethnicity in their everyday interactions until it was raised by someone else. A sense of belongingness both within one's ethnic community as well as in the wider community plays a significant role in how one constructs their identity. Caitlin felt a sense of belongingness both at home as well as in the wider community and therefore felt comfortable in either environment. Caitlin's experiences of growing up Chinese have been largely positive which perhaps explains her continued embracement of her Chinese heritage which included Chinese language retention—being Chinese was never a source of shame for her:

> Because inside, you're still Chinese—your roots are still Chinese, right? But being Australian just means that you can fit in with everyone and anyone. You should be very accepting of everything. But you yourself, you know, you're still Chinese.

Caitlin's Chinese roots were fundamental to her identity and her perception that to be Chinese means to speak the Chinese language was perhaps a reflection of her own upbringing. The Chinese language serves an important function not only as a tool that facilitates communication between Caitlin and her parents but as a tool to foster cultural understanding and transmission of values (Phinney et al., 2001).

Chung (2013) identified two other types of roles that children of immigrants may adopt with their parents—that of children as familial dependents who rely on parents for care giving and that of children as autonomous care takers who are not close to their parents and grow up detached from their parents. Familial dependents were found to have less empathetic understanding of their parents' cultural values and migration experiences than those who acted as cultural brokers. This was due to language barriers, lack of shared experiences, and their subordinate roles within the parent–child relationship with parents being strict authority figures. Fran is a second-generation Australian-born Chinese in her 20s who was raised by her grandparents due to some perceived discord with her parents whom she is not on speaking terms with. Fran's grandparents were effectively her 'parents' or primary care givers with strong views on Chinese language retention:

> Well to them [grandparents], 'You're Chinese; you have to speak Chinese. If foreigners see you, they expect you to speak Chinese'. [For a Chinese person who doesn't speak Chinese], they probably would consider them almost a disgrace. I know my view on this matter is a lot different from my grandparents, who think it's an absolute shame that they're not speaking Chinese. While they may not know a lot about China that they understand, but they just feel that the language part— losing that bit is an absolute shame. But with me, I think they shouldn't be blamed if they don't speak the language, or if they don't practice it— the Chinese culture, because there are various reasons for that.

Contrary to Chung's claim that familial dependents would be less empathetic of their parents' cultural values, Fran is accepting of her grandparents' views on language as a representation of Chineseness although she does not necessarily agree with them.

"Me and My Dad Don't Really Have Conversations"

The third role that children can adopt is that of autonomous care taker and, according to Chung (2013), this cohort is detached from their parents and more likely to be disdainful of their parents' culture. Their lack of appreciation of their parents' cultural upbringing can create family conflict and these children choose instead to assimilate into the host culture. Alice experienced roles of both familial dependent and autonomous care taker. Generational conflicts are an issue in every family but in immigrant families, there is also the issue of children's shift to a new language and a potential conflict derived from perceiving their parents as foreigners (Tannenbaum & Howie, 2002). Alice felt that her mother's cultural practices were at odds with Alice's desire to fit in with the Australian way of life. This discord was compounded by Alice's lack of command of the Chinese language which inhibited her relationship with her mother:

> Yes, it was very difficult. She didn't really understand what was happening to us and we couldn't speak to her properly I'd say my Chinese was the level of a ten-year-old. I don't think it was beyond that but we were at university. We were studying English literature and philosophy. Well, we could speak at that level in English but we couldn't speak to our mother at that level so we couldn't really explain to her what was going on really and she wouldn't have understood what was going on.

Generational conflict is a recurrent theme across cultures but in the case of the children of immigrants, it may sometimes be compounded by the lack of proficiency in a common language. 'Dissonant acculturation' may occur where the parents' knowledge of English is limited and they are unable or unwilling to learn English and their children refuse to speak the home language (Portes & Rumbaut, 2001). Emotional dissonance between generations, particularly, between the first- and second-generations is another key factor in the distance created between children and parents. Louie (2006) observed that the identities of second-generation Chinese were influenced by the lack of emotional connectedness and physical affection with their parents. It is not to say that they felt a lack of care from their parents as Asian parents express their love for their children through what they do, like support and sacrifice to provide an education, rather than what they say to them (Wu & Chao, 2005). Rather, when the only lines of communication between the second-generation and their parents is when parents 'command' them to do something, the emotional 'closeness' that the second-generation witness in families in the host culture is sadly lacking especially when identities of the second-generation are grounded in the local context rather than in their parents' countries of origin.

Ella is a second-generation Australian-born Chinese in her 60s. Her father migrated to Australia in the 1930s to establish the family business before being reunited with his wife who came to Australia after the Second World War. Ella spoke about her conflict with her mother and her way of avoiding that conflict: 'there were always arguments going on at home, and as young children, we decided, once we were very good in English at school, we actively spoke English to each other so that our mother couldn't understand what we were talking about.' Ella was emotionally detached from her mother which, in turn, distanced her from her cultural roots, at least, when she was growing up:

> I think my mother was probably typically Chinese. She liked to tell us all the time what we were doing wrong, how bad we were, and so I just resented it, I guess. And my mother used to

do things that were probably totally acceptable in China, but they stood out in Australia, and made me feel— I felt ashamed; I didn't want to be associated with that ... Well, I think my mother is totally different to me anyway, so she didn't care what people thought of her, and she did manage to communicate, but she never mastered [it], really, the basics of the English language, and so what my mother said, and how my mother expressed herself was always somehow like the stereotypes of, you know, the poor Chinese who couldn't pronounce their 'l's' and 'r's', and as a kid, I found— yeah, I was embarrassed; I wasn't proud.

Ethnic language is a hearable point of difference from the host language in Australia. Speaking and sounding Chinese was a source of embarrassment for Ella. To distance herself from her mother, Ella used language to create a barrier. In Alice's case, it was only later in life that she recognised the importance and value of being able to speak the Chinese language to communicate with her parents and being able to speak the Chinese language to engage in Chinese business opportunities. There are some key similarities between the two scenarios: Alice recognised the value in being able to communicate with her parents in their native tongue to avoid misunderstandings and when she was engaging in business in mainland China, she recognised the value of being able to communicate in Chinese to understand the environmental context and to promote her business opportunities:

> I think it's important to be able to speak the language. It enables you to establish contacts with China if you wanted to and Chinese people and fit in more - immerse yourself in the culture in China if you wanted to. And, sort of re-acquaint yourself or learn more about what wasn't passed on to you really. I mean, often your parents were just too busy and they don't have time to sit down and tell you things. And that was like my mother. She didn't tell us anything.

Arguably, Alice's motivations were largely practical and not because she either wished to embrace parental customs and values or wished to identify with the mainland Chinese. Ann, a second-generation Australian-born Chinese in her 20s who is more than 40 years younger than Alice, also reinforced the importance of language maintenance in China to be perceived as Chinese by Chinese people in China:

> Like if you do speak the language, it's easier to just go to China and fit in. Like I can go down the street and buy whatever I want. If I ask people a question, I don't need to [explain], like it's easier to fit in. There's like the taxi driver who was telling me off because I should keep my heritage and speak Chinese. I think it's very important to people in China that you keep a lot of the Chinese traditions and the language.

This was distinct from how Ann saw herself. Ann felt like an outsider when she visited China and she did not feel like she fitted in. Ann saw herself as first and foremost an Australian with a Chinese background with her ability to speak Chinese an incidental part of growing up rather than a defining feature of who she was. Irrespective of the motivations behind language loss and how one identified, the outcomes were palpable. Edward, a second-generation Australian-born Chinese in his 60s, lamented the breakdown of communication with his mother that continued to persist in his adult life:

> As I got older, I just sort of let the Chinese go, I guess, and tried to be like other kids. So, it got increasingly more difficult, I suppose, with my parents. It made it difficult conversing

with them, or even just discussing things that were going on. Dad was more conversant in English than Mum. Mum knew a few words, but not a lot. It's probably about as good as my Chinese, I suppose! I wasn't very close to my parents because of that issue. Even now, we don't tend to talk a lot, because again the same problem, Mum only speaks Chinese, and my Chinese is pretty bad, and it's not conversational. I just know a few words and that's about it. So, trying to converse with Mum, it's really difficult.

There are, however, other contexts where second language retention is difficult to maintain and language loss is not always planned. In the process of migration, the transmission of parental languages may be lost simply because parents may not have the time to spend cultivating language retention. Ben, also a second-generation Australian-born Chinese in his 20s, grew up in an environment where both parents spent most of his formative years working:

My Mum, she'd speak Cantonese to me. My Dad, he'd speak Vietnamese to me. But, my Cantonese and Vietnamese are really quite rudimentary because of a few factors like one, because I lived in a pretty Australian neighbourhood, there was no Cantonese or Vietnamese speaking kids around me. That's one reason, I guess. And the second one would be, they'd mostly be working most of the time while me and my little brother to some extent would be watching TV which is basically American TV.

Ben went further to remark on the lack of communication between his father and himself:

My Dad, he doesn't speak much English anyway. My Mum's English is better. Me and my Dad don't really have conversations. Yeah, it's a bit of a loss and a bit of a problem because it's hard to get points across, to argue...I wouldn't say I adopted any of my parents' views. From a young age, I always saw my Dad as like a country bumpkin type fella and my Mum, she's more intelligent than my Dad...It's kind of unfortunate, if not for like the cultural richness, also, there's a bit of a loss, it's a bit embarrassing as well knowing that you could have been tri-lingual or bi-lingual at least.

While Ben appears to be resigned about the lack of communication, it is arguably one of the key factors in loss of cultural heritage. Ben referred to his father as a 'country bumpkin type fella' which suggested that Ben perceived his father to be less worldly educated. One of the differences in upbringing between Ann and Ben was the amount of time invested by their parents in Chinese language cultivation. As Kibria (2002) points out, families vary in the extent to which they actively transmit ethnic cultural practices. In Ann's case, her father who was a university academic sent her to Chinese language school whereas in Ben's case, both his parents worked so that Ben and his siblings spent their time at home without cultivating second language retention and, arguably, with little intellectual stimulation from their father.

Portes and Rumbaut (2001) noted that in relation to language transmission, parental resolve and the resources committed to language retention play key roles. In an effort to transmit ethnic cultural practices, language is seen to be one of the key ways of maintaining a connection between second-generation children of immigrants with their parents and their community. One of the driving forces behind parental desire for their children to maintain a connection with their cultural heritage is ethnic pride and belongingness in their own community as opposed to that of the host society. Cathy's grandparents were born in China but her mother was born in Malaysia and her father was brought up in Singapore. Both her parents identified as Chinese as does Cathy, a second-generation Australian-born Chinese in her 30s, who grew up in the Northern suburbs of Melbourne. Cathy's father came to Australia to study at university but ended up opening a Chinese restaurant. There were few Chinese families in the Northern suburbs in the 1980s and Cathy experienced several racist encounters during her school years which eroded her sense of belonging in Australia. This sense of belonging also eluded Cathy's parents when living in the Northern suburbs where there were few Chinese families at the time. Cathy and her family were often exposed to incidences of racial hostility, which would have coloured their views towards their host community. So, Cathy's parents attempted to establish contacts with the Chinese community by sending Cathy to Chinese school in the Eastern suburbs. Cathy did not like Chinese school partly because she had no interest in learning Chinese and partly because she felt that her parents were not being themselves and were being ingratiating towards the Chinese in the Eastern suburbs of Melbourne who were purportedly wealthier than they were:

> I used to go to Chinese school in the Eastern suburbs and absolutely hated it. But, my Mum and Dad really loved it and because they used to be able to see all the Chinese parents. I didn't understand what was happening because they only spoke in Chinese. I didn't do well because how could I if I didn't understand what they were saying. Also, I saw what it did to my parents because they were trying to make friends so much. I didn't think they were being themselves so I found them a little ingratiating to them. I think they wanted to be a part of the community. They wanted to hang out with people that you know they felt that they could sort of relate to. But I think I always saw my parents as a bit different from the Eastern suburbs Chinese people. They used to talk about how wealthy the Chinese were in the East. We come from the North and we were very un-wealthy compared to, at least my parents used to say, compared to the Eastern suburbs ones.

Cathy disliked going to Chinese school possibly either because of perceived class differences where she could not identify with the Eastern suburbs Chinese or because of the stigma associated with being Chinese as manifested in the racism she encountered. Despite Cathy's parents resolve, Cathy did not develop her Chinese language skills and did not feel as comfortable in the language school environment as much as her parents did. As with Alice, over the life course, Cathy's idea of what it meant to be Chinese had changed. In their formative years, Alice perceived her Chineseness as a negative trait and Cathy, who appeared to be more conscious of how others behaved towards her, possibly a reflection of her levels of self-esteem, perceived that the community around her saw Chineseness as something negative. As adults, both Cathy and Alice have embraced their Chineseness and this appeared to be a common theme among the other participants in the study. In terms of ethnic language, Cathy did not feel that one was less Chinese because they did not speak Chinese. However, she did acknowledge that others might think otherwise. Alice, on the other hand, recognised the utility of being able to speak Chinese to do business in China. But, in terms of how she identified as Chinese, I would argue that Alice's ability to speak Chinese would not have altered that.

The reasons for language loss are complex but what appears to be a recurrent theme among participants in this study is the eventual realisation that second language retention is an important tool for communicating with people from one's cultural heritage for second-generation Australian-born Chinese. Family relationships do impact on language retention for second-generation Australian-born Chinese and this is intertwined with the social or environmental context.

Social Acceptability of Parental Languages

Ethnic identity shifts among the descendants of European immigrants seems to follow a process of assimilation to the point where ethnic identity becomes 'an optional leisure-time form of symbolic ethnicity' (Portes & Rumbaut, 2001, p. 149). This process of ethnic identity formation is influenced by socioeconomic status, degrees of acculturation in terms of linguistic and cultural similarities to the dominant group, the context of reception and the degree of discrimination experienced by the non-dominant group. Historically, for the Chinese in Australia, the process of ethnic identity shift was much more complex. Up until the abolition of the White Australia Policy, the Chinese were largely unwelcome and the experience of discrimination for the children of Chinese immigrants was reflected in their collective assignment to a subordinate group. As Ommundsen (2003) noted, because of systemic discrimination, a person of Chinese descent could not culturally be a citizen of Australia before the abolition of the White Australia Policy. Consequently, a Chinese person had the choice of cultural isolation or cultural self-denial and assimilation.

When language is seen to represent a cultural or ethnic group, it may sometimes be used to reject that group. One of the driving forces behind young second-generation Australian-born Chinese is the desire to fit in with the mainstream even if it means rejection of one's heritage via language loss. Peer influence is a major factor in immigrant children's maintenance or loss of their ethnic language (Luo & Wiseman, 2000). Social context plays a role in how an ethnic language manifests itself. The amount of social interaction with peers from the same group was also assumed to influence ethnic identity through greater use of the ethnic language (Phinney et al., 2001). At the same time, being surrounded by a native-speaking majority, foreign language use becomes private and is used by family and friends in private settings such as in the family home and at private gatherings (Portes & Rumbaut, 2001). Foreign language use becomes hidden and in extreme cases, it is also rejected. Frank, a second-generation Australian-born Chinese in his 20s, did not want to be identified as Chinese based on being able to speak Chinese:

> I actually don't like the sound of Chinese, and I don't like speaking it. I mean I know a few words and numbers or whatever, but when I speak it, I don't feel comfortable, and maybe it's because I haven't been speaking Chinese as a child earlier. But I feel like it just doesn't feel right for me to speak Chinese, and I don't have any desire to speak it. Maybe there's some sort of subconscious thing happening but I hope this delves into the assimilation thing. I think a part of me doesn't want to speak Chinese just because I don't really have any intention of living there or just being associated with Chinese-speaking people. I think I don't want to be known as, 'Oh yeah, he can speak Chinese; get him to speak with that Chinese person'. I like being known as that Australian guy who looks Chinese, but he can't speak Chinese. I

don't have a desire to speak Chinese, but I also feel like I just don't want to associate myself with the culture, because I don't really like it that much, or some parts of it.

Frank's comments reinforced a racialised notion of language. Kibria (2002) also remarks on the racialisation of ethnic traditions insofar as the distinct cultural symbols and practices of a particular ethnic group are incorporated into the generic 'Asian' label resulting in homogenisation of ethnic identities into 'an all-purpose Asian'. According to Luke and Luke (2000, pp. 51–52):

> Ascriptions of linguistic competence are commonly linked in people's minds to visible racial-ethnic markers: if you look Chinese you must be able to speak Chinese. When assumed linguistic competence fails to match visible 'obvious' ethnic identity, a sense of cultural in-groupness fractures and the ethnic English-only speaker can suddenly find her/himself repositioned outside the culturally distinct 'us'.

The racialisation of identity continues to be an issue as is evident in public displays of intolerance towards speaking languages other than English in public as experienced by some of the study participants. In Australia, there may not always be the same respect given to speaking languages other than English in public. There is an expectation that one's language is inextricably tied to their identity. For Luke and Luke (2000, p. 53), 'language acts as a "hearable" indicator of difference that is almost always used in conjunction with a reading of the speakers' bodily habitus, race and ethnicity often misclassifying identity following initial calculation based on visible racial difference'. Ann is a second-generation Australian-born Chinese in her 20s who is a university student. Ann felt a sense of discrimination for speaking Mandarin in public:

> I remember this one time on the train and I was speaking to my Mum in Mandarin and um, these people came on and they were like, 'why don't you speak in English?' or something like that. And that made me feel really like awkward especially because, you know, my English is pretty good. It's probably better than my Chinese. So, it made me feel very self-conscious after that.

Ann indicated that there was an expectation that people in Australia should be speaking English and remarked on how mainstream society frowned upon others not speaking in English:

> Sometimes, it's like a language thing. So, a lot of the time, if there's like a lot of international students whose English is not their first language and so among their friends, they'll speak Chinese or Cantonese or whatever. And then people will say, you know, why don't you learn English?

These experiences illustrate how language is intertwined with visible racial difference and, at the same time, demonstrate the double standards at play at many levels. Ann was reprimanded for speaking Mandarin and there was an assumption that she was a foreigner. If Ann was a Caucasian person speaking Mandarin, it is probable that she would not have been reprimanded. In situations where public displays of second language intolerance occur and different customs are measured by Eurocentric standards, it could be argued that second language loss is an inevitability. Language loss can have a catastrophic outcome in the sense that it has the potential to sever the ties that may exist to one's cultural heritage.

At the same time, there is potential risk of displacement from the host culture based on phenotype intertwined with ethnic language use. But as Luke and Luke (2000, p. 66) note, 'families are engaged in developing complex "third spaces" sites for the development of dynamic, hybrid cultural identities and practices'. Rather than language enabling identity formation or cultural membership, the focus is on how people use languages, discourses and texts to construct hybrid social identities or new cultural formations. As Edward, a second-generation Australian-born Chinese in his 60s, remarked:

> You could say that someone else who's learned to speak Chinese, I mean they don't become Chinese. It's hard to isolate just one aspect of it. I can't say that even if I did speak Chinese that I'd class myself as Chinese. I think the fact that I was born here— this is my country of birth, so I feel that I've got more of a belonging to Australia than China. You know, the Chinese country that I visit, I don't think I could live there, because it's so different to what I've experienced here.

Country of birth was what defined Edward's sense of belonging more than his ability to speak or not to speak Chinese. Irene, a second-generation Australian-born Chinese in her 20s, confirmed the importance of the functional aspect of language as a communication tool as opposed to its role in identity formation:

> I think it plays an important part [in identity], but I don't think it's the most important part. I feel like obviously for me it would be good to speak Chinese, but if you can communicate in any language, it's more about what you communicate rather than what language it is. If you're able to communicate in many different languages, that's great, because you can get your message out there in a lot of different ways, but it's more about the message rather than what you speak, if that makes sense.

Language loss may be related to the perceived stigma around parental language use and its association with ethnicity. Some of the experiences of the study participants suggest that speaking Chinese in public is frowned upon. Perceived public stigma around parental language use may be enough to deter one from speaking their parental language in public or to cause language loss. Family is a primary site of linguistic socialisation (Brubaker, 2013) and, in association with social context, plays an integral role in language loss or retention primarily among second-generation Australian-born Chinese. The first generation are more inclined to preserve their ethnic language and their ethnic culture whereas the second generation are more inclined towards the English language that is spoken by their peers, teachers and the mass media (Cheng & Kuo, 2000). Furthermore, knowledge of parental languages has rarely lasted past the third generation in the US (Portes & Hao, 1998) and most third- and later-generation children speak only English at home (Alba et al., 2002).

Discussion

The key findings of this chapter demonstrate that ethnic language retention or loss is affected by both community interactions and perceived attitudes as well as parental expectations. Generational status also plays a role in ethnic language retention with first- and second-generation Australian-born Chinese grappling with communication issues compared to later generations where these language issues are no longer pertinent. As with phenotype, ethnic language is perceived to be a significant identity marker. However, unlike phenotype, ethnic language is malleable insofar as it can be discarded at will. The ability to decide whether or not ethnic language retention is central to one's identity formation is consistent with the 'liquid' nature of life (Bauman, 2007). How one makes the decision to retain parental languages is dependent on a series of factors both within the home and in the wider community.

It is inevitable that language vitality diminishes across generations when it is not supported in the wider, largely monolingual society (Louie & Edwards, 1994). Historically, in the US, bilingualism was perceived to be a negative. According to Portes and Rumbaut (2001), by the 1920s, academics considered the continued use of foreign languages as a sign of the limited intellectual capacity of immigrants. Unaccented English was privileged at the time 'as a sign of full membership in the national community' (p. 117) with key political figures such as Theodore Roosevelt denouncing foreign language use and multiculturalism in general. Roosevelt particularly targeted German Americans at the time. It was not until the 1960s that bilingualism was positively associated with cognitive development and academic performance.

In Australia, the privileging of the English language while not overt was a by-product of a relatively homogeneous settler society up until the first half of the twentieth century coupled with neglect of the Aboriginal population and due in part to the implementation of the White Australia Policy. At the start of post-war migration, Australia was almost stridently monolingual with the then Immigration Minister Arthur Calwell calling for 'complete assimilation of migrants into the Australian way of life' (Ozolins, 1993, p. 1). At the time, Australia felt at odds with the influx of non-English speaking background (NESB) migrants and felt a general unease with its proximity to Asia. In terms of languages, wartime conflict with Japan and Germany had led to a decline in the learning of these wartime enemy languages and suspicion of speakers of these languages in Australia (Ozolins, 1993). In Australia in the 1950s and 1960s, there was also a general lack of differentiation between Chinese and Japanese people and a common schoolyard taunt 'Chinese, Japanese, dirty knees, look at these', reflected a lack of distinction in terms of levels of disdain directed towards people of Asian appearance. For Luke and Luke (2000, p. 49), 'race often supplants language as identity marker, transforming a tacit sense of "us" into "us and them"'.

After the Second World War, it was fair to say that the push towards the assimilation of immigrants and the racism directed against people of Asian appearance impacted on ethnic language retention among Australian-born Chinese. Many of the study participants refrained from speaking Chinese for fear of being seen as different to the point that language loss was inevitable. This reluctance to speak Chinese in public was also evident among younger study participants which suggests that the stigma associated with foreign language-speaking persists across time.

In spite of the perceived stigma, ethnic language has been shown to be a key marker of ethnic identity for second-generation Australian-born Chinese particularly in the formative years when they were often traversing two cultures. Ethnic language is a salient marker of culture and language loss can lead to cultural practices not being passed on leading to a decline in ethnic identity (Lai, 2016; Phinney et al., 2001) particularly for the second generation. The extent to which it continues to be a marker of ethnic identity is dependent upon the nature of familial ties and expectations as well as the nature of community interactions. Family situation and communal context as well as generation play important roles in determining whether children will retain their parental language (Alba et al., 2002). With authoritarian parent–child relationships, loss of ethnic language and lack of connection to the parental country of origin, the second-generation may not interact favourably with the home life created by their parents. According to Louie (2006, p. 373), the home is a symbolic connection to the parents' country of origin and for the second-generation, home can also be a representation of 'a place in the past' mediated by their parents. It is the parents' responsibility to make the meanings of that past known or not known. Similarly, a key element of identity preservation is the transmission of cultural artefacts and customs that represent being Chinese. Parents are instrumental in transmitting these customs to their children (Hiller & Chow, 2005). If there is a lack of parent–child dialogue and loss of ethnic language, there is also lack of knowledge of the parental homeland and of family histories and customs. The loss of ethnic language amongst the second-generation as reflected in a lack of Chinese fluency coupled with the parents' lack of fluency in English makes communication with parents about complex issues difficult and contributes to the distancing between children and parents (Louie, 2006). As this study demonstrates, loss of parental language and resultant communication breakdown was a common outcome for the majority of second-generation Australian-born Chinese.

By the third generation, ethnic language retention played less of a role in ethnic identity as English became the lingua franca. Ethnic language was not always perceived to be a measure of one's ethnicity and sometimes it was only used as a tool for communication rather than identification. Other markers of ethnic identity such as blood relations and participation in cultural activities were shown to be relevant in ethnic identity construction. Over the life course, ethnic identity was seen to be fluid.

Ethnic identity construction is largely based on self-perceptions but how one sees themselves is not always aligned to how others see them. Ang (2001) notes that, although there are many different Chinese identities, there is still a hegemonically constructed idea that 'not speaking Chinese' is a sign of lack of authenticity as a

Chinese. Some of the study participants also adopted the view that to be a 'real' Chinese, one needed to speak the language. However, Ann, a second-generation Australian-born Chinese in her 20s, remarked 'I really appreciate the fact now that I can speak Mandarin. But I don't think like my friends who can't speak Chinese are necessarily less Chinese than I am.' Many of the study participants were mainly conversant in English in the public domain. If they were also conversant in Chinese, this was usually confined to the home environment. However, the propensity to speak or not to speak Chinese did not fundamentally alter their sense of Chineseness.

Much of the discussion on ethnic language maintenance has focused on the second generation, the social context in which they have grown up as the children of immigrants and the generational conflicts that comes with living in two worlds. For the first generation, immigration often involved loss at many levels: loss of significant people and culture; loss of familiarity and for the second generation, loss of mother tongue. The immigrant's identity was formed in the old culture and by the old language and to change one's language not only affected everyday life, it affected self-identity and the ability to communicate and pass on cultural heritage to following generations. For the second generation, this study supports the idea of ethnic language as an identity marker. However, as has been shown, language is often used as a tool for communication (Brubaker, 2013) rather than as a tool for the transmission of cultural values and traditions. While the study participants spoke about the capacity to communicate with their parents and indeed with other people on their visits to mainland China by having the ability to communicate in a common language, their acculturation to Australia was also significant. By the third generation, much of the language issues faced by the second generation were irrelevant. This did not mean that they were less Chinese given that they adopted other representations of Chinese identity such as participation in cultural festivities.

What it means to be Chinese is a fluid concept and the role that language has in shaping that identity is also fluid. As this research shows, Australian-born Chinese fashion their identity in a multitude of ways (Bhabha, 1990) and Chinese language as an identity marker and a means of communication becomes less relevant for the third generation and beyond. There is a three-generation process in terms of preservation of the parents' language (Alba et al., 2002; Portes & Hao, 1998). According to this model, the immigrant generation learns as much English as he/she can but speaks the mother tongue at home; the second generation may speak the mother tongue at home but shifts to unaccented English at school and at work; and by the third generation, English becomes the home language and effective knowledge of the parental tongue disappears (Portes & Hao, 1998). The reasons for parental language retention are varied and while it may be perceived by some, both internally and externally, as a marker of ethnic identity, this research demonstrates that ethnic language use is often used as a tool for communication but not necessarily a tool for the transmission of cultural values and traditions. By the third generation and beyond, the construction of Chineseness is fashioned with or without knowledge of the ethnic language.

References

Alba, R., Logan, J., Lutz, A., & Stults, B. (2002). Only English by the third generation? Loss and preservation of the mother tongue among the grandchildren of contemporary immigrants. *Demography, 39*(3), 467–484. https://doi-org.ezproxy.lib.monash.edu.au/, https://doi.org/10.1353/dem.2002.0023

Ang, I. (2001). *On not speaking Chinese: Living between Asia and the West*. Routledge.

Bauman, Z. (2007). *Liquid times: Living in an age of uncertainty*. Polity Press.

Bhabha, H. K. (Ed.). (1990). *Nation and narration*. Routledge.

Brubaker, R. (2013). Language, religion and the politics of difference. *Nations and Nationalism, 19*(1), 1–20. https://doi.org/10.1111/j.1469-8129.2012.00562.x

Cheng, S. H., & Kuo, W. H. (2000). Family socialization of ethnic identity among Chinese American pre-adolescents. *Journal of Comparative Family Studies, 31*(4), 463–484. Retrieved from https://search.proquest.com/docview/60093440?accountid=12528

Chung, A. Y. (2013). From caregivers to caretakers: The impact of family roles on ethnicity among children of Korean and Chinese immigrant families. *Qualitative Sociology, 36*(3), 279–302. https://doi.org/10.1007/s11133-013-9252-x

Cornell, S. (1996). The variable ties that bind: Content and circumstance in ethnic processes. *Ethnic and Racial Studies, 19*(2), 265–289. Retrieved from https://search.proquest.com/docview/1036476222?accountid=12528

Eriksen, T. H. (2010). *Ethnicity and nationalism: Anthropological perspectives* (3rd ed.). Pluto Press.

Hiller, H. H., & Chow, V. (2005). Ethnic identity and segmented assimilation among second-generation Chinese youth. *Sociological Studies of Children and Youth, 10*, 75–99. https://doi.org/10.1016/S1537-4661(04)10005-6

Kibria, N. (2002). *Becoming Asian American: Second-generation Chinese and Korean American identities*. The John Hopkins University Press.

Lai, H.-L. (2016). Understanding ethnic visibility through language use: The case of Taiwan Hakka. *Asian Ethnicity*, 1–18. https://doi.org/10.1080/14631369.2016.1171130

Louie, V. (2006). Growing up ethnic in transnational worlds: Identities among second-generation Chinese and Dominicans. *Identities: Global Studies in Culture and Power, 13*(3), 363–394. https://doi.org/10.1080/10702890600838118

Louie, K., & Edwards, L. (1994). Chinese for Dinkum Aussies. *Asian Studies Review, 18*(2), 53–62. https://doi.org/10.1080/03147539408712995

Luke, A., & Luke, C. (2000). The differences language makes: The discourses on language of inter-ethnic Asian/Australian families. In I. Ang, L. Law, S. Chalmers, & M. Thomas (Eds.), *Alter/Asians: Asian-Australian identities in art, media and popular culture*. Pluto Press.

Luo, S.-H., & Wiseman, R. L. (2000). Ethnic language maintenance among Chinese immigrant children in the United States. *International Journal of Intercultural Relations, 24*(3), 307–324.

Ommundsen, W. (2003). Tough ghosts: Modes of cultural belonging in diaspora. *Asian Studies Review, 27*(2), 181–204. https://doi.org/10.1080/10357820308713374

Ozolins, U. (1993). *The politics of language in Australia*. Cambridge University Press.

Phinney, J. S., Romero, I., Nava, M., & Huang, D. (2001). The role of language, parents, and peers in ethnic identity among adolescents in immigrant families. *Journal of Youth and Adolescence, 30*(2), 135–153.

Pieterse, J. N. (1994). Globalisation as hybridisation. *International Sociology, 9*(2), 161–184. https://doi.org/10.1177/026858094009002003

Portes, A., & Hao, L. (1998). E Pluribus Unum: Bilingualism and loss of language in the second generation. *Sociology of Education, 71*(4), 269–294. Retrieved from http://search.proquest.com/docview/60063522?accountid=12528

Portes, A., & Rumbaut, R. G. (2001). *Legacies: The story of the immigrant second generation*. Berkeley: University of California Press.

References

Smolicz, J. J. (1980). Language as a core value of culture. *RELC Journal, 11*(1), 1–13. Retrieved from http://search.proquest.com/docview/61096873?accountid=12528

Smolicz, J. J., & Secombe, M. J. (2003). Assimilation or pluralism? Changing policies for minority languages education in Australia. *Language Policy, 2*(1), 3–25. Retrieved from http://search.proquest.com/docview/62236495?accountid=12528

Smolicz, J. J. (1992). Minority languages as core values of ethnic cultures: A study of maintenance and erosion of Polish, Welsh and Chinese languages in Australia. In W. Fase, K. Jaspaert, & S. Kroon (Eds.), *Maintenance and loss of minority languages* (pp. 277–305). John Benjamins Publishing Company.

Smolicz, J. J., Secombe, M. J., & Hudson, D. M. (2001). Family collectivism and minority languages as core values of culture among ethnic groups in Australia. *Journal of Multilingual and Multicultural Development, 22*(2), 152–172. https://doi.org/10.1080/01434630108666430

Souchou, Y. (2009). Being essentially Chinese. *Asian Ethnicity, 10*(3), 251–262. https://doi.org/10.1080/14631360903189633

Tannenbaum, M., & Howie, P. (2002). The association between language maintenance and family relations: Chinese immigrant children in Australia. *Journal of Multilingual and Multicultural Development, 23*(5), 408–424. https://doi.org/10.1080/01434630208666477

Wu, C., & Chao, R. K. (2005). Intergenerational cultural conflicts in norms of parental warmth among Chinese American immigrants. *International Journal of Behavioral Development, 29*(6), 516–523. https://doi.org/10.1080/01650250500147444

Chapter 5
Performing Chineseness

In the process of ethnic identity construction, perceptions and actions of others both within the home and outside the home count. How these external perceptions and actions impact on self-perceptions is influenced by one's sense of belonging and agency. Sense of agency is, in turn, affected by generational, historical, spatial and socio-economic factors. Just as feelings of Chineseness are affected by external factors, so too are actions or the ways in which Chineseness is performed. This chapter examines the creative ways in which Chineseness is performed whether it be in the simple act of sharing of food, in active participation with other Chinese community members through associations and activities, in lifestyle choices like marriage and education or in visits to the 'homeland'. There are different meanings of Chineseness in the contemporary world and the Chinese diaspora, and it is open to interpretation (Hibbins, 2005). What is evident in the performance of Chineseness is the level of control or agency one has in choosing how to display their Chineseness as well as an acknowledgment of what constitutes Chineseness even if one chooses not to identify with these signifiers.

In 'doing' Chinese, one needs to understand how the social and environmental context can both promote and constrain one's ability to exercise agency. One's sense of identification with their culture of origin is based on a shared sense of history and tradition (Alvarez & Helms, 2001). Being in an ethnic minority position, it is possible that one may feel less powerful. According to Alonso (1994), the construction of status and power in societies are influenced by class, gender, age, sexual orientation and ethnicity. With the White Australia Policy still in place after the Second World War and before its legal abolition in 1973, Australian-born Chinese were arguably lacking in social 'status and power'. Ang (1993) speaks about the 'corporeal malediction' of Chineseness and it was from this situational context that the Australian-born Chinese were navigating everyday life in the 1960s and 1970s.

As cultural diversity in Australia increased from the 1970s onwards, the situational context experienced by Australian-born Chinese study participants changed and continues to evolve. Consistent with Bauman's (1996) perspectives on 'liquid' life, some Australian-born Chinese were now exercising increased agency in constructing their identity. Bauman (2001) recognises that in times of 'liquid' modernity, identity is not a 'private matter' and individuality is socially produced. It is not so much how to obtain and maintain an identity but which identity we choose and how we adapt to changing identities (Bhabha, 1996). One becomes aware of a need for having an identity when they have trouble answering the questions, 'who am I' or 'where do I belong'? Bauman (1998) Control over one's life or control over one's identity is dependent upon the ability to move at will as opposed to being bound to a place. The social hierarchy is no longer marked by fixed identities and the degree of freedom to select one's identity and to hold it for as long as they desire becomes the hallmark of social advancement or success. It is the activity of choosing more than what is being chosen that matters. Lack of fixity also has other ramifications over time. For Portes and Rumbaut (2001, p. 166), 'not only are self-identities malleable, but their relationships with other aspects of adaptation also change'.

Chineseness can be a racial identity but, as some indicated, their physical traits are not normally dwelt upon. If they are to become an issue, it is usually when someone else draws it to their attention. For some, although there is a recognition of their Chinese heritage, there are no active moves to display their ethnicity. That is, they tend to identify as Australian with a Chinese background at most. Ann, a second-generation Australian-born Chinese, is happy to acknowledge her Chinese background but identifies more with her Australian upbringing:

> I think it's sort of a background thing. Like it's not something that I think has influenced a lot of my personality or who I am. But, it's definitely there, like I wouldn't erase it or anything like that. I don't think it's part of my values or my aspirations or anything like that. I don't think it's really informed that side. But, it is sort of where I come from. I think the way I think about issues in the world and that kind of thing is more of a Western influence than a Chinese influence. I think that's why I would say I identify as more Australian. I think it's more just, like I do think about it but, I wouldn't tell everyone I'm a Chinese-Australian, unless the Chinese part was relevant to what I was saying.

Similarly, a sense of being Australian is a recurrent theme among second-generation Australian-born Chinese like Cameron:

> People see me as an Aussie: the accent, where I was born. They don't take into account race and the colour of your skin. They see me as an Aussie—as an Australian. It's probably happened more from when I've got to high school and upwards, as opposed to when I was a child. When you were a child, you had yellow skin, you were Chinese, you're not one of us. When you were young and adolescent, you think differently to how you think as an adult. You try and combine what's good about Australia and what's good about Chinese in me — to have the good aspects of both. That's how I would identify myself.

It appears from Cameron's comments that his identity, as perceived by others, is Australian but he is also exercising some choice. It is precisely this ability to choose that underlies the ways in which Chineseness is performed by the Australian-born Chinese in this study. This chapter examines the manifestation of Chineseness through food, membership of Chinese community associations, participation in Chinese events and activities, ancestor worship, marriage, education and 'homeland' visits. At the same time, this chapter contextualises the way Chineseness has been performed and how this has impacted on choice.

You Are What You Eat

Food is central to the performance of Chineseness whether it be around the dishes consumed, the practice of using chopsticks or the bringing together of family members around the table. There are a multitude of factors at play in the dining experience and each factor on its own is not necessarily unique to Chinese identity. Nonetheless, the communal dining experience is an opportunity to bring families together and to some extent, reinforce a sense of solidarity and identification as a unit. Denise, a second-generation Australian-born Chinese in her 60s, commented on the importance of food and other cultural traits in her sense of Chineseness but acknowledged that they were not unique to Chinese people:

> We are very thingy about food. But then food as a sort of a way of joining the community - it's not unique to Chinese. It's also in a lot of other cultures. The Italians have it. The Greeks have it. I suppose the food is the part that we really relate to most. There's a lot of attitudes which I think are much more Chinese - which maybe we're not so enamoured of - this thing about image. There's huge elements of, I suppose what they call face, which really is sort of not quite keeping up with the Joneses. But then as we expanded and met other people and had much more exposure to other cultures, you realise that other cultures have that attitude too.

The act of sharing food around a communal dining table is not uniquely Chinese but the process had the effect of creating a common ground and a sense of belonging. This is an important process for those study participants who may have experienced discrimination in the community and lack of a sense of belonging. Gabrielle, a fourth-generation Australian-born Chinese in her 40s, and Ella, a second-generation Australian-born Chinese in her 60s, both recognised the importance of food as a representation of their Chineseness. In both cases, it was the only avenue available to them to express their Chinese identity. Gabrielle is of mixed heritage and two key signifiers of being Chinese, that is, phenotype and language, eluded her. Gabrielle's sense of belonging and the happy memories associated with sharing food with her relatives were central to her identity. Gabrielle embraced the culture and history represented in family dinners. To Gabrielle, these family dinners represented Chineseness:

> For me, mostly it's about family. It was always about the big family, and family get-togethers, and I've never met anyone that wasn't nice or generous. It's about aunts and uncles who aren't blood relatives. It's about meals—large meals, great food. [Laughs] I think it's belonging— you know, that sense of belonging to something that's bigger that has culture and history that runs back through the ages that's bigger and more extensive than, perhaps, our own lives, and so we can sort of attach ourselves to something that goes way back.

For Gabrielle, family gatherings were a source of happiness and belonging and to which she identified strongly. In efforts to assimilate to mainstream society, Ella grew up rejecting most of the Chinese traditions imparted by her parents. However, Chinese food was one of the few ways that Ella could express her Chineseness later in life. Ella related the importance of food to family relationships:

> I would say that the most important Chinese custom is the food. Because even though we wanted to eat Australian food and any other kind of food, we were always interested in food. As soon as we left home, we came back every holiday, and we'd always want to know how to cook this or how to cook that. But when we were home, we never wanted to watch; we never wanted to cook; we never wanted to do a thing. But as soon as we left home, we all wanted to be able to cook Chinese food. And I think that for me, that is my Chineseness—my love of Chinese food, and that's what I've passed onto my boys as well. The only thing, because I couldn't speak Chinese to them, but they always had Chinese food. And the older I've got, what I naturally cook and naturally want to eat 90 per cent of the time is Chinese food. So, coming together, this is the importance of the family I think that also revolves around food.

Food serves as a bonding mechanism among family members because of the shared nature of the dining experience. Heather, a third-generation Australian-born Chinese in her 40s, had a traumatic experience growing up and was teased mercilessly by her schoolmates because of her Chinese appearance. During this traumatic period, Heather felt unsupported by her mother. Because of her negative experiences, Heather shunned her Chinese heritage and consequently, had little knowledge of Chinese culture. Now that Heather had come to terms with her Chinese identity, Chinese food had become the common link used to foster a bond with her mother and reflect on her identity:

> What does being Chinese mean to me? I think it just means accepting my heritage, and I do accept my heritage a lot more now, and I'm more interested in finding out about it. It's always about the food; the whole family embraces the food. Being Chinese is all about going with my Mum to Chinatown and eating everything in sight. They used to eat everything back then…Whereas for me, I just find that really revolting. But she loves it, and that's the thing. For her, it probably has positive memories of her childhood, whereas I just think, 'Where's the meat on it? It's bones'. [Laughs] Oh, and things like fish heads and eating eyeballs. To me, that's what being Chinese is about, eating really weird food that no-one else would want to eat.

Their visits to Chinatown served to cement their relationship. Chineseness was associated with traditional Confucian values like the centrality of family and the non-expression of feelings (Hibbins, 2005). In Heather's case, her mother exemplified that lack of outward emotion towards her daughter so the opportunity to bond with Chinese food was important to Heather. This recognition of Chinese food and the process of eating and sharing it in a communal setting as a powerful indicator of Chineseness continued to persist across time.

The importance of food as a signifier of identity can also come down to the ingredients used. For Isabelle, a second-generation Australian-born Chinese in her 60s, the ingredients used in her mother's cooking were a representation of being Chinese that Isabelle strived to reject when she was younger:

> I mean I'm aware I'm Chinese, and probably when I was growing up, I didn't want to be. I chose to be more Westernised. I mean some of the food - I wish Mum would have cooked in butter rather than oil, and, 'Why can't we have milk in our tea and sugar in our tea?' We

were having all these good things, but, [I thought], 'Why doesn't Mum fry in fat rather than in oil?'

Isabelle acknowledged that ingredients in her Chinese diet may have been healthier options but, in her youth, she was more concerned with assimilating to a Western way of life. Similarly, Ann, a second-generation Australian-born Chinese, was self-conscious of being different as a child and made attempts to hide her food practices to assimilate with mainstream society:

> I remember in Year 2, we had like a breakfast day and the teacher went around like asking "what do other people eat for breakfast?" Like she didn't ask me but she asked another person and she said, 'like rice porridge' or something and the teacher was like 'oh, we won't be having that at our breakfast day', kind of not in a mean way. And then when she asked me, I was like 'I eat cereal' but I didn't. I just thought it's easier just to fit in.

Food was also used as a mechanism to re-claim one's Chinese identity. Cathy, a second-generation Australian-born Chinese in her 30s, became proud of her Chinese heritage after initially rejecting it:

> I'm very proud to be Chinese now. So, I like to identify as being Chinese all the time. I work in different offices across the Eastern suburbs. There are a lot of Chinese people there and I like to tell everybody the only reason why they can eat good dumplings for lunch is because of my people, that sort of thing. But, having said that, I've got my own version of being Chinese. I was born here, I was brought up here you know. My parents also changed their ideas of being Chinese.

Cathy's experiences have shaped her version of being Chinese and the person that she is today:

> My version is that I like the food, it's the best and also, even though I don't have my own family and stuff, feelings of family are quite specific, I think. I think everybody's feelings are but I associate it with being Chinese.

Food as a representation of Chineseness or other ethnic identities transcends generations and time. Study participants of all ages have acknowledged the centrality of Chinese food in the manifestation of Chineseness. On the whole, the type of food traditionally eaten in the family home was perceived as an indicator of ethnicity in a broad sense both within the home and outside of it. For Brenda, a third-generation Australian-born Chinese of mixed heritage in her 30s, her families' way of doing Chinese through food reinforced her sense of difference from the mainstream:

> I haven't been brought up with the Anglo-Saxon culture, like that sort of surrounding me, but it's not what I have at home. So, there's a sense of it being kind of separate and different. When you go to school and all the other kids are eating very plain lunches and you've got all these ethnic foods, kind of you do stand out because you're the minority. So, growing up, you kind of feel like a bit of a minority, you feel different because you're not a white person.

As children, these study participants were intent on trying to fit in with the mainstream and the perception that food was a source of differentiation was testament to the extent to which ethnicity pervaded many aspects of everyday life. However, with increasing cultural diversity, intercultural mixing, the introduction of fusion food and the broadening of people's palates, the boundaries manifested by food are becoming increasingly blurred. Nonetheless, it was not just about the type of food eaten but the process behind eating Chinese food that was perceived to represent Chineseness.

The simple act of sharing food was something that could differentiate one cultural practice from the next. Emily, a second-generation Australian-born Chinese in her 20s has a boyfriend of Anglo-Celtic origin who was raised with different meal etiquette:

> My boyfriend always looks at me funny when I keep asking to share something at a restaurant, because he's so used to ordering your own serving. You don't ask for other people's food, but when my parents and I go out, it's always, 'Okay, let's order this and this, and we'll share it'. It's always a discussion of what everyone else wants to eat, but when it comes to eating with my boyfriend and his family, it's always that it doesn't matter if we're ordering the same thing. You are eating for yourself; you're ordering for yourself. Don't worry about everyone else—that it's unusual to care like that.

In terms of everyday life, if one were to visit to a local Chinese restaurant, one might observe a unique table configuration with large groups of people gathered on a round table with a 'lazy Susan' strategically placed in the centre to enable the sharing of food. Cutlery would also be replaced by chopsticks. This process in which food was ingested was also perceived to be a representation of Chinese cultural practices. Caitlin, a second-generation Australian-born Chinese in her 40s, operated a Chinese restaurant with her husband and had observed the way in which her customers interacted with food:

> There is a cultural element there as well. There's the real village element, which I just have no idea about, and then there's just the cultural element of just using chopsticks. You know, I see kids coming around here; they can't use chopsticks, you know. I mean I think you should use chopsticks. The characters of being Asian, that when I see them coming in like that, I'd probably say that if I see an Asian person who's not speaking Chinese [and] they're not using chopsticks, they have no idea about their own culture. I don't think they're Asian.

Chopsticks do not represent Chineseness alone but they do play a role in an overall image of Chineseness. Chopsticks also vary from one Asian ethnicity to the next. Caitlin extended her belief system to her cousin noting that physical appearance alone did not guarantee that one was perceived to be Chinese. For Caitlin, enacting Chineseness was an important part of one's claim to be Chinese:

> My cousin, he's just Western all over. There's nothing Chinese about him at all, apart from his appearance. He's Chinese, purely because of his looks. But is he real Chinese? That's why I say 'fake Chinese' because when he comes back, and he's in our family environment; you know, we're doing our Chinese things like eating together—you know, sharing food with your bowls and all this sort of stuff, and he feels awkward doing this.

The act of sharing food around a communal table reinforces family relationships and, in some cases, creates connections where they may not otherwise exist. Emily, a second-generation Australian-born Chinese in her 20s, acknowledged the differences between the ways in which Chinese people dined compared to the wider community. For Caitlin, a second-generation Australian-born Chinese in her 40s, the use of chopsticks and sharing food were integral to the 'true' Chinese experience.

For Australian-Chinese, food and the way in which it was shared and eaten were strong representations of their Chinese heritage. For some, it seemed to be the only way that they could demonstrate their belonging to this cultural group. The act of using chopsticks or of eating Chinese food did not make someone Chinese. It was the whole process of sitting around the dinner table in a restaurant or at home with relatives, sharing Chinese food, eating rice, and using chopsticks that was a common memory for many and one which bound them together. Food traversed generations and was an accessible way of displaying ethnic identity when other markers may not have been apparent or were rejected in the past.

Chinese Community Associations as Centres of Chineseness

Chineseness was also performed through the establishment and maintenance of Chinese Community Associations. Two study participants, Doris and Albert, were active members of their local Chinese Community Associations. Doris was a fourth-generation Australian-born Chinese in her 50s with mixed heritage—her mother was Anglo-Celtic. Albert was also a fourth-generation Australian-born Chinese but in his 60s. The Chinese Community Associations, of which they were a part, housed museums that represented the history of Chinese immigration to Australia. Multi-generation Australian-born Chinese who had ancestors that came to Australia during the Gold Rush boom in the nineteenth century or who lived in Australia in the first part of the twentieth century were able to identify with this representation of Chineseness. This representation of Chineseness generally reflected the experiences of Chinese from the Southern provinces of China. One could argue that participants whose families migrated to Australia after the White Australia Policy was abolished were a different cohort in terms of their reasons for migration, their socio-economic status and their level of education among other factors. Therefore, they may have been less likely to identify with these cultural representations. This does not devalue these cultural representations but highlights the diverse ways in which Chineseness is constructed and the diversity of the Chinese diaspora. There is no single way of imagining China and 'to be or not to be Chinese becomes a question with different answers depending on different contexts' (Chu, 2008, p. 204). Chineseness is plural in nature and the question becomes what is privileged or institutionalised (Chu, 2008), for example, Maoist China, modern China, or ancient China?

The establishment of local Chinese Community Associations served as a mechanism to demonstrate and maintain collective forms of Chinese cultural heritage. However, their relevance to the Chinese community was influenced by both generational and historical factors. Whether the second generation maintains its cultural participation depends on their parents but also social factors like ethnic visibility and residence in a high immigrant community. Caitlin, a second-generation Australian-born Chinese in her 40s, was once an active member of her local Chinese Community Association, an Association where her grandfather was one of the original committee members. Her family would socialise with members of this community and participate in cultural festivals. While it was not a high immigrant community, the Association was a meeting place for the Chinese community in the area and hence, the Chinese were ethnically visible. The Association originally represented an older generation of Chinese from the Taishan-speaking region of China who had been living in Australia for the last forty to fifty years. According to Caitlin, the younger generation was not interested in attending the Association gatherings because they were 'boring' and there was 'nothing else there to do' apart from having lunch.

Caitlin recognised the disparities between and expectations of different members of the Chinese community when she reflected on how younger, Mandarin-speaking Chinese students could not relate to the Chinese Community Association that was originally set up by her parents' generation. The Chinese community has evolved and there is a constant need to reconstruct, re-make and update identities (Bauman, 1998). Chinese Community Associations evolved as membership changed and were one way of representing Chineseness but they cannot be fixed or static just as cultures are not static, fixed or homogeneous (Nagel, 1994).

Membership of such Associations is a way of endorsing one's Chineseness. Albert noted that the Association's Constitution stated that members were to be Chinese but he believed that membership of this Association was open to those who believed in the Chinese culture:

> We had some people who really objected because they're actually married to a Chinese or they might have been married to a Chinese and they actually consider themselves to be more Chinese than actually Caucasian. So this is going back to your question, if you consider yourself to be Chinese and you believe in the Chinese culture and like the Chinese social aspects of life then we accept them as a member. It's your own perception and it's all in the culture and all in the family structure and it's all in the way you can consider yourself Chinese.

Doris also remarked that one can be Chinese, honorary or otherwise, by being associated with the local Chinese Community Association, by participating in cultural activities, by marriage or birthright. Doris was active in her community and fostered Chinese connections:

> Being associated with every Chinese association here in Bendigo, as I said, I have a Chinese doctor and a Chinese acupuncturist, and the new group I have been associated with and the old group I was associated with and I was invited to be part of the Executive on the Museum. We donate our business for a fund raiser to the community, to the Bendigo Chinese Association (BCA). So, we assist in every possible way.

Albert commented on how membership of his Association had been expanded to include people of Caucasian background. Doris also remarked on how participation in cultural events organised by her Community Association was also open to non-Chinese. The focus is on a mixing of a range of cultures rather than their separateness (Pieterse, 1994). At the same time, there were those that would question this principle of inclusion. Emily, a second-generation Australian-born Chinese in her early 20s, saw the enacting of Chineseness by Westerners as an anomaly:

> I think it is quite often physical, because I mean you've seen different people who have adopted Chinese values, say a Westerner trying to learn from Buddhism and become a Buddhist monk. There's still quite a leap, in a sense, that ethnicity and culture I think are quite bound up in what it means to be Chinese. It's something that Chinese people hold dear, and I don't think many other people want to adopt necessarily.

Both Doris and Albert also resided in regional or rural towns where, according to their experiences, the Chinese community was held in high regard. There was a sense of pride expressed in their cultural heritage and unlike some of their city counterparts who experienced schoolyard taunts, their experiences growing up were not imbued with negativity towards their cultural heritage. Albert commented on how some of his 'white' friends were envious of his social life and Doris remarked on how the wider community embraced the annual Chinese New Year Festival organised by her Chinese Community Association.

Membership of and participation in Chinese Community Associations was one way of performing Chineseness. Not all would agree that appearance did not matter. However, consistent with Bauman (2001), identities are transient and can be adopted and discarded at will. Non-Chinese members of Chinese Community Associations may choose to identify with the Chinese community when they are engaging with ethnically Chinese people and participating in Association activities. However, they were also able to adopt another identity outside these spaces. It is a form of cultural hybridisation where individuals have multiple identities and they are able to adopt several organisational options simultaneously (Pieterse, 1994).

Chinese New Year and Doing Chinese

Just as one can join a Chinese community association, participation and celebration of key cultural events in the Chinese calendar are sometimes used to represent one's affiliation with Chineseness. Ann is a university student and a second-generation Australian-born Chinese in her 20s. Ann's family celebrated special occasions like Chinese New Year with a low-key family dinner:

> Usually, like for Chinese New Year, we'll have one dinner. My grandma does make 'zongzi' like for the Dragon Boat Festival. And then we'll have moon cakes for Mid-Autumn Festival. It's something I noticed that my friends whose family background is from mainland China tend to celebrate the festivals less than say people with a Chinese-Malaysian background. [With] the little traditions and certain aspects to it, they will follow to a tee kind of thing and we'll be like, oh we've had dinner altogether, that's fine.

Also, Ann did not generally participate in public cultural festivities. For Ann, such activities did not necessarily represent Chinese people:

> I think they are quite an accessible way for people who aren't Chinese to understand Chinese culture because it's like fun and festive. There's like lots of traditions and stuff. It's easier to make people understand like that aspect. But, at the same time, I don't think it really reflects what Chinese people are like. It's just the way they like celebrate this festival.

Perhaps this was indicative of a lack of need to follow tradition to maintain one's ethnic identity or perhaps it is not something that was a priority for Ann's family. Unlike some others, Ann's extended family in Australia was relatively small so it may account for the absence of large-scale family celebrations. Alan, a second-generation Australian-born Chinese in his 30s, similarly acknowledged some Chinese cultural practices but they were not central to his values:

> So, you do red packets but it's not such a big deal. We don't follow the bit [with] relatives and that kind of thing, not that we had that many around. Not just your immediate family but your extended family if you are more traditional. And we didn't really practice that. Even now we don't practice that. The expectation to give red packets to my sister, for example, who is married – we don't really follow that. I think there are some things like I think ancestral worship to me would form part of someone who I would view as more Chinese.

Red packets are small red envelopes filled with money that are usually given during Chinese New Year and other auspicious occasions. Red represents happiness and good fortune and recipients of red packets are wished a peaceful and safe new year. For Alan, his identity centred around his religious beliefs:

> Our identity comes for us more as Christians, like from a religious perspective more so than the cultural perspective. As Christians, we kind of think that the values we hold sometimes are still congruent with Chinese values but sometimes they're not. And so, you know that's why we don't practice ancestral worship and those types of attitudes.

Alan also identified as an Australian and was cognisant of his Chinese background, at the same time recognising that Chinese culture was not fixed. Because Alan's identity was primarily based on his religious affiliation, his Chinese background was incidental. Alan deemed Asian culture to be so diverse and wide-ranging which might explain in part its lack of bearing on his identity:

> I see myself as Australian with a Chinese background. You can't ignore that and having certain events throughout the New Year festivals and those kinds of things tend to remind you of where we live and where we shop. My wife and I, we shop at Springvale and still eat out at Chinese restaurants. The good thing about Chinese or Asian culture is that you're not fixed because there is not just one Asian culture.

Unlike Ann and Alan, for some Australian-Chinese, these Chinese cultural festivities were an opportunity to embrace their Chineseness even if these cultural festivities did not resonate with other Chinese people. Each year, Doris and her extended family participated in the annual Easter Parade in her regional town. The highlight of the parade was the Chinese display of the Sun Loong, the world's longest imperial Chinese dragon organised by her local Chinese Community Association. Doris was actively involved in the celebrations and her grandchildren performed in the Blossom Dances. The event is a major tourist attraction and promotes an exotic image of the Orient that appeals to the West. Chu (2008) calls this process, cultural commodification. In the process of participation, one can gain recognition and agency. As Hangen (2005, p. 51) observes, 'there is a risk of underestimating the agency of those who accept racial identities'. Doris presumably saw the value in promoting a particular brand of Chinese culture and while it may not be the motivating force behind her actions, it had the effect of reinforcing an essentialised Chinese image.

Doris is proud of her Chinese heritage and by embracing these public Chinese celebrations and fostering this tradition in her grandchildren, she is able to stay connected to the Chinese community in her regional town. In one sense, the fostering of such tradition reinforces a particular imagined community much like the ANZAC tradition and culture institutions like the Country Women's Association and the RSL. The exotic Chinese image reinforced in cultural festivals and events may not resonate in the minds of the younger study participants but it is important for Doris and it is a conscious decision on her part to use these exotic images as part of her identity. Such exotic images are also perceived to be representative of Chinese culture in the public domain. Other markers of ethnic identity like phenotype and language elude Doris so it is possible that Doris has limited options when it comes to constructing her Chinese identity. Doris' mother is Caucasian but it is her father's Chinese heritage that Doris is drawn to It could be argued that Doris' authenticity as Chinese is not genuine. However, as this study demonstrates, Chineseness is perceived and understood in a multitude of ways and it is the decisions that one makes that play an important role in defining who one is.

Like Doris, Gabrielle, who is a fourth-generation Australian-born Chinese in her 40s with both German and Chinese heritage, actively celebrated key Chinese cultural festivals. Her family life was surrounded by Chinese culture although her family was estranged from her German relatives. As she explained:

> All my mum's family we didn't have anything to do with, so my whole family, my life growing up and my culture was all around Chinese culture. Chinese New Year's, Chinese birthdays and family celebrations and so forth were all done, mostly at my Aunt's house. We did a lot of those celebrations, and all my family's associates were Chinese also, and so we'd have lots of friends and family who would come to celebrations who were Chinese as well.

While there may be a resistance towards behaving in a Chinese way in terms of participation in cultural celebrations, there is an implicit acknowledgment that such celebrations are a representation of one's Chineseness. Gillian, a third-generation Australian-born Chinese in her 60s, considered herself an Australian and while she did not participate in many cultural events, she believed that they represented aspects of Chinese culture:

> I think I see myself more as an Australian, part China. I still like to keep some of the culture in that sense. We don't celebrate Chinese New Year like other families do. They may go out and give red packets, but we don't do that. We'd just celebrate Christmas and even that's sort of gone a bit by the way, but mainly it's birthdays really, now. My mother-in-law still celebrates Chinese traditions, like at a certain time of the year, you go to the cemetery, and they have their festivals and that, and we don't.

Some of the participants acknowledged that their understanding of Chineseness was not necessarily 'authentic' but rather a hybrid version. Hybridity is not necessarily about one voice seeking cultural supremacy over another but is what can be described as a 'third space' (Bhabha, 1996). Cathy is a second-generation Australian-born Chinese in her 30s who grew up in the working-class suburbs of Melbourne. Her parents owned a Chinese restaurant and spent the bulk of their time running the family business. Apart from Chinese school, the family was not surrounded by many other Chinese families so Cathy would formulate her ideas of Chineseness and associated customs around what she learnt from her parents:

> I was taught I must always respect my elders and not to question them which is a bit different from the way my school friends were brought up. I assumed that was a Chinese custom and later found out that that was linked to Confucianism. We always used to celebrate Chinese New Year and still do every year. We don't celebrate as fulsomely as they do in China. I was never exposed to all the full traditions of Chinese New Year but we always celebrated it. I felt like a lot of my life when I was young was related to being Chinese. A lot of it had to do with my behaviour. A lot of it was about being respectful, particularly to my family and it was also the face-saving.

David, a second-generation Australian-born Chinese university student in his early 20s, commented on how his family had adapted to living in Australia and combined their Chinese values with Australian values. David embraced both cultures in equal measure:

> I was born in Australia and I see myself as an Australian, but still I have a Chinese background, and we should embrace the strengths of our culture. Chinese New Year is a really important time. Everybody in China goes back to their families. It's about the only time the whole family gets together in the whole year, and so I see that as a really important time, and I really embrace those values: family, of getting together in celebration, of kind of harmony and stuff like that. They stand for something that I'd like to continue, and in the future, I'd love to pass that on, whether it's to my cousins or maybe to my children.

In summary, participation in Chinese cultural events and activities represented a particular version of Chineseness that resonated with some but not others. Both Ann and Alan, second-generation Australian-born Chinese, acknowledged that these cultural events and activities represented aspects of Chinese culture but did not invest a lot of energy in participation. Ann and her family celebrated key dates in the Chinese calendar with family dinners but she felt that festival celebrations like Chinese New Year did not reflect what Chinese people were like. Alan recognised that the giving of red packets of money on Chinese New Year was a signifier of Chinese culture but did not subscribe to this activity because he was more cognisant of his religious identity. Alan also noted that Chinese or Asian culture was not fixed. Some of the other study participants also adopted a positive attitude towards Chinese cultural events. Cathy, a second-generation Australian-born Chinese in her 30s, celebrated Chinese New Year with her family every year as did Gabrielle, a fourth-generation Australian-born Chinese in her 40s. Doris, a fourth-generation Australian-born Chinese was also actively involved in Chinese cultural events. On the other hand, Gillian, a third-generation Australian-born Chinese in her 60s, did not celebrate Chinese New Year.

Central to these performances of Chineseness was not so much the acts themselves but the belief that these acts helped to define what it was to be Chinese. How the family embraces Chinese cultural events coupled with the strength of the family bond influences the continuation of such traditions.

Marrying Chinese

For Australian-born Chinese, there is often the expectation from their parents that they carry on Chinese culture by marrying someone of Chinese heritage. This was particularly evident for the second-generation Australian-born Chinese s born in the 1950s. After the Second World War, and with the White Australia Policy still in force, the population demographic in terms of immigrant mix was quite different to what it became after the policy was abolished. Ella, a second-generation Australian-born Chinese in her 60s, commented on her upbringing:

> Being Chinese for us was awfully boring. We were supposed to marry someone who didn't smoke, drink or gamble. And we thought, 'Gee, that's boring'. And the idea— well that was Mum's idea, that one day when we'd finished our education, she was going to take us to Hong Kong and find us husbands, and we used to think that that was hilarious, because that was never going to happen, and it never did, of course, but it didn't stop her from telling us that that was what was going to happen.

Growing up with parents who want their children to adhere to traditional patterns of behaviour and to participate in the homeland imaginary does not mean that the second-generation will adopt these practices (Louie, 2006). If the first-generation are dogmatic and rigid in their adherence to traditional patterns of behaviour, generational conflict is likely to occur (Hiller & Chow, 2005). Ella's mother followed Chinese tradition in her own marriage. She was married to the eldest son of his family and therefore was traditionally expected to play the role of matriarch in that family. Although it did not work out that way after they migrated to Australia, Ella's mother continued to embrace the ideas that she had brought from China. According to her daughter, she was dogmatic about who her children married. Her ideas about marriage conflicted with her daughter's ideas. For Ella's mother, it was important that her daughters married a Chinese man. Her wishes effectively homogenised the Chinese man in the process. Ella spent some time living in the US and pointed out the differences between Chinese men and the inappropriateness of homogenising them. She reflected on the similarities between American-born Chinese and those born in Australia as opposed to Chinese men from elsewhere:

> I felt that Chinese were very conservative, and they had certain expectations of their wives, or of a Chinese woman, or of a woman, that I could not fulfil, because I was so Australian, and I did not feel as if I had anything in common with Chinese men. When I went to San Francisco, I met people like myself—you know, American-born Chinese. I found them very interesting, because the Chinese man to me was someone who I had nothing in common with, from Hong Kong—we didn't speak the same language, really, or have the same sense of humour. But in California, I met really cool American-born Asian men, and I went out with a few. I saw them as ABC's like myself, so we had something in common.

Some participants felt that they had to marry someone of Chinese heritage, not only to please their parents, but also in the belief that it was an expectation in the wider Chinese community. Cathy is a second-generation Australian-born Chinese in her late 30s. Experiences of racism were an everyday occurrence at the time including racist taunts directed at the children in the schoolyard and at the family in the wider community. This may have impacted her parents' views of the wider host society and the desire for their children to marry another Chinese person. The expectation from her parents to marry a Chinese person was influenced by their distrust of the wider community and possibly their desire at one stage to return to Malaysia. Cathy's family also lived in the Northern suburbs of Melbourne where the population was generally in the lower socio-economic ladder and with fewer Chinese families in the area, they may have felt isolated. Their experiences of racism would have reinforced their desire for their daughter to marry someone with a similar ethnic background. When Cathy was in her 20s, she was involved in a relationship with a Malaysian Chinese man with the relationship eventually ending partly because she was not deemed Chinese enough:

> I remember when we were in that relationship, I remember, because I always considered myself to be extremely Chinese, and then I realised when I was with his family, who were very nice people, that I wasn't Chinese enough. And this is not saying this is Chinese culture but it's the way that I saw it. I don't think I was submissive enough. I remember we had a house and everything, and he would tell me off for not cleaning well enough and say that I was really lucky because he would help with the household chores and I should be so lucky to find anybody else who would do that. You and I think that's funny now. But, at the time, I remember thinking "Oh, you know, that's right. I should be so lucky because my Dad didn't help with household chores either." But, then when I left that relationship I realised that was really an attitude that was specific to him and it had to do with the way that he saw women and their role.

Cathy was perhaps not perceived as Chinese enough because she did not defer to her husband as her mother would have a generation ago. Cathy was an educated woman with career aspirations so this may have conflicted with her expected primary role as a 'homemaker'. Cathy initially believed that by marrying a Chinese man, she would somehow be doing something that would reinforce her Chineseness. Ironically, Cathy's sense of belonging in Australia increased because of her experiences within the Chinese community and in one sense her separation from that community. Cathy was married to a Chinese person in her twenties but the relationship ended because Cathy felt she was not Chinese enough. After the split, Cathy started to feel like she belonged to Australia more than any other place.

The path to identity formation is not necessarily an easy one particularly for those Australian-born Chinese whose parents struggled to adapt to their new environment. Harry, a third-generation Australian-born Chinese in his 50s, remarked on the pressure he had from his parents to marry a Chinese woman in order to have a 'pure Chinese' family. Harry was faced with enormous pressure to marry a Chinese woman from an early age because Harry's mother could not speak English:

> One of the hardest things that I had to deal with growing up as a child was both my brothers had married Anglos. My brothers always said to me, 'Mum and Dad are so understanding letting us marry Anglos', but they didn't know, because my parents just pushed it on me from about 7 or 8 years of age, 'You've got to marry a Chinese', because my Dad on behalf of my Mum would say, 'You've got to marry a Chinese, because your Mum can't communicate with your sisters-in-law. And they pushed and pushed, and said, 'We want to have a pure'— I didn't like what they were saying. They said, 'You want to have a pure Chinese family; you've got to marry a Chinese'. And I had this burden on me all my life. I've rebelled all my

life and it was very difficult, even as a teenager, to go out with an Anglo girl, because my parents objected.

Marrying a Chinese person does not, however, make someone more Chinese. In Harry's case, the fundamental consideration may have been the fostering of communication more than anything else, an issue dealt with at length in the last chapter. Ian, a third-generation Australian-born Chinese in his 60s, acknowledged the expectations of first-generation parents for their children to marry within their culture but noted that it did not necessarily follow that that culture would be maintained:

> I'm sure all Asian parents of that generation were thinking they'd marry within the race. But how can you expect that when you bring your family to another country? There's going to be some sort of cross-marriage at some level. My daughter married an Australian, and my older son married a Malaysian girl. It's up to them. And, my sister married an Australian, and my younger brother married an Australian. So, my older sister and I married Asians; it just happened that way. A lot of my friends sound very Chinese. I don't see myself as Chinese. I think the ethics of my parents are part of me, so even though I don't follow the customs, the way I act and deal with people is related to how my parents brought me up.

For Albert, a fourth-generation Australian-born Chinese in his 60s, marrying someone of the same background presumably alleviated any potential complications:

> In those days, my uncles and my father used to go back to Hong Kong to find a wife. Because you know the grandparents always want their kids to marry someone in the same culture, same race. Not because they are racist it's just that in those days they considered that it saved complications. Because in those days Chinese have a lot of certain beliefs and it's good to marry someone who has the same beliefs.

One might expect that the pressure to marry someone of the same ethnicity may diminish over the generations as well as in postmodern Australia with its diverse population mix. Certainly, some among the study participants were partnered with non-Chinese people. However, there were still occasions when some of the younger study participants experienced disapproval towards mixed relationships. Emily, a second-generation Australian-born Chinese in her early 20s, encountered such an occasion:

> And there was this time my boyfriend and I were just holding hands at the bus stop, and this Chinese man walked past, and he expressed disapproval about us; he kind of tutted and just muttered something under his breath quite angrily. For Asian families, I think it's more particular, that as a minority, marrying a Chinese is still kind of important.

Cameron, a second-generation Australian-born Chinese in his late 20s, recognised that he may have had a filial duty to carry on his parents' culture:

> I did have the dream: your great grandparents were Chinese; your parents were Chinese; I'm Chinese and I would marry and I'll keep continuing with that line, because I'm the last male in my family and that sort of thing. But life's too short for thinking like that.

Based on marriage expectations espoused by the study participants, these views did not appear to have diminished over time for the second-generation. Younger second-generation Australian-born Chinese continued to confront what they perceived to be their parents' preferences of Chinese marriage partners or their community's expectations around their life path in terms of marriage. Ann is a second-generation Australian-born Chinese university student in her 20s and lamented how her life path was potentially mapped out for her:

> I think sometimes I feel frustrated that like we're all painted with the same brush – that I will be associated with people that I'm nothing alike to just because we look the same. I think that with some Chinese people, there's this attitude of, 'oh, I'm just going to get a stable job and get married and have kids' and they don't really think about things like politics or like issues because it's a bit too hard or they just don't think that it concerns them. And I think that, I don't think it's necessarily like that thing that's specific to Asian people. But I think because there's less of us, if people are like that, they'll just associate that with me and that makes me feel a bit uncomfortable.

Implicit in Ann's comments was a traditional way of viewing one's life course, and while not confined to Chinese families, it was evident in some of the comments made by the study participants. Within that traditional trajectory was this idea of marrying within one's culture. As Ella pointed out, her mother's idea of marrying a Chinese man fallaciously homogenised Chinese men who varied depending upon their cultural experiences. The act of marrying another Chinese person was not as simple as Ella's mother might have expected. Marrying another Chinese person did not make someone more Chinese, as Ian explained, even if the first-generation believed this to be the case. And while there may still be an underlying assumption that marrying within the same ethnic group would continue the 'blood line', for younger participants like Emily and Cameron, it was not a key consideration.

Educational Achievement

Like marriage within the same ethnic community, educational achievement was one of the expectations that parents have of their children and it was perceived to be more so in Chinese immigrant families. The meaning of success was found to differ between parents and their children. Parents' meaning of success seemed oriented towards middle-class status and recognition for the family whereas for young people, success was not just about academic achievement but about being happy and proud of who they were (Pang et al., 2015). Growing up with such expectations was not always well received by the study participants. Cathy felt initial resentment at first but with the benefit of hindsight, she was grateful for her parents' actions:

> I really resented it. But I'm grateful now. At the time, I felt that a lot of things such as the ability to be creative in other ways were suppressed. And, I grew up with non-Chinese, non-Asian children who had very different types of lifestyles. So, I used to compare myself to that and feel very stuck. But, now I look back and I'm very grateful. But at the time, I didn't like it.

Other traits that Cathy associated with being Chinese related to her work ethic and acknowledgment of being Chinese:

So, if somebody has quite a strong work ethic, not being married to the job but quite a strong work ethic, and they happen to look Chinese, I'd sort of associate that with being Chinese. Also if they are, I went through a stage of being very ashamed of being Chinese of which now I'm ashamed that I was ashamed to feel Chinese, if they are comfortable with themselves and identify with being Chinese.

Parents are only one source of cultural transmission as peers and other social networks influence behaviour. However, parents may also influence their children's social networks by influencing their choice of friends (Killian & Hegtvedt, 2003). In terms of her experiences outside the home, Cathy remarked on how her social life was curbed by her parents because they prioritised her studies. Cathy felt that her parents were selective in Cathy's friendship choices and discriminated against her 'white' friends:

> They were very strict about my studies - that I had to get certain marks, that I wasn't allowed to socialise very much. So, every time I got a party invitation, you know my parents, actually my Mum particularly wanted to get a letter from the Mum of the child who was inviting me. She didn't like it that I had so many white friends. Yes, she had a lot of problems with it. And there were only two other Asian girls in my class from Year 7 and I was friends with the two of them. She much preferred me to hang out with those girls rather than my best friend, the one I was telling you about who is not at all Asian.

Discrimination on the part of the first-generation immigrant may be due to a suspicion of the host society driven, in part, by experiences of discrimination. Cathy's parents owned a Chinese restaurant and encountered occasions where they were subjected to racism including a rock being thrown through their restaurant window inscribed with words to the effect of John Howard being right. This was during the 1980s when John Howard, a Liberal MP, suggested that the proportion of Asian immigration was higher than what the public preferred. The mismatch between parents' and children's ideals and perceptions may have more to do with how they adapt to the new environment than with differences in cultural norms and customs (Hua, 2008). Cathy's parents did not feel that they belonged in Australia:

> It sounds really terrible [but] they used to say that they didn't want me to be friends with white people and I remember just thinking that was strange and it's going to be hard. But a part of me just assumed I wouldn't stay in Australia as well because they always talked about how much they didn't enjoy Australia and so I think I sort of felt like that as well. And I just assumed that I would go and live in Singapore [or] Malaysia.

Cathy's parents also felt that white friends would not have the same values as Chinese friends in terms of educational achievement, at least, not in the Northen suburbs of Melbourne. While Cathy felt that her parents did not feel a sense of belonging in Australia which, in turn, influenced their attitudes towards raising their children, Isabelle, who is a second-generation Australian-born Chinese in her 60s, felt that her parents were more accepting of living in Australia and could see the benefits of being in Australia as opposed to being in China. However, Isabelle's parents migrated to Australia at a different time to Cathy's parents. Isabelle's father came to Australia as a 12-year-old possibly in the 1920s or 1930s and her mother came to Australia in 1948. Cathy's father, however, came to Australia in the 1960s to study at university and her mother arrived not long after before they married. It may be possible that, for Cathy, her father's level of education may have had a direct bearing on his expectations for his children's education and that, for Isabelle, the values of the day were for women to get married and have children. There are, of course, other situational factors that impact on life course and experiences. In any case, Isabelle's parents seemingly put marriage before education:

> I also see that Chinese parents, by and large, are quite ambitious. I mean I see all those sorts of traits. And perhaps the so-called 'tiger mum' is a bit— a more extreme kind. But generally, unlike a lot of people— I suppose this is the only difference. It was thought of here that when you grew up, you got married, so you didn't have to go to university, and I remember applying for jobs and getting them, and I was saying, 'I really do want to go to university'. And they said, 'What do you want to do that for? You're going to get married', and all this sort of thing. But my mother always said, 'You should have an education' so it wasn't that. But on the other hand, she had all the other characteristics: 'You must get married; you must defer to your husband', and all that sort of thing. But she did encourage and support women having an education—being educated.

This is probably a reflection of the environment in which Isabelle grew up—fewer women growing up in the 1950s were tertiary-educated compared to younger women today. Over time, education was still regarded as an important pursuit in Chinese families even if they have assimilated to the culture of the host society. David, a second-generation Australian-born Chinese university student in his early 20s, noted how his parents had adapted to living in Australia but still maintained traditional values when it came to education:

> My parents have been in Australia for about 25 years now, and their views have changed a lot. But my parents are very pushy about going to university and studying. When I was in Year 12, I said to my Dad, 'I want to be a carpenter'. That did not go down well with him. But then other things, like my grandparents, they went to China for six months, and they let us use their apartment when we were 18. There was like fifteen 18-year-olds, all of us up in the apartment with drinks and stuffing around until like two or three in the morning. A lot of Chinese families wouldn't let them do that.

Marriage and education are two ways in which the first-generation can hope that their children will use to maintain and perpetuate their Chineseness. These performances are arguably more pronounced for the second-generation who are often placed in a position of balancing a number of cultural expectations compared to subsequent generations. Second-generation Australian-born Chinese were often expected to behave in certain ways in terms of marriage and education and this was sometimes met with resistance. Only with the benefit of hindsight and maturity did some of the second-generation study participants begin to understand the driving forces behind their parents' expectations. As time goes by, appreciation of one's cultural heritage seemed to increase and this is manifested in visits to the homeland.

Going Home

One way that study participants sought connections with their Chinese heritage was through visits to the homeland. The homeland is arguably an extension of one's social world and one's relationship with the homeland may play a significant role in identity construction. Actual experiences with the ancestral homeland can be sparse and when they do occur, the experiences of the second-generation are invariably different to those of their parents given that their experiences are grounded in the local context and given that contextual changes take place over the course of time. If the second-generation felt that the traditions in the home were 'foreign', that sense of foreignness may be heightened by visiting the homeland as a tourist (Louie, 2006). Not only is it likely that the homeland of their parents has changed, the second-generation may experience reactions from 'other Chinese' that question their authenticity as Chinese.

When Faye, who is a second-generation Australian-born Chinese of mixed background, visited her father's home town in Malaysia, the locals did not believe that she was of Asian background: "Not just a local but they couldn't see that I had any Asian background. I kept my name, my father's name and they would see my name and say things like 'How do you have that name?', as if to tell me that your husband must be Chinese because clearly you have no Asian background."

Sometimes one's perception of the homeland as a place of belonging may be at odds with the real-life experiences when one visits the homeland. What the individual imagines the homeland to be may sometimes be based on family memories or mythologised ideas of what the homeland is. In travelling to Malaysia, Faye thought of it as a home coming and was quite disappointed that the locals did not recognise her connection to what she perceived as the homeland: "For me, there was a kind of symbolic homecoming that afterwards I kind of thought, it's like I felt like I was coming home but home wasn't there to receive me in a way. I mean it is what it is, isn't it?"

One assumption that was sometimes made was that the homeland was an homogeneous place where diasporic Chinese could return to and feel at home. According to Luke and Luke (2000), the presumption of a fixed, singular culture or identity is an essentialist perception. And as Hsu (1991, p. 227) remarks, 'seldom, however, does a Chinese clearly define China as a nation or as a culture'. Emily could not identify with the local Chinese population in Northeast China. Instead, asked about how she felt growing up in Australia, Emily felt an affinity with Australia more so than with China:

> I felt just the same, and I think that's part of why I wasn't interested in Chinese, even though my parents got in a Taiwanese teacher for me and a few other kids. It was so foreign for us trying to just speak this funny language. We were ABC; there was no need for us to speak Chinese here. We grew up with 'Sesame Street' and 'Barney' and all that. It was not part of our culture; I was Australian—it was as simple as that.

Ann who is also a second-generation Australian-born Chinese in her 20s had a somewhat different background to Emily insofar as her parents were both born in China and migrated to Australia, her father in 1989 and her mother in 1991. Ann's grandparents also migrated to Australia in the mid-nineties. Of all the study participants, Ann would presumably be the one with the closest ties to the homeland. According to Ann, her parents saw themselves as Chinese but were happy that they moved to Australia because there was greater transparency in how things operated. Her grandparents who also lived in Australia did yearn to return to China but acknowledged that the environmental conditions in China were not conducive to their health. Within this family context, Ann acknowledged her Chinese heritage but saw it as something in the background rather in the foreground of her identity. This was in spite of her family's close ties and connections with China:

> I think that there are some people who kind of have their Asian or like Chinese heritage at the forefront of their identity and they're in all the Asian clubs and like they only have Chinese friends or Asian friends. But, I think that I am more associated with people who it's not their whole identity, and it's like part of them and that they have a lot of other interests and I think those other interests, that's how I relate to people more.

And when asked if she had a connection with the homeland when she visited China:

> Well I do but at the same time, I think I feel more like an outsider when I'm there. Like I don't feel like I fit in really. I'd rather just say that I am Australian. I just think that's easier than, like I don't think people should care necessarily about where I come from. So, I don't want to make it like at the forefront.

Although Ann had close ties to the homeland, her experiences were grounded in the local context and therefore, her identity was shaped by these experiences as well. Ann also did not feel the need to display her Chineseness. And what Ann considered was the homeland was not necessarily the same as what other study participants in this research considered to be the homeland which brings us to the issue of context. David was talking about embracing Chinese values but he would not call himself Chinese:

> Me and my brother don't really see ourselves as Chinese. We see ourselves as Australian. Like we are of Chinese background, and we accept that but we don't consider ourselves to be Chinese. We didn't grow up in China …. I certainly don't see myself as a Chinese person because I don't think I have the cultural awareness. Being from a Chinese family, my parents still adopt a lot of the values and a lot of the customs, and you pick it up through them, and through the Chinese community as well, and you embrace that. But it doesn't mean you're Chinese …My personal values and my ideals are based on my experiences growing up in Australia, and what I believe to be right and wrong. My values are very Australian-based.

According to Bauman (1996), the 'home' is not 'imaginary' but 'postulated'—it is about having a home, not in a physical sense, but an urge to feel at home, to recognise one's surroundings and belong there. When study participants visited the 'homeland', they may have been searching for a connection based on pre-conceived ideas about what that connection might entail. What seemed to happen in the process of searching for such a connection was the realisation that the connection and sense of belonging was in Australia.

Parents may also be instrumental in driving impressions of the homeland that serve to inspire their children to visit and sometimes with misleading ideas of what to expect. In her analysis of whether ethnic identity matters, Chandra (2006) dispels some myths—the myth of common ancestry and the myth of common region of origin. Accordingly, common ancestry cannot be a defining feature of ethnic groups since individuals often belong to different ethnic groups even if they have a common ancestry. The study participants had relatives who came from China in previous generations but they also had parents or grandparents from South-east Asia, Vietnam, South Africa and other places. In terms of the myth of common region of origin, the perception of a common homeland presupposes the existence of a group but what constitutes this group cannot be defined by that region of origin. First-generation parents who migrated from China to Australia in the 1940s are not the same as those that migrated to Australia in the 1980s. 'Ethnic identities can change even in the short term as individuals combine and re-combine elements from their fixed set of attributes differently' (Chandra, 2006, p. 420). The participants in this study had varying ways of negotiating relationships with significant others in the context of different social environments. In their visits to the homeland, what they imagined that homeland to be varied. And whilst there is some commonality in their ethnic groupings and region of origin, there were many differences thus reinforcing the notion that identity is both fluid and dynamic. One of the common themes emerging from the participants' visits to their homeland was a feeling that they were just visiting tourists rather than locals thus reinforcing the myth of the homeland. The Chinese diaspora does not have to return to a homeland to reinforce their ethnic consciousness and this is possible when the Chinese community is able to recreate a Chinese community outside the original homeland (Safran, 1991).

Discussion

This chapter demonstrates that Chineseness is manifested in a variety of ways. The critical point to be made in the performance of Chineseness was the act of choosing ways of doing Chinese rather than what was actually chosen. Environmental conditions, social and historical context and familial relationships have played a significant role in how Chineseness was enacted. The level of agency one has in shaping their identity was evident in the way study participants were able to 'pick and choose' aspects of their identity. The opportunity to pick and choose signifies freedom (Bauman, 1998). Underpinning the diverse ways in which Chineseness is performed is the level of agency one has in being able to pick and choose individual representations of Chineseness. 'Freedom' to choose must always be understood in the context in which choices are being made. As context changes from one individual to the next, so too does the level of agency and control. As has been demonstrated in this chapter, there were diverse ways in which Chineseness was done and they did not always resonate with all. What was important though, was that such actions resonated with the actors themselves and about finding a voice (Bhabha, 1996). This is consistent with the view that ethnic identities are situational in character and are not fixed or permanent but malleable (Verdery, 1994).

Ethnic groups are defined from the perspective of their members and the ethnic character of a social encounter depends on the situation and is not absolute (Eriksen, 2010). Intergenerational relations and the situational context in which they occur are important factors in the construction of identity. Parents play an active role in socialising their children by defining and interpreting their symbols, culture and ethnicity to their children (Cheng & Kuo, 2000; Sabatier, 2008). While parents are active agents in socialising their children, it is only their interpretation of the symbols and meaning of their culture and ethnicity that is being conveyed. Families interpret and transmit ethnic culture differently. Ethnic culture may be transmitted through several means including art, dress, religion, beliefs and customs (Cheng & Kuo, 2000). For the study participants, parental perceptions have been instrumental in influencing how Chineseness is performed.

The role of parents in the transmission of culture may also be undermined with increasing exposure to external social settings and with the cognitive development of children. Cheng and Kuo (2000) recognise the differences in the way ethnic families project their ethnicity, the degrees to which they exercise control and the way they express their ethnic identity. When some of the study participants perceived their parents to be too controlling and dogmatic in imposing their expectations on their children, conflict was often the outcome. In their study of second-generation Vietnamese American cultural behaviours, Killian and Hegtvedt (2003) found that children who were embarrassed by their parents' ethnic ways were more likely to assimilate as American.

Our perception of how others see us affects how we see ourselves. Further, how we see ourselves is not always aligned to how others see us. The dichotomy between how we see ourselves and how others see us, however, continues irrespective of the passage of time and the shift towards a globalised world. Ben noted, 'I'm probably more Chinese to other people than I am to myself'. Ethnic identity is a product of both external and internal definitions. Ethnic groups become agents in their own construction, shaping and re-shaping their identities based on history, culture and pre-existing constructions (Cornell, 1996). Over the course of time when the social environment changes, our identity may also change (Hale, 2004). Most scholars agree that ethnic groups are not fixed or given but are historically emergent and vary over time (Brubaker, 2009; Yans, 2006). Further, 'ethnicity, race, and nationhood are not things in the world, but perspectives on the world' (Brubaker, 2009, p.32). These include ways of identifying oneself and others and creating classifications in culturally specific ways. As this chpater has shown, how individuals have dealt with intergenerational relations, educational expectations, being a member of an ethnic minority, exposure to Chinese customs and values, contact with the wider Chinese community, marriage expectations and homeland experiences are testament to the diversity of factors that shape our identity. When the study participants were aware of being in an ethnic minority position and were exposed to racism, they were more inclined to assimilate to the host society and less inclined to adopt parental customs and traditions. This effectively limited their understanding of their parents' culture which may explain in part the limited way in which Chineseness was performed.

Irrespective of situational context, there seemed to be a universal acceptance that Chinese food and the process of eating it was a true demonstration of doing Chinese. There was general acceptance among the study participants that the centrality of food and the way in which it was shared was an 'authentic' display of Chineseness. Most of the study participants experienced the process of family gatherings involving Chinese food and chopsticks. Simple acts like eating rice daily with chopsticks may be signifiers of Chinese culture (Ngan, 2008). There were happy memories associated with sharing food in this manner and this seemed to have transcended generational differences. Historically, many of the older study participants grew up in environments where they were the ethnic minority and it was not uncommon for them to try to assimilate with the dominant culture at the time and to reject Chinese heritage. However, Chinese food seemed to be a mainstay.

The process of eating and sharing Chinese food was a readily accessible means of encapsulating Chineseness and sometimes it was the only way of performing Chineseness especially for those Australian-born Chinese who actively rejected their Chinese heritage in the first place as they were growing up. The process, in itself, did not make someone Chinese. However, it was and continues to be a part of everyday life and the memories associated with that experience were what helped one to distinguish themselves from others. For later generations, it was sometimes the only way in which Australian-born Chinese could do Chinese.

Like food, participation in Chinese community associations was another way of engendering Chineseness. In one study of second-generation Vietnamese American Cultural behaviours, those involved in the ethnic community have higher social capital and parents who display cultural behaviours have children who are more involved in ethnic networks (Killian & Hegtvedt, 2003). However, traditional Chinese community associations were becoming less popular among young Australian-born Chinese as with other formal organisations. For the study participants who were active members of their local Chinese community association, these associations also housed Chinese museums that documented the history of Chinese settlement in their respective regions. In doing so, they were a representation of Chineseness that is not relevant to all Chinese. In one sense, these museums were like time capsules reflecting the life and hardships encountered by early Chinese immigrants settling into a country where they were an ethnic minority and where assimilation to mainstream society was expected. Contemporary migrants do not necessarily undergo a process of assimilation and, in an era of globalisation, no longer need to sever ties with their 'homeland' (Nagel, 1994). The socio-economic circumstances in which contemporary Chinese migrants come to live in Australia may also be different in terms of education levels. Some of the younger study participants had parents who were university-educated compared to the parents of the older study participants who did not have the same educational opportunities in the earlier part of the twentieth century. In addition, some of the earlier first generation parents originated from farming cultures in rural areas of China whereas contemporary Chinese migrants tended to fit into the skilled migration category.

In the case of marriage, the essentialisation of Chineseness based on phenotype was evident in some of the comments made by study participants of their parents' expectations. Marrying Chinese was perceived as a way of preserving the 'bloodline'. The underlying assumption of ethnic commonality in Chinese people is inherently flawed. A 'catch-all term' for ethnic minorities ignores the complexities and different circumstances and experiences that people have (Andrews, 2016). There are different ways of being Chinese but there still exists this notion that identity embodies ethnicity and nationality (Chu, 2008). As Chu (2008, p. 199) notes, 'identity today is polyglot, multiethnic, migrant, made from elements that cut across various cultures'. This is not to say that essentialisation is inherently wrong. Strategic essentialism may be used for political leverage (Sathian & Ngeow, 2014; Veronis, 2007) as was the case with annual Chinese New Year events on cultural calendars.

There was also a stereotypical image that persists of Chinese students being the 'model minority'. Whether this stereotype was justified is not the point. What several second-generation Australian-born Chinese study participants experienced was an expectation from their parents that they focus on their studies and these sentiments seem to have transcended time to some extent. One of the reasons for migration is arguably for advancement and in the case of first-generation Chinese immigrants, education was one way of ensuring advancement.

In one's search for belonging or identity, some of the study participants had travelled to what they perceived to be the 'homeland'. It is an action that can either reinforce a sense of Chineseness or reinforce what one is not. Sometimes it might entail a mythologised idea of what the homeland entails, an idea that may have been formulated by the memories of the first-generation when they left the homeland many years ago. Nonetheless, for some of the study participants, it was almost like a rite of passage to discover their roots. Some of the older study participants also made trips back to China and the overarching feeling was a sense of being a tourist. Again, it is not so much the outcome as it is the belief in a connection and the choice to investigate that connection that counts.

In the performance of Chineseness, the fundamental consideration is one's ability to choose and to exercise agency more than what is being chosen and this was evident in this study. Given that level of agency varied, there were diverse ways in which Chineseness was enacted and not all study participants performed Chineseness in the same way.

References

Alonso, A. M. (1994). The politics of space, time and substance: State formation, nationalism and ethnicity. *Annual Review of Anthropology, 23*, 379–405. Retrieved from http://www.jstor.org.ezproxy.lib.monash.edu.au/stable/2156019

Alvarez, A. N., & Helms, J. E. (2001). Racial identity and reflected appraisals as influences on Asian Americans' racial adjustment. *Cultural Diversity & Ethnic Minority Psychology, 7*(3), 217–231. https://doi.org/10.1037/1099-9809.7.3.217

Andrews, K. (2016). The problem of political blackness: Lessons from the black supplementary school movement. *Ethnic and Racial Studies, 39*(11), 2060–2078. https://doi.org/10.1080/01419870.2015.1131314

References

Ang, I. (1993). To be or not to be Chinese: Diaspora, culture and postmodern ethnicity. *Southeast Asian Journal of Social Science, 21*(1), 1–17. https://doi.org/10.1163/030382493x00017

Bauman, Z. (1998). Identity—Then, now, what for? *Polish Sociological Review, 123*, 205–216. Retrieved from http://www.jstor.org.ezproxy.lib.monash.edu.au/stable/41274679

Bauman, Z. (2001). Identity in the globalising world. *Social Anthropology, 9*(2), 121–129. https://doi-org.ezproxy.lib.monash.edu.au/https://doi.org/10.1017/S096402820100009X

Bauman, Z. (1996). From pilgrim to tourist—Or a short history of identity. In S. Hall & P. du Gay (Eds.), *Questions of cultural identity* (pp. 18–36). Sage.

Bhabha, H. K. (1996). Culture's in-between. In S. Hall & P. du Gay (Eds.), *Questions of cultural identity* (pp. 53–60). Sage Publications Ltd.

Brubaker, R. (2009). Ethnicity, race, and nationalism. *Annual Review of Sociology, 35*, 21–42. https://doi.org/10.1146/annurev-soc-070308-115916

Chandra, K. (2006). What is ethnic identity and does it matter? *Annual Review of Political Science, 9*, 397–424. https://doi.org/10.1146/annurev.polisci.9.062404.170715

Cheng, S. H., & Kuo, W. H. (2000). Family socialization of ethnic identity among Chinese American pre-adolescents. *Journal of Comparative Family Studies, 31*(4), 463–484. Retrieved from https://search.proquest.com/docview/60093440?accountid=12528

Chu, Y-W. (2008). The importance of being Chinese: Orientalism reconfigured in the age of global modernity. *Boundary 2, 35*(2), 183–206.

Cornell, S. (1996). The variable ties that bind: Content and circumstance in ethnic processes. *Ethnic and Racial Studies, 19*(2), 265–289. Retrieved from https://search.proquest.com/docview/1036476222?accountid=12528

Eriksen, T. H. (2010). *Ethnicity and nationalism: Anthropological perspectives* (3rd ed.). Pluto Press.

Hale, H. E. (2004). Explaining ethnicity. *Comparative Political Studies, 37*(4), 458–485. https://doi.org/10.1177/0010414003262906

Hangen, S. (2005). Race and the politics of identity in Nepal. *Ethnology, 44*(1), 49–64. Retrieved from https://search.proquest.com/docview/60047551?accountid=12528

Hibbins, R. (2005). Migration and gender identity among Chinese skilled male migrants to Australia. *Geoforum, 36*(2), 167–180. https://doi.org/10.1016/j.geoforum.2003.10.003

Hiller, H. H., & Chow, V. (2005). Ethnic identity and segmented assimilation among second-generation Chinese youth. *Sociological Studies of Children and Youth, 10*, 75–99. https://doi.org/10.1016/S1537-4661(04)10005-6

Hsu, C.-Y. (1991). A reflection on marginality. *Daedalus, 120*(2), 227–229. Retrieved from http://www.jstor.org/stable/20025381

Hua, Z. (2008). Duelling languages, duelling values: Codeswitching in bilingual intergenerational conflict talk in diasporic families. *Journal of Pragmatics, 40*(10), 1799–1816. https://doi.org/10.1016/j.pragma.2008.02.007

Killian, C., & Hegtvedt, K. A. (2003). The role of parents in the maintenance of second generation Vietnamese cultural behaviors. *Sociological Spectrum, 23*(2), 213–245. https://doi.org/10.1080/02732170390132217

Louie, V. (2006). Growing up ethnic in transnational worlds: Identities among second-generation Chinese and Dominicans. *Identities: Global Studies in Culture and Power, 13*(3), 363–394. https://doi.org/10.1080/10702890600838118

Luke, A., & Luke, C. (2000). The differences language makes: The discourses on language of inter-ethnic Asian/Australian families. In I. Ang, L. Law, S. Chalmers, & M. Thomas (Eds.), *Alter/Asians: Asian-Australian identities in art, media and popular culture* Pluto Press.

Nagel, J. (1994). Constructing ethnicity: Creating and recreating ethnic identity and culture. *Social Problems, 41*(1), 152–176. https://doi.org/10.2307/3096847

Ngan, L. (2008). Living in-between: Hybrid identities among long-established Australian-born Chinese in Sydney. *Chinese Southern Diaspora Studies Journal, 2*(1), 127–135.

Pang, B., Macdonald, D., & Hay, P. (2015). Do I have a choice?" The influences of family values and investments on Chinese migrant young people's lifestyles and physical activity participation in Australia. *Sport, Education and Society, 20*(8), 1048–1064. https://doi.org/10.1080/13573322.2013.833504

Pieterse, J. N. (1994). Globalisation as hybridisation. *International Sociology, 9*(2), 161–184. https://doi.org/10.1177/026858094009002003

Portes, A., & Rumbaut, R. G. (2001). *Legacies: The story of the immigrant second generation.* University of California Press.

Sabatier, C. (2008). Ethnic and national identity among second-generation immigrant adolescents in France: The role of social context and family. *Journal of Adolescence, 31*(2), 185–205. https://doi.org/10.1016/j.adolescence.2007.08.001

Safran, W. (1991). Diasporas in modern societies: Myths of homeland and return. *Diaspora, 1*(1), 83–99. https://doi.org/10.1353/dsp.1991.0004

Sathian, M. R., & Ngeow, Y. M. (2014). Essentialising ethnic and state identities: Strategic adaptations of ethnic Chinese in Kelantan, Malaysia. *Asian Studies Review, 38*(3), 385–402. https://doi.org/10.1080/10357823.2014.936361

Verdery, K. (1994). Ethnicity, nationalism, and state-making: Ethnic groups and boundaries: Past and future. In H. Vermeulen & C. Govers (Eds.), *The anthropology of ethnicity: Beyond 'Ethnic groups and boundaries'* (pp. 33–58). Het Spinhuis Publishers.

Veronis, L. (2007). Strategic spatial essentialism: Latin Americans' real and imagined geographies of belonging in Toronto. *Social & Cultural Geography, 8*(3), 455–473. https://doi.org/10.1080/14649360701488997

Yans, V. (2006). On "Groupness". *Journal of American Ethnic History, 25*(4), 119–129. Retrieved from https://search.proquest.com/docview/216445706?accountid=12528

Chapter 6
Conclusion

Overview

The central focus of this book was to investigate how Chineseness was perceived, constructed and understood by multi-generation Australian-born Chinese. Ethnicity is generally perceived to be a core feature of identity for first-generation immigrants and presumably, this is passed on to the second generation and beyond. For ethnicities with both visual and 'hearable' markers of difference, such markers of difference tend to feature prominently in identity construction. In the case of the Chinese in Australia, phenotype or visible physical features as well as ethnic language were generally regarded as obvious markers of difference. Historically, Chineseness was viewed in a relatively one-dimensional way based on these obvious markers of difference. This study has shown that Chineseness in postmodern society is not one-dimensional but nuanced in multiple ways. Not only is Chineseness multi-faceted it is a 'liquid' entity that changes over time and space.

In the case of the Chinese diaspora in Australia, the Chinese migrated to Australia from many countries, resulting in a diverse array of cultural, economic and political backgrounds. The environment and society in which the first generation initially settled in Australia has also changed over time and this, in turn, has impacted on the second and later generation experience growing up in Australia. Individual identities also evolve in relation to situational factors. Individual identities are, thus, malleable and shaping them is easier than trying to keep them in shape. According to Bauman (2000), liquidizing powers have shifted from the system to society, from politics to life experiences and from the macro to micro level. To be successful, the idea is to be oneself and not like all the rest with difference and not sameness being the best (Bauman, 2003). People are haunted by the problem of identity (Bauman, 2005). Those at the top of the power pyramid, to whom space and distance are superfluous and home can be anywhere, are the ones who can choose from what is on offer and change at will. Those at the bottom are the ones who try to cling to a sole identity and keep it from falling apart.

There have been occasions in Australia's history where political parties sought to influence the process of identity ascription with a drive towards homogeneity and by manipulating public information. For Bauman (2007: 16), 'fear of a phantom enemy is all the politicians have left to maintain their power'. In terms of ethnicity, phenotype was often used as a marker of identity on the erroneous assumption that race was a fixed phenomenon. The 'White Australia' policy was enacted to restrict the number of Chinese and other 'non-white' immigrants from settling in Australia. The Australian Government was intent on maintaining a level of homogeneity among its citizens up until the dismantling of the Policy and this was arguably based largely on physical appearance. In recent times, when politicians and the media use terminology such as 'Islamic terrorists', 'African gangs' and 'boat people', they may be contributing to homogenised views about refugees, asylum seekers and Muslims. This has the potential effect of creating fear and misunderstanding among the community.

In the global arena, local politicians have the eyes of the rest of the world cast on them so, in that sense, power and politics may become separated (Bauman, 2007). In the modern state, political control was available to those in power. However, with the advent of globalisation that underpins postmodern society, politics remains local but uncontrolled in the global space. Despite past mutterings to re-create homogeneous collectivities with shared histories, customs, language or other features, postmodern Australia is a conglomerate of multiple identities that interact and evolve dynamically. Diasporas are more mobile and spread across many spaces. Individuals are not necessarily driven by nation state sentiments alone and, in the case of the Chinese diaspora, their diverse backgrounds mean that their influences are broader and more far-reaching than their physical borders.

Identities are also diverse and influenced by situational factors. As this book demonstrates, Chinese identity is multi-faceted and its characteristics differ from one individual to the next. It is the individual and not the social institution who determines the outcomes (Bauman, 2000). Borders are drawn before the traits are identified and once identified, they are used to reinforce the border (Barth, 1969). A focus on the uniqueness of the cultural traits within ethnic groups wrongly presupposes that they stand in isolation. Groups are in continuous contact with one another and are multi-faceted. The reality is that cultural traits neither define the ethnic group nor are they necessarily unique to that group.

Given that Chineseness is not fixed, a new level of complexity is introduced when attempting to answer questions around the importance of visual features and ethnic language retention as markers of identity and whether Chineseness is 'inescapable'. These questions imply homogeneity in what constitutes Chineseness and it is a static condition. What has been established in this book is that Chineseness means different things to different people and it may be conceptualised differently over the life course of an individual. Inescapability implies that Chineseness is a negative concept and therefore, needs to be escaped. This book has shown that Chineseness is constructed in a multitude of ways and is not necessarily viewed as a negative trait; instead, it may also be wholeheartedly embraced. The emergence of hybrid forms of Chineseness as demonstrated in the way multi-generation Australian-born Chinese enact their ethnic identities aligns with Bauman's model of a 'liquid' life. The diversity in the ways in which Chineseness is perceived, constructed and understood also supports the idea that traditional core features of ethnic identity are not sufficient enough to define the Chinese diaspora as an entity in itself.

Informed by ideas of 'liquid modernity' and hybrid and segmented identities, this book explored how multi-generation Australian-born Chinese perceived, constructed and understood their Chineseness. In so doing, it challenged essentialist views of identity as authentic, homogeneous and unchanging. This study recognised that situational context was a fundamental determinant in identity construction and it supports a pluralist view of identity as fluid, heterogeneous and changing (Barth, 1969; Bauman, 2000).

The Chinese population in Australia is culturally diverse and Chineseness is not a singular category with a fixed content (Ang, 2001). This book has demonstrated the diverse ways in which Chineseness was constructed among both younger and older multi-generation Australian-born Chinese. In terms of population diversity and levels of cultural tolerance in Australia, the circumstances in the first three decades after the Second World War were vastly different to the circumstances in the decades after the abolition of the White Australia Policy and the introduction of multiculturalist policies. This affected how Australian-born Chinese constructed their identity. Arguably, the shifting landscape has coincided with increased agency in identity construction.

There are other studies on multi-generation Australian-born Chinese, most notably the works of Lucille Ngan, Chan Kwok-bun and Carole Tan. Ngan and Chan (2012) focused only on research data from long-established Australian-born Chinese who were born in Australia and whose family had resided in Australia (or resided outside of China) for over three generations. Their historical past stemmed back to the Gold Rush era and the introduction of the Immigration Restriction Act in 1901. The cohort in the current study not only included long-established Australian-born Chinese but also younger second-generation Australian-born Chinese from a wider range of diasporic Chinese groups. By broadening the study cohort, this book was able to build on the understanding of the Chinese in Australia in the postmodern context of globalisation.

A majority of informants in Tan's (2004) original research were also Australian-born descendants of Chinese migrants who arrived in Australia prior to or during the years of the White Australia Policy. Tan did not fully investigate how Chineseness was interpreted and negotiated by Australian-born Chinese and was satisfied that their 'racial' ancestry was sufficient for 'being Chinese'. In contrast, this book has primarily focused on the diverse ways in which Chineseness is constructed and understood, thereby moving beyond fixed, collectivist 'racial' representations of Chineseness that were common at the height of the White Australia Policy.

There are numerous studies both locally and internationally that focus on the second-generation immigrant and their relationship with the host society. However, there are fewer studies that target second-generation Australian-born Chinese and even fewer that examine the multi-generation Australian-born Chinese experience across time and space. In Australia legislation was enacted to specifically exclude Chinese immigrants. The only other country enacting legislation designed to exclude

Chinese labourers was the United States with the Chinese Exclusion Act of 1882. With the White Australia Policy in place for at least the first sixty-odd years of the twentieth century, national identity was centred on being 'white' and Anglo (Walton et al., 2018). In line with Anderson's (1983) conceptualisation of the nation-state, Australia was imagined as 'white' and shaped by 'race'. The study participants growing up during this period were faced with the realisation that they were outside the realm of the Australian imagined community. With the shift from a 'white' Australia to a multicultural Australia from the 1970s onwards, one might imagine a cultural change in the Australian landscape.

Walton et al. (2018) argued that, since the 1970s, the political shift from a 'white' Australia to a multicultural Australia has not coincided with any changes in Australia's cultural imaginary as being 'white' and Anglo. Accordingly, 'cultural diversity is still viewed as "other" coming from "elsewhere" (that is, "other" than Britain)' (p. 133). The implication is anything 'other' is somehow perceived to be inferior to the dominant imaginary. Further, being the 'other' assumes a degree of negativity. In the case of Australian-born Chinese, their ethnic identity can be seen in a positive light as demonstrated often in the ways it was enacted. While this study has demonstrated evidence of the 'othering' process, it has also demonstrated the resilience of Australian-born Chinese to be active agents in their self-identification and to embrace Chineseness as a core feature of their identity rather than as something to be rejected. The shift away from Chineseness as a negative, inescapable trait to a trait that is central to one's self-identification demonstrates how individuals have the power to determine outcomes over the social institution (Bauman, 2000). This study has shown that ethnic identity construction among Australian-born Chinese reflected the shift from a static, monological approach to a dialectical, liquid approach towards identity construction (Bauman, 2000). Contrary to Walton et al. (2018), this self-determination in ethnic identity construction must also be seen in the context of the environmental and social changes resulting from increased cultural diversity in Australia's population flowing from multiculturalist policies since the 1970s.

While this study has highlighted Chineseness as a core attribute to identity construction among Australian-born Chinese, it has also demonstrated the other end of the spectrum where Chineseness was not always considered central to the identity of Australian-born Chinese study participants or they were ambivalent about their Chineseness (Benton & Gomez, 2014). There were several reasons why Australian-born Chinese considered themselves 'Australian' as opposed to Chinese. This included a perceived stigma associated with being Chinese, a desire to be 'white', a desire to assimilate to mainstream culture and to fit in, or exposure to mainstream culture with little reinforcement of one's cultural heritage. It may be one factor or it may be a series of factors that result in an outcome where 'Australian' identity is fully embraced instead of a Chinese identity. What it does indicate is that identity cannot always be bound by physical or cultural traits alone. As Barth (1969) noted, ethnic identities are situational and based on both ascription and self-ascription rather than the cultural attributes one may have. In the study of ethnic identity, it is the individually-determined cultural differences marking boundaries that is significant and not the analyst's idea of those differences.

A broader understanding emerged when the Australian-Chinese experience was compared with that of the global Chinese diaspora, in particular in the US and United Kingdom. From an historical perspective, both Australia and the United States are similar in terms of being settler societies. In addition, from the commencement of white settlement in Australia, affinity with British identity was strong. As evidenced in this book, the Australian-born Chinese have had distinct experiences compared to the US and UK counterparts.

This book is also unique insofar as it is one of the few studies that included 'mixed race' Australian-born Chinese who identified as Chinese in the study cohort. The study of 'mixed races' is an entity in itself and often treated separately. Why these study participants chose to highlight their Chinese identity was not the focus of this study but was nonetheless significant because it demonstrated that phenotype was not necessarily a defining feature of being Chinese given that some of these participants did not have typically Chinese physical features. In the case of 'mixed race' study participants, it can be shown that the postmodern world is so complex and mixed that it can no longer be studied through the lens of fixed identifications or ethnic group formations (Brubaker, 2002; Jenkins, 2008). There is a mixing of a range of cultures rather than cultures being separate (Bhabha, 1990; Pieterse, 1994). With the possibility of having multiple identities comes the creation of the 'third space' of hybridity (Ang, 2001; Bhabha, 1990). One can no longer expect to treat ethnic identities as absolute and fixed, thus challenging the authenticity of one-dimensional views of Chineseness.

Phenotype and Identity

Ethnic identity construction was examined in terms of the concepts of being, feeling and doing Chinese. Two of the main signifiers of an ethnic group's identity, phenotype and ethnic language maintenance, were prime measures of being and feeling Chinese. Phenotype or visible physical features and ethnic language are obvious markers of difference (Martin, 2003) between Chinese people, specifically Australian-born Chinese, and the host society. The emphasis placed on these two features as measures of ethnic identity was dependent upon social and environmental conditions intertwined with a host of variables. Despite the power of visible features and language in in constructing ethnic identity, individuals constructed their identities that suited them. How the individual reacted to the essentialisation of ethnic identity was largely dependent upon their social context, social capital and family relationships. The stronger the social or family relationships, the more likely the individual would exercise agency (Rosenthal & Feldman, 1990) in arriving at a hybridised identity that embraced rather than rejected their Chineseness. What was evident was the diversity of characteristics that defined a Chinese identity and the complexity of what it meant from one individual to the next. The category of Australian-born Chinese was also fraught with complexity given that family origins were wide-ranging, the situational context varied and changed over time and individual identity itself was unique. The outsider perspective on Chinese identity was sometimes incompatible with the insider perspective. Nonetheless, the propensity to homogenise Chineseness based on visible appearance and languages spoken were two key criteria evident in perceived social constructions of Chineseness.

As demonstrated in Chapter Three, biology does matter when it comes to how Australian-born Chinese see themselves. These experiences are not confined to Australian-born Chinese but are arguably evident for other non-Anglo groups in Australia or those groups that have visible features that are not consistent with the dominant Anglo-Celtic majority. According to Barth (1969), our sense of identity is developed by acting in the world and interacting with others rather than being invented by ourselves. The problem lies in identity being formed on the basis of misinformation or macro controls of that information. The manipulation of public information prevents one from displaying individual identity and reduces one's knowledge of other people (Barth, 1994). As Brubaker (2004a) contends, 'groupism' can be problematic but ethnic groups continue to be treated as entities.

After the Second World War, the Australian Government was intent on boosting population numbers but favoured immigrants of European background over immigrants from China. Up until that time, the White Australia Policy was used as a tool to exclude Chinese immigrants and in doing so, it had the effect of representing Chinese people as a maligned group. The Australian-born Chinese study participants growing up in 1950s to 1970s Australia were often collectively categorised on the basis of phenotype and experienced discrimination accordingly. Phenotype was perpetuated and reinforced as a marker of identity among Australian-born Chinese and this was explicated through experiences around the racialisation of identity (Matthews, 2000), the perceived stigma of being Chinese, the fostering of stereotypes (Song, 2003; Zhou, 2014) and of being the 'perpetual foreigner' (Cheryan & Monin, 2005).

The focus on phenotype in identity construction (Bailey, 2000; Yue, 2000) can also work to exclude Australian-born Chinese from the category of being Chinese. This may be evident with Australian-born Chinese of mixed parentage who identify as Chinese but others may not accept them as Chinese. Some met with incredulity when they expressed themselves as Chinese. This book has shown the inefficacies of essentialising Chineseness based on physical appearance alone and how this has impacted Australian-born Chinese, especially those of mixed heritage. Also, the notions of 'half-Chinese' or 'part Chinese' are fallacious insofar as such they are not physically quantifiable. Rather, there should be a recognition of multiple, concurrent identities where individuals are free to choose which ones to use at any given moment in time. This is more so as it pertains to postmodern society where populations are increasingly mobile and ethnicities have become increasingly blended.

The construction of Chineseness based on phenotype had a pervasive influence on the way in which Australian-born Chinese saw themselves. As school-age children, encounters with bullying and name-calling were commonplace particularly for those who were attending school during the 1960s and the 1970s. Australia's cultural imaginary at the time was grounded on being 'white' and Anglo (Dunn et al., 2004; Walton et al., 2018). The impact that name-calling had during their school years varied in relation to the perceived support they had. Those who did not feel that they had support from either their family or friends tended to resent their Chineseness and were intent on assimilating to the mainstream population. This resentment manifested in the rejection of Chinese cultural practices and language. But the resentment was short-lived and Chineseness was readily embraced in adulthood. For those who felt supported by family and/or friends, any negative experiences they may have encountered in the school playground had little impact on their sense of well-being and belonging.

Some as adults were quick to disassociate themselves from their Chinese identity. They were fearful of being grouped together with other Chinese groups such as 'the mainland Chinese buying up real estate', a 'boat people' or 'international Chinese students'. This fear was founded on the racialisation of identity and the resultant stigma associated with being Chinese (Jenkins, 1994), with the perpetuation of negative stereotypes, and the possibility of being labelled a 'perpetual foreigner'. This fear has reinforced the precariousness of being Chinese and it being contingent upon macro influences (Lo, 2000). Depending on the social and political context, these fears traversed time especially if they were reinforced within the family.

Phenotype as an identity marker is also pervasive in the US. American history, like Australian history, is rooted in a mythology around the white settler experience of migration to seek a new life and to build a new nation. According to Tuan (2002), white ethnics could exclusively claim this collective memory of the pioneering experience unlike African Americans brought on slave ships and Native Americans forced to incorporate into this American life. While Asian immigrants also arrived voluntarily, they experienced exclusion and rejection which was similar to the experiences of the Chinese in nineteenth century Australia and well into the twentieth century. Asian Americans were thus not seen as 'real' Americans and their experiences of early migration were erased from collective memory. "Cultural authenticity" is something that Asian Americans must also involuntarily contend with as they become more removed from the immigrant generation. They can be deemed inauthentically American as well as not being seen as Chinese enough. Contemporary Asian Americans continue to face challenges in identity construction in the face of an environment where the centrality of race is key.

To Speak or not to Speak Chinese

Just as the way one looks affected identity construction, the way one sounds or the language spoken played a role in identity formation. For some Australian-born Chinese, there was a belief that knowledge of parents' native language was a sign of authenticity as a Chinese person. In addition, like phenotype, speaking Chinese in public was also associated with negativity just as there was stigma about being Chinese. Some of the study participants actively chose not to speak or learn their parents' language and instead, chose to assimilate as much as possible to the host culture. They were not able to manipulate their physical appearance but they were able to control their spoken language.

Ethnic language retention was a key marker of ethnic identity for second-generation Australian-born Chinese especially in their formative years when they were often traversing two cultures—that of their parents and the host country. First-generation Chinese immigrants were more inclined to speak in their native language in the first instance and the second-generation were expected to communicate in their parental native language. Consistent with Portes and Hao (1998), ethnic language was an important signifier of ethnic identity for first- and second-generation Australian-born Chinese but became less important as a marker of ethnic identity by the third- and fourth-generation. Second-generation Australian-born Chinese were largely preoccupied with fitting in with the mainstream population and showed little interest in retaining their parents' language because it did not fit in with mainstream culture. The act of rejecting parental language represented the rejection of parental culture or ethnicity. As speaking Chinese in public was frowned upon, many second-generation Australian-born Chinese expressed disdain towards speaking Chinese in public. Few grasped the opportunity to learn Chinese formally. Some did not communicate readily with their parents as they were growing up and for those who did communicate, the preferred language spoken was English and not Chinese even when their parents spoke to them in Chinese.

Not all refused to learn or speak their parents' native language. The younger cohort of second-generation Australian-born Chinese whose parents came from mainland China did not express any qualms about speaking Chinese. For them, speaking Chinese to their parents was just a part of everyday life. Their parents were well-educated and who openly embraced their ethnicity.

Loss of ethnic language contributed to communication difficulties between first- and second-generation Chinese Australians. Cultural differences between generations also contributed to communication difficulties. Not only does the transmission of customs become problematic, the cultural differences between the first generation grounded in their home country and the second generation grounded in the host society can inadvertently lead to communication breakdown. These cultural differences may be reflected in differences in parenting roles and may manifest in emotional dissonance and disconnect with the homeland.

By the third and later generations of Australian-born Chinese, loss of the mother tongue was often absolute. In Australia, despite opportunities to study second languages in the school system as well as multi-language signage and interpreter services being available, multi-generation Australian-born Chinese invariably spoke the dominant language. In these situations, English was also the main language spoken at home. Yet, multi-generation Australian-born Chinese were often viewed as Chinese immigrants, which indicates the persistence of essentialised ways of defining Chinese identity and 'identity denial' (Cheryan & Monin, 2005). By the third generation, ethnic language maintenance played less of a role in ethnic identity construction among Australian-born Chinese. The immigrant generation learns as much English as they can but speak the mother tongue at home; the second generation may speak the mother tongue at home but shifts to unaccented English at school and at work; and English becomes the home language for the third generation and knowledge of the parental tongue disappears (Alba et al., 2002; Portes & Hao, 1998).

Part of the process of native language loss may be attributed to the dominance of the English language since it is the lingua franca in Australia.

In this book, the role of ethnic language as a transmitter of cultural practices and values was juxtaposed against the idea that ethnic language was primarily a functional tool of communication between the first- and second-generation. There was little doubt that knowledge of the parental language was an important tool for second-generation Australian-born Chinese to communicate with their parents, particularly if their parents spoke little English, if any at all. However, ethnic language was not always be a measure of one's ethnicity. While ethnic language maintenance has many functions, its function was limited. Rather than it being a tool for the transmission of cultural values and traditions and a marker of ethnic identity, ethnic language was often a tool for communication only. Other ethnic identity markers were more relevant in ethnic identity construction. Many in this study refused to communicate with their parents in Chinese or expressed little interest in retaining the parental language. Having little knowledge of the parental language did not, however, lessen their Chinese identity even if that was the initial intention.

There is also a fundamental anomaly in the importance of native language retention being a signifier of identity in circumstances where ethnic language serves neither a communication role nor a tool for transmitting cultural practices and values. Where many Chinese dialects spoken, language was not the common denominator and this was evident with the changing face of Chinese immigration. Many could not identify with other Chinese people because of the language barrier resulting from the incompatibility of dialects spoken. For the trained listener, the difference is evident but for the untrained, the foreignness of the language spoken was enough to categorise the individual into a specific group. The dichotomy between the insider and outsider perspective was demonstrated when it came to the spoken language. This shows that language as a marker of identity is largely based on it being a hearable sign of difference. Like phenotype, native language was essentialised with little regard for the nuances of dialect.

The Enactment of Chineseness

As has been demonstrated by the ways in which Chineseness has been performed by Australian-born Chinese, 'doing' Chinese is a part of everyday life and varies from person to person depending upon the level of agency one has. The situational context, which affects identity construction, is continually evolving and therefore, individual self-perceptions are bound to evolve (Bauman, 1996). For some Australian-born Chinese, eating Chinese food and the way it is ingested is integral to their sense of Chineseness. For others, participation in Chinese cultural events or celebration of important dates in the Chinese calendar that makes them uniquely Chinese. On the whole, Chineseness is enacted in a myriad of ways and it can be a core feature or a peripheral one depending upon the situational context. This ranged from lifestyle decisions like choice of marriage partners and educational pursuits to participation in

Chinese community associations and celebration of Chinese festivals. Chineseness was also embraced in everyday practices like the sharing of meals or in conscious decisions to connect with the 'homeland' through visits to China.

Food and its sharing seemed to be universally accepted and recognised as an important feature of Chineseness across both generations and time. As with participation in Chinese community associations or engagement with Chinese festivals, food and the way it was ingested was something that could be controlled irrespective of how one looked or what languages they spoke. Eating Chinese food with chopsticks and engaging in large family meals as a group indicated a demonstration of doing Chinese. While the act of large family gatherings around the dinner table was not unique to Chinese people, it nevertheless often featured prominently in the everyday lives of Australian-born Chinese and was sometimes the only obvious display of Chineseness for some.

Some of these actions were generation-specific while others transcended time. Choice of marriage partners, for example, was more of an issue for second-generation Australian-born Chinese whose parents expressed desire for their children to marry within their culture. This was based on the presumption that communication would be easier and the intended spouse would also reflect the same values and traditions as the parents. However, there was also evidence that relationship with someone of a similar ethnicity and culture to their parents failed, as they were not Chinese enough. This indicates that ethnicity on its own was not necessarily a criterion for forming a common ground. Group boundaries are in a constant state of flux. For the third generation and beyond, there was not such a strong push towards marrying someone of the same ethnicity.

The complex ways of and, at times, reluctance towards embracing Chinese identity has been demonstrated in this book but the affirmation of being Chinese has also been demonstrated in equal measure. There is a common belief that ethnic minorities may choose either to assimilate, integrate or reject the mainstream culture of the host society. However, this implies that one's ethnicity is not equal to the mainstream and that it is not valued in the same way. As this book demonstrated, Chineseness was not necessarily perceived as a negative trait by Australian-born Chinese.

Family relationships built on mutual respect and solid support networks have the capacity to override any negative impacts associated with racialisation of identity and consequently Chineseness is embraced rather than rejected. Social changes brought on by multiculturalist policies since the 1970s have also played a role in the extent to which Australian-born Chinese embraced their Chineseness. From a generational perspective, third and later generations seemed to embrace their brand of Chineseness more readily. This was reflected in their active participation in Chinese cultural events and festivals. Some of the older second-generation Australian-born Chinese who may have rejected their Chineseness in their youth, were now lamenting the loss of their native language and were more accepting of their cultural heritage. For younger second-generation Australian-born Chinese, their Chinese identity was just part of who they were. Their Chineseness was integral to their everyday lives without question.

For Australian-born Chinese, this book demonstrated the pervasiveness of phenotype on self-perceptions. There was also a certain precarity in their sense of identity and belonging. In the face of this uncertainty, Australian-born Chinese have by and large exercised agency in the way in which they have adapted their identity to create hybridised identities embracing their Chineseness. For Lo (2000, pp. 167–168), 'the discursive and provisional use of race is based on "strategic essentialism"—a paradoxical situation whereby essentialist ideas are consciously mobilised by marginalised communities as a form of empowerment.' This was demonstrated in the ways in which Chineseness was enacted. As this book has shown the multi-generation Australian-born Chinese have created hybrid identities that reflect a dialectical approach to their Chineseness, either central or peripheral but always there.

In sum, there is continuity and change in the importance and influence of visual markers, ethnic language and cultural performance in the construction and experience of identity among Australian Chinese. Equally significant are the historical, social and political changes in the host society, including multicultural policies and the evolution of a more inclusive society. Even as phenotype and language use are critical in the construction of identity, their relevance is negotiable depending on parental origin, individual generation, geography of residence and time. As a result Chineseness is embraced or rejected in multitude and complex ways across space, generation and time.

References

Alba, R., Logan, J., Lutz, A., & Stults, B. (2002). Only English by the third generation? Loss and preservation of the mother tongue among the grandchildren of contemporary immigrants. *Demography, 39*(3), 467–484. https://doi.org/10.1353/dem.2002.0023

Anderson, B. R. O. G. (1983). *Imagined communities: Reflections on the origin and spread of nationalism*. Verso.

Ang, I. (2001). *On not speaking Chinese: Living between Asia and the West*. Routledge.

Bailey, B. (2000). Language and negotiation of ethnic/racial identity among Dominican Americans. *Language in Society, 29*(4), 555–582. https://doi.org/10.1017/S0047404500004036

Barth, F. (Ed.). (1969). *Ethnic groups and boundaries: The social organization of culture difference*. Little, Brown and Company.

Barth, F. (1994). Enduring and emerging issues in the analysis of ethnicity. In H. Vermeulen & C. Govers (Eds.), *The anthropology of ethnicity: Beyond 'ethnic groups and boundaries'* (pp. 11–32). Het Spinhuis Publishers.

Bauman, Z. (2003). Educational challenges of the liquid-modern era. *Diogenes, 50*(1), 15–26. https://doi.org/10.1177/039219210305000103

Bauman, Z. (1996). From pilgrim to tourist—or a short history of identity. In S. Hall & P. du Gay (Eds.), *Questions of cultural identity* (pp. 18–36). Sage.

Bauman, Z. (2000). *Liquid modernity*. Polity Press.

Bauman, Z. (2005). *Liquid life*. Polity Press.

Bauman, Z. (2007). *Liquid times: Living in an age of uncertainty*. Polity Press.

Benton, G., & Gomez, E. T. (2014). Belonging to the nation: Generational change, identity and the Chinese diaspora. *Ethnic and Racial Studies, 37*(7), 1157–1171. https://doi.org/10.1080/01419870.2014.890236

Bhabha, H. K. (Ed.). (1990). *Nation and narration*. Routledge.

Brubaker, R. (2002). Ethnicity without groups. *European Journal of Sociology, 43*(02), 163–189. https://doi.org/10.1017/S0003975602001066

Brubaker, R. (2004). *Ethnicity without groups*. Harvard University Press.

Cheryan, S., & Monin, B. (2005). Where are you really from? Asian Americans and identity denial. *Journal of Personality and Social Psychology, 89*(5), 717. https://doi.org/10.1037/0022-3514.89.5.717

Dunn, K. M., Forrest, J., Burnley, I., & McDonald, A. (2004). Constructing racism in Australia. *Australian Journal of Social Issues, 39*(4), 409–430. https://doi.org/10.1002/j.1839-4655.2004.tb01191.x

Jenkins, R. (1994). Rethinking ethnicity: Identity, categorization and power. *Ethnic and Racial Studies, 17*(2), 197–223. https://doi.org/10.1080/01419870.1994.9993821

Jenkins, R. (2008). *Rethinking ethnicity* (2nd ed.). SAGE.

Lo, J. (2000). Beyond happy hybridity: Performing Asian-Australian identities. In I. Ang, S. Chalmers, L. Law, & M. Thomas (Eds.), *Alter/Asians: Asian-Australian identities in art, media and popular culture*. Pluto Press Australia Ltd.

Martin, J. (2003, September 20). The global hierarchy of race: As the only racial group that never suffers systemic racism, whites are in denial about its impact. *The Guardian*, 1.23.

Matthews, J. (2000). Violent visions and speechless days: Corporeality and the politics of image. In I. Ang, S. Chalmers, L. Law, & M. Thomas (Eds.), *Alter/Asians: Asian-Australian identities in art, media and popular culture*. Pluto Press Australia Ltd.

Ngan, L.L.-S., & Chan, K.-b. (2012). *The Chinese face in Australia: Multi-generational ethnicity among Australian-born Chinese*. Springer.

Pieterse, J. N. (1994). Globalisation as hybridisation. *International Sociology, 9*(2), 161–184. https://doi.org/10.1177/026858094009002003

Portes, A., & Hao, L. (1998). E Pluribus Unum: Bilingualism and loss of language in the second generation. *Sociology of Education, 71*(4), 269–294. Retrieved from http://search.proquest.com/docview/60063522?accountid=12528

Rosenthal, D. A., & Feldman, S. S. (1990). The acculturation of Chinese immigrants: Perceived effects on family functioning of length of residence in two cultural contexts. *The Journal of Genetic Psychology, 151*(4), 495–514. https://doi.org/10.1080/00221325.1990.9914635

Song, M. (2003). *Choosing ethnic identity*. Polity Press.

Tan, C. (2004). *'Chinese inscriptions': Australian-born Chinese lives*. (Doctoral dissertation) Retrieved from https://monash.hosted.exlibrisgroup.com/MON:au_everything:catau21188237990001751

Tuan, M. (2002). Second-generation Asian American identity: Clues from the Asian ethnic experience. In P. G. Min (Ed.), *The second generation: Ethnic identity among Asian Americans* (pp. 209–237). Altamira Press.

Walton, J., Priest, N., Kowal, E., White, F., Fox, B., & Paradies, Y. (2018). Whiteness and national identity: Teacher discourses in Australian primary schools. *Race Ethnicity and Education, 21*(1), 132–147. https://doi.org/10.1080/13613324.2016.1195357

Yue, M.-B. (2000). On not looking German: Ethnicity, diaspora and the politics of vision. *European Journal of Cultural Studies, 3*(2), 173–194.

Zhou, M. (2014). Segmented assimilation and socio-economic integration of Chinese immigrant children in the USA. *Ethnic and Racial Studies, 37*(7), 1172–1183. https://doi.org/10.1080/01419870.2014.874566

Uncited References

Ang, I. (2000). *Alter/Asians: Asian-Australian identities in art, media and popular culture*. Pluto Press.

Ang, I. (2011). Ethnicities and our precarious future. *Ethnicities, 11*(1), 27–31. https://doi.org/10.1177/1468796811010010205

Ang, I., Law, L., Chalmers, S., & Thomas, M. (Eds.). (2000). *Alter/Asians: Asian-Australian identities in art, media and popular culture*. Pluto Press.

Anthias, F. (2001). New hybridities, old concepts: The limits of 'culture'. *Ethnic and Racial Studies, 24*(4), 619–641. https://doi.org/10.1080/01419870120049815

Barbour, R. S. (2001). Checklists for improving rigour in qualitative research: A case of the tail wagging the dog? *British Medical Journal, 322*(7294), 1115–1117. https://doi.org/10.1136/bmj.322.7294.1115

Bashi, V. (1998). Racial categories matter because racial hierarchies matter: A commentary. *Ethnic and Racial Studies, 21*(5), 959–968. Retrieved from https://search-proquest-com.ezproxy.lib.monash.edu.au/docview/210227355?accountid=12528

Bauman, Z. (1995). Searching for a centre that holds. In M. Featherstone, S. Lash, & R. Robertson (Eds.), *Global modernities* (pp. 140–154). Sage Publications Ltd. Retrieved from https://search-proquest-com.ezproxy.lib.monash.edu.au/docview/60042055?accountid=12528

Bauman, Z. (1997). The making and unmaking of strangers. In P. Werbner & T. Modood (Eds.), *Debating cultural hybridity: Multi-cultural identities and the politics of anti-racism* (pp. ??). Zed Books.

Bauman, Z. (2006). *Liquid fear*. Polity Press.

Berthoud, R. (1998). Defining ethnic groups: Origin or identify? *Patterns of Prejudice, 32*(2), 53–63. https://doi.org/10.1080/0031322X.1998.9970255

Bhabha, H. (1988). The commitment to theory. *New Formations, 5*(1), 5–23.

Bhabha, H. K. (1994). *The location of culture*. Routledge Classics.

Billig, M. (1995). *Banal nationalism*. Sage.

Bowen, G. A. (2008). Naturalistic inquiry and the saturation concept: A research note. *Qualitative Research, 8*(1), 137–152. https://doi.org/10.1177/1468794107085301

Brannick, T., & Coghlan, D. (2007). In defense of being "native": The case for insider academic research. *Organizational Research Methods, 10*(1), 59–74. https://doi.org/10.1177/1094428106289253

Brubaker, R. (2001). The return of assimilation? Changing perspectives on immigration and its sequels in France, Germany, and the United States. *Ethnic and Racial Studies, 24*(4), 531–548. https://doi.org/10.1080/01419870120049770

Brubaker, R. (2005). The 'diaspora' diaspora. *Ethnic and Racial Studies, 28*(1), 1–19. https://doi.org/10.1080/0141987042000289997

Brubaker, R. (2014). Beyond ethnicity. *Ethnic and Racial Studies, 37*(5), 804–808. https://doi.org/10.1080/01419870.2013.871311

Brubaker, R., & Cooper, F. (2004). Beyond "identity." In R. Brubaker (Ed.), *Ethnicity without groups* (pp. 28–63). Harvard University Press.

Carnoy, M., & Rhoten, D. (2002). What does globalization mean for educational change? A comparative approach. Guest editorial essay. *Comparative Education Review, 46*(1), 1–9. Retrieved from http://www.jstor.org/stable/10.1086/324053

Children of the Revolution. (2003, December 26). *The Sydney Morning Herald*. https://www.smh.com.au/national/children-of-the-revolution-20031226-gdi1qx.html (DUPLICATE entry??).

Christian Research Association. (2010, June). *Factors in declining church attendance*. Retrieved from https://cra.org.au/factors-in-declining-church-attendance/

Collins, P. (1998). Negotiating selves: Reflections on 'unstructured' interviewing. *Sociological Research Online, 3*(3). Retrieved from https://search.proquest.com/docview/38615641?accountid=12528

Dirlik, A. (1999). Bringing history back in: Of diasporas, hybridities, places, and histories. *Review of Education, Pedagogy, and Cultural Studies, 21*(2), 95–131. https://doi.org/10.1080/107144 1990210202

Eide, E. (2010). Strategic essentialism and ethnification. Hand in glove? *Nordicom Review, 31*(2), 63–78. Retrieved from https://search.proquest.com/docview/848679644?accountid=12528

Eidheim, H. (1969). When ethnicity is a social stigma. In F. Barth (Ed.), *Ethnic groups and boundaries* (pp. 39–57). Little, Brown and Company.

Fase, W., Jaspaert, K., & Kroon, S. (Eds.). (1992). *Maintenance and loss of minority languages*. John Benjamins Publishing Company.

Fillmore, L. W. (1991). When learning a second language means losing the first. *Early Childhood Research Quarterly, 6*(3), 323–346. https://doi.org/10.1016/S0885-2006(05)80059-6

Hage, G. (1994). Locating multiculturalism's Other: A critique of practical tolerance. *New Formations*, 19–34.

Hall, S., & du Gay, P. (Eds.). (1996). *Questions of cultural identity*. SAGE Publications.

Hammersley, M. (2001). On 'systematic' reviews of research literatures: A 'narrative' response to Evans & Benefield. *British Educational Research Journal, 27*(5), 543–554. Retrieved from https://www.jstor.org/stable/1501950

Hanson, P. (2016). Pauline Hanson's 1996 maiden speech to parliament: Full transcript. (2016, September 15). *Sydney Morning Herald*. Retrieved from https://www.smh.com.au/politics/federal/pauline-hansons-1996-maiden-speech-to-parliament-full-transcript-20160915-grgjv3.html

Harris, A. (2009). Shifting the boundaries of cultural spaces: Young people and everyday multiculturalism. *Social Identities, 15*(2), 187–205. https://doi.org/10.1080/13504630902778602

Hester, S., & Francis, D. (1994). Doing data: The local organization of a sociological interview. *The British Journal of Sociology, 45*(4), 675–695. Retrieved from http://www.jstor.org/stable/591889

Hsu, R. Y. (1996). "Will the model minority please identify itself?" American ethnic identity and its discontents. *Diaspora: A Journal of Transnational Studies, 5*(1), 37–63. https://doi.org/10.1353/dsp.1996.0004

Huat, C. B. (2009). Being Chinese under official multiculturalism in Singapore. *Asian Ethnicity, 10*(3), 239–250. https://doi.org/10.1080/14631360903189609

Humphrey, C. (2012). Dilemmas in doing insider research in professional education. *Qualitative Social Work, 12*(5), 572–586. https://doi.org/10.1177/1473325012446006

Il Giornale Italiano. (1932). The acme of refinement, good taste and courtesy as shown by our detractors when "truth" is untruthful. Retrieved from https://trove.nla.gov.au/newspaper/article/83028371

Joseph, C. (2009). Postcoloniality and ethnography: Negotiating gender, ethnicity and power. *Race, Ethnicity and Education, 12*(1), 11–25. https://doi.org/10.1080/13613320802650907

Jupp, J. (1995). From 'White Australia' to 'part of Asia': Recent shifts in Australian immigration policy towards the region. *The International Migration Review, 29*(1), 207–207. Retrieved from http://search.proquest.com/docview/215278965?accountid=12528

Jupp, J. (2009). Immigration and ethnicity. *Australian Cultural History, 27*(2), 157–165. https://doi.org/10.1080/07288430903165303

Kabir, N. (2006). Representation of Islam and Muslims in the Australian Media, 2001–2005. *Journal of Muslim Minority Affairs, 26*(3), 313–328. https://doi.org/10.1080/13602000601141281

Khatri, R. B., & Assefa, Y. (2002). Access to health services among culturally and linguistically diverse populations in the Australian universal health care system: Issues and challenges. *BMC Public Health, 22*(1), 1–14. https://doi.org/10.1186/s12889-022-13256-z

Khoo, S.-E. (1995). Language maintenance amongst the second generation. *People and Place, 3*(4), 9–12.

Lentin, A. (2017). (Not) doing race: 'casual racism', 'bystander antiracism' and 'ordinariness' in Australian racism studies. In M. Boese & V. Marotta (Eds.), *Critical reflections on migration, 'race' and multiculturalism: Australia in a global context* (pp. 125–142).

References

Leong, G. (2000). Remembering Chinese. *Journal of Australian Studies, 24*(65), 58–68. https://doi.org/10.1080/14443050009387586

Levine-Rasky, C. (Ed.). (2002). *Working through whiteness: International perspectives.* State University of New York Press.

Lim, S.-L., Yeh, M., Liang, J., Lau, A. S., & McCabe, K. (2008). Acculturation gap, intergenerational conflict, parenting style, and youth distress in immigrant Chinese American families. *Marriage & Family Review, 45*(1), 84–106. https://doi.org/10.1080/01494920802537530

May, S., Modood, T., & Squires, J. (2004). *Ethnicity, nationalism, and minority rights.* Cambridge University Press.

Menand, L. (1995). Blind date: Liberalism and the allure of culture. *Transition, 67,* 70–81.

Mirsky, J. (1991). Language in migration: Separation individuation conflicts in relation to the mother tongue and the new language. *Psychotherapy: Theory, Research, Practice, Training, 28*(4), 618–624.

Modood, T., Squires, J., & May, S. (2004). *Ethnicity, nationalism and minority rights.* Cambridge University Press.

Mu, G. M. (2014). Heritage language learning for Chinese Australians: The role of habitus. *Journal of Multilingual and Multicultural Development, 35*(5), 497–510. https://doi.org/10.1080/01434632.2014.882340

Neckerman, K. M., Carter, P., & Lee, J. (1999). Segmented assimilation and minority cultures of mobility. *Ethnic and Racial Studies, 22*(6), 945–965. https://doi.org/10.1080/014198799329198

Ngan, L. (2008). Methodological issues in studying the identity of long-established Australian-born Chinese. *Migration & Identities, 1*(2), 133–150.

Oakley, A. (2002). Social science and evidence-based everything: The case of education. *Educational Review, 54*(3), 277–286. https://doi.org/10.1080/00131910220000016329

Ommundsen, W. (2002). Of dragons and devils: Chinese-Australian life stories. *JASAL, 1*(1), 67–80.

Ommundsen, W. (Ed.). (2001). *Bastard moon: Essays on Chinese-Australian writing.* Otherland.

Pauwels, A. (2005). Maintaining the community language in Australia: Challenges and roles for families. *International Journal of Bilingual Education and Bilingualism, 8*(2–3), 124–131. https://doi.org/10.1080/13670050508668601

Pieterse, J. N. (2001a). The case of multiculturalism: Kaleidoscopic and long-term views. *Social Identities, 7*(3), 393–407. https://doi.org/10.1080/13504630120087235

Pieterse, J. N. (2001b). Hybridity, so what? The anti-hybridity backlash and the riddles of recognition. *Theory, Culture & Society, 18*(2–3), 219–245. https://doi.org/10.1177/026327640101800211

Portes, A., & Schauffler, R. (1994). Language and the second generation: Bilingualism yesterday and today. *International Migration Review, 28*(4), 640–661. Retrieved from http://www.jstor.org/stable/2547152

Qin, D. B. (2006). 'Our child doesn't talk to us anymore': Alienation in immigrant Chinese families. *Anthropology and Education Quarterly, 37*(2), 162–179. Retrieved from https://search.proquest.com/docview/838989635?accountid=12528

Quah, S. R. (2009). Performing Chineseness in multicultural Singapore: A discussion on selected literary and cultural texts. *Asian Ethnicity, 10*(3), 225–238. https://doi.org/10.1080/14631360903189583

Rapley, T. J. (2001). The art(fulness) of open-ended interviewing: Some considerations on analysing interviews. *Qualitative Research, 1*(3), 303–323. https://doi.org/10.1177/146879410100100303

Rosenthal, D. A., & Feldman, S. S. (1992b). The relationship between parenting behaviour and ethnic identity in Chinese-American and Chinese-Australian adolescents. *International Journal of Psychology, 27*(1), 19. Retrieved from http://ezproxy.lib.monash.edu.au/login?url=http://search.ebscohost.com/login.aspx?direct=true&db=bth&AN=5775983&site=ehost-live&scope=site

Schonpflug, U. (2001). Intergenerational transmission of values: The role of transmission belts. *Journal of Cross-cultural Psychology, 32*(2), 174–185. Retrieved from https://search.proquest.com/docview/230109604?accountid=12528

Seale, C., & Silverman, D. (1997). Ensuring rigour in qualitative research. *European Journal of Public Health, 7*(4), 379–384. Retrieved from https://search.proquest.com/docview/61545132?accountid=12528

Smolicz, J. J. (1981). Core values and cultural identity. *Ethnic and Racial Studies, 4*(1), 75–90. Retrieved from https://search.proquest.com/docview/61048768?accountid=12528

Song, M. (2004). Introduction: Who's at the bottom? Examining claims about racial hierarchy. *Ethnic and Racial Studies, 27*(6), 859–877. https://doi.org/10.1080/0141987042000268503

Suttner, R. (2012). Understanding non-racialism as an emancipatory concept in South Africa. *Theoria: A Journal of Social and Political Theory, 59*(130), 22–41. https://doi.org/10.3167/th.2012.5913002

Sydney Living Museums. (201?). Chinese on the Goldfields. Retrieved from https://sydneylivingmuseums.com.au/stories/chinese-goldfields

Sylvain, R. (2014). Essentialism and the Indigenous politics of recognition in Southern Africa. *American Anthropologist, 116*(2), 251–264. https://doi.org/10.1111/aman.12087

Tabar, P., Noble, G., & Poynting, S. (2010). *On being Lebanese in Australia: Identity, racism and the ethnic field*. Lebanese American University Press.

Tajfel, H. (1981). *Human groups and social categories: Studies in social psychology*. Cambridge University Press.

Tan, C. (2006). 'The tyranny of appearance': Chinese Australian identities and the politics of difference. *Journal of Intercultural Studies, 27*(1–2), 65–82. https://doi.org/10.1080/07256860600607660

Tan, C. A. (2000). Boundaries, border-crossings and gatekeepers: Issues relating to the formation of identity amongst young Chinese Australians in the 1920s and 1930s. This paper has been accepted for publication in an edited book by Henry Chan and Regina Ganter entitled.

Tan, C. A. (2001). *Chinese families down under: The role of the family in the construction of identity, 1920–1960*. Paper presented at the International Conference "Migrating Identities: Ethnic Minorities in Chinese Diaspora" held by the Centre for the Study of Chinese Southern Diaspora, ANU, 26–28 September 2001.

Travers, M. (2009). New methods, old problems: A sceptical view of innovation in qualitative research. *Qualitative Research, 9*(2), 161–179. https://doi.org/10.1177/1468794108095079

Umana-Taylor, A. (2004). Ethnic identity and self-esteem: Examining the role of social context. *Journal of Adolescence, 27*(2), 139–146. https://doi.org/10.1016/j.adolescence.2003.11.006

Vermeulen, H., & Govers, C. (1994). *The anthropology of ethnicity: Beyond "Ethnic groups and boundaries."* Het Spinhuis Publishers.

Vertovec, S., Cohen, R. & Nagel, C. (2001). Migration, diasporas, and transnationalism. *Political Geography, 20*(2), 247–256. Retrieved from https://search.proquest.com/docview/38970930?accountid=12528

Wallace, K. M. (1984). The use and value of qualitative research studies. *Industrial Marketing Management, 13*(3), 181–185. Retrieved from https://search.proquest.com/docview/204593587?accountid=12528

Washington, E. (n.d.). Chinese on the Goldfields. Retrieved from https://sydneylivingmuseums.com.au/stories/chinese-goldfields

Werbner, P. (1997). Essentialising essentialism, essentialising silence: Ambivalence and multiplicity in the constructions of racism and ethnicity. In P. Werbner & T. Modood, *Debating cultural hybridity: Multi-cultural identities and the politics of anti-racism*. Zed Books.

Wu, F. H. (2002). *Yellow: Race in America beyond black and white*. Basic Books.

Wu, S.-M. (1995). Maintenance of the Chinese language in Australia. *Australian Review of Applied Linguistics, 18*(2), 105–136. Retrieved from http://search.proquest.com/docview/85626902?accountid=12528

Yang, W. (1994). I ask myself, am I Chinese? *Art & Asia Pacific, 1*(2), 89–95.

Yue, M.-B. (2009). Beyond ethnicity, into equality: Re-thinking hybridity and transnationalism in a local play from Hawai'i. *Cultural Studies, 23*(5–6), 775–794. https://doi.org/10.1080/09502380903132363

References

Zevallos, Z. (2003). That's my Australian side': The ethnicity, gender and sexuality of young Australian women of South and Central American origin. *Journal of Sociology, 39*(1), 81–98. https://doi.org/10.1177/0004869003039001321

Zhang, D. (2010). Language maintenance and language shift among Chinese immigrant parents and their second-generation children in the U.S. *Bilingual Research Journal, 33*(1), 42–60. https://doi.org/10.1080/15235881003733258

Milton Keynes UK
Ingram Content Group UK Ltd.
UKHW021958170124
436211UK00005B/150